CHILDREN AND FAMILIES AFFECTED BY ARMED CONFLICTS IN AFRICA

IMPLICATIONS AND STRATEGIES FOR HELPING PROFESSIONALS IN THE UNITED STATES

Joanne Corbin, Editor

NASW PRESS

National Association of Social Workers
Washington, DC

Cheryl Y. Bradley, *Publisher*
Sarah Lowman, *Project Manager*
Juanita Doswell, *Proofreader*
Bernice Eisen, *Indexer*

Cover by Eye to Eye Design Group
Interior design and composition by Electronic Quill
Printed and bound by Victor Graphics

First impression June 2012

Library of Congress Cataloging-in-Publication Data

Children and families affected by armed conflicts in Africa : implications and strategies for helping professionals in the United States / edited by Joanne Corbin.
p. cm.
Includes bibliographical references and index.
ISBN 978-0-87101-442-9
1. Children and war—Africa. 2. War and families—Africa. 3.War victims—Services for—Africa. 4. War—Psychological aspects. 5. Psychic trauma in children. I. Corbin, Joanne.
HQ784.W3C489 2012
303.6'6083096—dc23

2012010113

Printed in the United States of America

Contents

Acknowledgments

Many individuals have contributed to this book from the initial conceptualization to the completed manuscript. The conceptualization of this book began with my research on families affected by armed conflict in Uganda. I had the privilege of listening to the experiences of African children and adults whose lives have been shaped by armed conflict. They shared their experiences of violence, survival, and re-establishing their lives. I also heard the stories of Africans who emigrated from these contexts of armed conflict and were living in the United States; these were stories, they stated, no one knew about in the United States and no one asked. At the onset of my research in Uganda, a physician cautioned me that in doing this work I would "scratch many wounds." I have kept this comment in mind each day that I worked with these children, families, and service providers. I hope that the readers of this book become increasingly aware of the many wounds that individuals from contexts of armed conflict may carry every day of their lives. I am honored to have heard these stories and deeply appreciative to all who shared their journey with me. I am also extremely grateful for my colleagues in Uganda who contributed to this book and my understanding of the historical, political, and cultural issues, especially Stella Ojera, Father Remigio Obol, and Archbishop John Baptist Odama.

I wish to thank my colleagues at Smith College School for Social Work for providing advice and encouragement during the development of this book. Dean Carolyn Jacobs was a strong supporter of the book and the conference on children in armed conflict that was the catalyst for this book.

Many individuals were involved in the fine details of preparing this book. The work of student research assistants contributed immeasurably to this work through the extensive fact checking and reference finding; I am deeply appreciative of the tireless work of Deborah Ahove from Smith College and Cory Telman from University of Massachusetts Amherst. Neil Bilotta, graduate of Smith College School for Social Work, compiled the acronyms and terms. I wish to thank Allen Woods and Julie Abramson for their careful attention to detail during the content editing phase. I am grateful for Laura Wyman's support with copying and correspondence. It has been a pleasure to work with the editors of NASW: Lisa M. O'Hearn, John Cassels, and Sarah Lowman. Thank you all for your shepherding of this project and bringing it to completion.

And, finally, my heartfelt appreciation goes to my family and friends who have encouraged me in this project from the first moment.

Abbreviations and Acronyms

DDR	disarmament, demobilization, and reintegration
DDRR	disarmament, demobilization, reintegration, and rehabilitation
FAC	formerly abducted children
FARC	Fuerzas Armadas Revolucionarias de Columbia
ICC	International Criminal Court
IDP	internally displaced person
LTTE	Liberation Tigers of Tamil Eelam or Tamil Tigers
LRA	Lord's Resistance Army
LURD	Liberians United for Reconciliation and Democracy
NGO	nongovernmental organization
PTSD	posttraumatic stress disorder
UNHCR	United Nations High Commissioner for Refugees
UPDF	Uganda People's Defence Force—Uganda's Army

Introduction

Joanne Corbin

The purpose of this book is to inform social workers and other helping professionals in the United States about the context and realities of children and families affected by armed conflict in Africa and the strategies used to support them and to increase the awareness and knowledge that social workers bring to their work with individuals from these areas who are currently in the United States. This book focuses on armed conflict experiences in Africa, and most of the practice examples are based on the armed conflicts in Uganda and Rwanda. The focus on children and families affected by armed conflict in Africa is important for four reasons. First, although armed conflict affects children and families throughout the world, Africa is one region that is disproportionately affected by armed conflict and thus deserves singular attention. Second, although the percentage of immigrants, refugees, and asylum seekers from Africa is small in comparison to the total foreign-born population in the United States, it is a growing population. Third, the traditional African worldview that influences health and well-being is different from the Western worldview predominant in U.S. social services. Fourth, there are few social work books or articles that focus solely on the psychosocial issues of African children and families affected by war in Africa. It is important that practitioners understand the experiences that children and families from areas of armed conflict in Africa bring to social services, health services, and educational settings and reflect on what this may imply for helping professionals in the United States working with this population.

The objectives of the book are to

- increase awareness and knowledge of the nature of children and families' involvement in armed conflicts in Africa;
- increase awareness of the psychosocial interventions being used in several contexts in Africa among U.S. practitioners and to enhance their capacity to incorporate these strategies into their work;
- increase knowledge of the ways exposure to violence and trauma affects individual, family, social, and community functioning and the impact on recovery;
- understand the theories used in interventions with children and families affected by trauma experiences and identify the effective practices that have been researched;
- increase the cultural competence of U.S. practitioners working with refugee and immigrant populations from conflict-affected areas in Africa by examining the social and cultural understandings of mental health through selected exemplars;
- increase practitioners' ability to implement social services and programs among resettled and relocated populations that meet basic human needs and support the development of human capacities.

Background

Each day, the news informs us of wars and armed conflicts throughout the world. Many individuals' lives are defined by armed conflicts that last for years. Although the total number of armed conflicts has decreased in the world since the 1990s and the number of international and interstate wars has decreased, the number of intrastate wars has increased. These intrastate wars are more likely in Africa and Asia: Africa experiencing 40 percent of the armed conflicts worldwide and Asia 37 percent. Since the 1990s, the United States has seen an increase in the number of individuals coming from African countries affected by war as immigrants, refugees, and asylum seekers. The African population in the United States is a small percentage of the foreign-born population; however, it is an increasing one with an experience that is culturally different from that of Western society. Some individuals are involved as combatants, others as victims, and others as witnesses to the violence. Often, individuals fall into all three categories. Social service professionals at state and local agencies, medical facilities, mental health centers, and schools are likely to encounter individuals having such backgrounds. Therefore, it is important for social service professionals to become better informed about the situations of armed conflict that people may be coming from and the experiences that they may have been exposed to.

The need for a book that addressed these issues was identified as a result of a conference that was held at Smith College School for Social Work in 2005 on Children in Armed Conflict: Implications for U.S. Clinical Practice. The conference brought social workers, researchers, and policy developers with a range of backgrounds on this issue together to discuss critical issues for working with children and families affected by armed conflict. These issues involved the effects of armed conflict on the lives of individuals in these areas, the strategies that were used to cope, importance of cultural compatibility of the interventions, and the demographic information on Africans who are arriving in the United States from countries affected by armed conflict. This conference evolved from research on the effects of armed conflict on children who had been abducted by the Lord's Resistance Army (LRA) in northern Uganda. A critical aspect of this work for the editor was the importance of working with individuals affected by armed conflict, not working on them. The research, conference, and this book grew out of dialogue with practitioners in this field and with American and African practitioners who have worked in armed conflict in Africa. This book presents the perspectives of Africans who discuss the political, economic, cultural, social, and spiritual elements of life that have been affected by war.

The chapters in the book discuss topics of relevance for children and families affected by armed conflict in Africa and use the context of the LRA conflict in Uganda and Rwandan genocide as exemplars. However, the themes that are emphasized are global in nature, such as the nature of armed conflict and its impact on families; the impact of trauma on children, families, and communities; the importance of developing interventions that support an individual's worldview of well-being; the cultural and social adjustment of individuals immigrating to the United States; and the clinical implications of populations from areas of armed conflict moving to the United States. Therefore, the overarching themes and practice implications may apply to children and families affected by armed conflict from other regions.

Organization of the Book

The book is organized into three sections. The first section, What We Know, includes chapters 1, 2, and 3 and focuses on the increase in individuals coming to the United States from regions of armed conflict in Africa and experiences of children and families in war-affected communities in Africa. Authors provide contextual information about the experiences of armed conflict in Africa and the experiences of individuals and families resettling in the United States. The second section, African Experiences and Responses, chapters 4, 5, and 6, describes psychosocial and healing approaches used in African contexts of armed conflict. Contributors use firsthand experience to describe the basic needs of the population, the complexity of the children and families' lives, the challenges in gender relationships, and expectations for psychosocial healing and well-being. The third section, Practice Implications for Social Workers, chapters 7, 8, and 9, discusses practice issues related to war-affected populations. Theories that shape these practices are identified. These chapters also explore African cultural and traditional practices that might lend themselves to being integrated in U.S. social work practice. A Conclusion summarizes the key themes, highlights the practice implications for helping professionals, and identifies future areas of practice and research with children and families living in the United States who have been affected by armed conflict in Africa.

Overview of the Chapters

In chapter 1, Joanne Corbin explores the increase in the number of individuals coming to the United States from countries experiencing armed conflict in Africa. This information establishes the need for helping professionals to increase their knowledge and skills with this population. From 1990 to the present there has been a decrease in the overall number of armed conflicts but an increase in the number of intrastate conflicts. There has been a corresponding increase in the number of African individuals coming to the United States from countries that have experienced armed conflict. The resettlement patterns for immigrants have expanded, with implications that most counties in the United States have African populations. This chapter highlights the importance of U.S. helping professionals understanding the impact of these data on their work and the sociocultural characteristics of these populations.

One of the most concerning issues on the global scene is the involvement of children under 18 years of age in armed conflict. In chapter 2, Jo Becker presents the context of children involved in armed conflict. Most armed conflicts worldwide involve children under 18 years of age, and children's involvement in armed conflict is a growing phenomenon. Understanding the ways that children become connected to the armed forces or armed groups can help U.S. social service providers understand the day-to-day economic and political challenges facing many families. The author uses examples of individual children she has met to describe their experiences within these armed groups.

In chapter 3, Eugenie Mukeshimana describes the firsthand experience of coming to the United States after living through the Rwandan genocide. Mukeshimana explains the fears and challenges of surviving through the genocide and the loss of family, friends, and community; the challenge of finding a way out of a country in the political instability of the aftermath; and resettling in a foreign country. The biopsychosocial perspective is used to frame the experiences of an individual in resettlement and the strategies to support that individual. The chapter will help practitioners reflect on how social service delivery and individual interventions can support the needs of newly arrived populations.

In northern Uganda, the strategies for working with children, families, and communities affected by armed conflict involves addressing violence and increasing the capacity of individuals to work for peace. In chapter 4, Reverend Father Remigio C. Obol examines the concept of peace in the Acholi population, the ways that peace has been damaged in the armed conflict, and strategies for retuning to peace. The chapter identifies key concepts in the Acholi culture and African culture that support peace and are important for individual and collective well-being.

In chapter 5, Stella Ojera describes the psychosocial approach to working with children affected by armed conflict in northern Uganda. The cultural and contextual issues that shape the development of psychosocial approaches are described. The components of the center-based approach and community-based approach are discussed. The important role of community involvement and agency collaboration is highlighted. The psychosocial approach is a common approach used in many countries in Africa; several examples are included.

In chapter 6, Theresa S. Betancourt and colleagues Sarah E. Meyers-Ohki, Sara N. Stulac, Christine Mushashi, Felix R. Cyamatare, and William R. Beardslee examine locally defined constructs of mental health for conflict-affected communities in Rwanda. This chapter describes a research study designed to develop knowledge and understanding of Rwandan conceptualizations of mental health issues that affect family functioning. The findings from the study were used to create a family-based intervention to strengthen family functioning. The chapter highlights the importance of culturally congruent interventions and significant participation of the community.

In chapter 7, Joan Granucci Lesser provides the groundwork for working with individuals affected by trauma. She begins by providing an understanding of the major concepts in trauma work including trauma, acute stress disorder, posttraumatic stress disorder, cultural trauma, collective memory, and vicarious traumatization. Throughout her discussion of the impact of trauma on individuals, Lesser pays attention to the importance of the political, social, and cultural worlds of individuals who have experienced trauma. She uses a developmental perspective for conducting psychosocial assessments, looking at the types of trauma symptoms that are seen during childhood, early adolescence, and late adolescence. Lesser offers a description of the techniques that have been used to help individuals recover and heal from trauma.

In chapter 8, Joanne Corbin explores the conceptual integration of African cultural orientation into the Western psychological approaches to intervene with trauma. Cultural worldviews influence how individuals and communities understand experiences, respond to these experiences, and develop interventions. Two traditional African ceremonies are examined to understand the implications for healing from the psychological and social effects of armed conflict. Ways of working with trauma from a Western perspective may be culturally incongruent to individuals from a traditional African perspective. Key beliefs and values of the African worldview are presented.

In chapter 9, Joanne Corbin explores the importance of using an ecological framework for assessing the areas of strengths and vulnerabilities that African individuals and families from contexts of armed conflict have experienced. The challenges for practitioners working with populations affected by armed conflict are identified.

The conclusion of the book provides a summary of the key themes that are presented in the chapters and identifies implications for practice. It also provides recommendations for further development in practice and research areas.

Conclusion

The goal of this book is to help practitioners expand their understanding of the contextual issues affecting children and families affected by armed conflict in Africa through the book's focus on Uganda and Rwanda. It is hoped that the content prompts helping professionals to increase their knowledge of the effect of armed conflicts on client populations; expand the questions that become part of assessments; deepen their understanding of the significance of cultural worldviews; and increase their awareness and knowledge of integrating aspects of culture, where appropriate, into the interventions used with armed conflict–affected populations.

SECTION 1

What We Know

The chapters in this section provide an overview of the African populations immigrating to the United States with experiences of armed conflict and raise awareness of the experiences of two specific African populations affected by armed conflict. The chapters in the section draw attention to the complexity of factors affecting African populations affected by armed conflict and the necessity for social workers to be informed about and attend to the micro and macro aspects of practice to address the needs of this population effectively.

Chapter 1 describes recent immigration patterns from Africa and provides a backdrop for understanding the direct and indirect effects of armed conflict on these new arrivals and their social and cultural networks. Chapter 2 focuses on child soldiers, one group affected by armed conflict in Africa, and helps service providers begin to grasp the enormity of their experiences, consider support that is needed to support positive reentry into society for these individuals, and recognize the strengths that those who have survived bring with them. Chapter 3 presents a personal experience of immigrating to the United States as a result of the Rwandan genocide and provides an in-depth understanding of the challenges facing African individuals and families from contexts of war. Seeing this experience through the eyes of a social worker allows helping professions to be more aware of the needs of people coming from such experiences; understand how the process of immigrating can be filled with loss, confusion, and unpredictability; and understand what is needed to improve this experience of new arrivals.

1

Africans Coming to the United States from Contexts of Armed Conflict:
Relevance for Helping Professionals

Joanne Corbin

The number of African immigrant, refugees, and asylum seekers immigrating to the United States has increased dramatically over the past 30 years. Although this number is small, at 4 percent of the U.S. population, it represents an increase of 400 percent since the 1970s (Wilson, 2009). Most of these new arrivals are coming from countries that have experienced political and armed conflicts. Those new arrivals not directly involved in such conflicts as combatants or civilian casualties are often indirectly affected by the breakdown of political, economic, and social infrastructures that affect the entire country. These new arrivals from Africa bring experiences of conflict in addition to histories, cultures, and worldviews that are different from those of the helping professionals they will encounter in the United States.

Social workers and other helping professionals need to prepare themselves to address the unique concerns and needs of this population. Such efforts will require an understanding of the historical, political, and economic factors that clients have experienced prior to immigrating to the United States. Most literature about social services and immigrant issues focuses on the category of immigrants as a whole or for major population groups, yet the population of African new arrivals with experiences of armed conflict requires help from professionals who have knowledge of their specific needs and unique cultures. This chapter provides such information to support the capacity of helping professionals to provide culturally aware assistance to such immigrants, thereby strengthening their ability to successfully engage these clients in services.

First, the demographic and resettlement patterns of African immigration to the United States will be reviewed as will the reasons for African emigration.

This chapter will then present information about the African worldview, religious beliefs, and cultural practices so that social workers can draw on such knowledge to work more effectively with African clients.

U.S. Demographics

My interest in understanding more about the demographic patterns of new arrivals (immigrants, refugees, asylum seekers) from Africa began when I learned that approximately half of all new arrivals in the mid-2000s to my home state, Massachusetts, were from Africa (see Table 1-1). Data from the same source indicate that up to 38 percent of these new arrivals from Africa resettled in western Massachusetts, where I reside (Office of Health and Human Services-MA, 2011). These data provided me with insight about a population of which I had not been aware. I was then motivated to investigate the specific needs of African refugee and asylum seekers.

Similar patterns in demographics exist in the national data on African immigrants, refugees, and asylum seekers. During the period 1983 to 1992, African immigrants to the United States accounted for 2 percent to 3 percent of the immigrant population to the United States (U.S. Department of Justice, 1992, as cited in Kamya, 1997, p. 155). This percentage increased 5 percent to 9 percent from 2000 to 2006 (Jefferys, 2007). African refugees specifically have accounted for 9 percent to over 50 percent of all refugees coming into the United States in the late 1990s and early 2000s (Office of Refugee Resettlement [ORR], 2004a). African asylum seekers have accounted for 18 percent to 28 percent of all asylum seekers coming into the United States (U.S. Department of Homeland Security [DHS], 2008). Overall, the current percentage of the U.S. foreign-born population from Africa is small at 4 percent (Wilson, 2009), but this percentage has steadily increased from .4 percent of the foreign-born population in the 1960s to 2.5 percent in the early 2000s (U.S. Census Bureau, 2002).

The growth in the African foreign-born population in the United States parallels the growth in the overall U.S. foreign-born population. In 2003, the U.S. population was approximately 283 million (U.S. Census Bureau, 2003); the foreign-born population was 33.5 million, 11.7 percent of the total U.S. population (Larsen, 2004), the highest percentage since 1900, when the percentage of the foreign-born population was 14.7 percent (Gibson & Lennon, 1999).

Reasons for Increased African Immigration to the United States

The first reason for the increase in African migration to the United States is that more individuals are joining family members who have become permanent U.S. residents. During the 1980s and 1990s, there were changes in

TABLE 1-1: African Refugee and Asylum Seekers Arrivals in Massachusetts

Year	Annual Total—All arrivals	Annual Total—Arrivals from Africa	% Arrivals from Africa
2000	2,240	564	25
2001	1,895	495	27
2002	1,006	164	16
2003	1,190	462	39
2004	1,731	955	55
2005	1,601	721	45
2006	1,100	483	44
2007	1,032	453	44
2008	1,419	313	22
2009	2,120	272	13

Source: Office of Health and Human Services-MA, 2011.

family-sponsored immigration applications, making it easier for individuals emigrating from other countries to join family members in the United States; greater opportunities were also available for individuals to emigrate from countries that were underrepresented in the United States (DHS, n.d.).

A second reason is that many African immigrants have sought to advance their educational goals and professional skills. Takougang and Tidjani (2009) explained that African immigrants in the 1960s and 1970s sought to complete their education and planned to return to use their skills in African countries that were gaining independence from colonial rule. This is consistent with Kamya's (1997) study of African immigrants, in which he found that 85 percent were emigrating for educational purposes. However, beginning in the 1980s many African immigrants to the United States were choosing to remain in the United States and find other ways of supporting families and communities in their countries of birth (Takougang & Tidjani, 2009). In addition, changes in U.S. immigration legislation during the 1980s and 1990s made it easier for students and professionals to remain in the United States (DHS, n.d.).

A third reason for African immigration is the social, economic, and political upheavals in many African countries. The number of legal residents, refugees, and asylum seekers coming to the United States from African countries increased due to the conflicts in that region. Singer and Wilson (2007) identified three distinct migration periods to the United States. The first was the Cold War period from 1980 to 1991, which focused largely on refugees from the dissolution of Soviet republics. The second was the Balkans period from 1992 to 2000, when refugees were fleeing the breakup of Yugoslavia and its successor states. The third is the "civil conflict period" of the late 1990s to the present. This period consists of refugees coming as a result of the political and civil conflicts in Africa and Asia (Singer & Wilson, 2007). African immigration to the United States has by and large occurred during this period.

Supporting this pattern, Hume and Hardwick (2005) studied the resettlement of refugees from African countries in Portland, Oregon, beginning in the 1980s and found that they were fleeing war and persecution in Ethiopia or present-day Eritrea, Sudan, Somalia, Liberia, Democratic Republic of the Congo (DRC), Chad, Sierra Leone, and Togo. Violence, fueled by a struggle for control of resources like minerals or oil and battles for political power, has affected everyone living in these regions. Worldwide, Africa has 39 percent of the world's armed conflicts[1] (Ploughshares, 2010). Unfortunately, civilians are increasingly involved in such conflicts as combatants or victims of attacks on neighborhoods, schools, and hospitals (UN Security Council, 2005). Children are a particularly vulnerable group as those under 18 years of age have been forced or coerced to become combatants in three-fourths of the world's armed conflicts (Human Security Center, 2005, pp. 35, 113).

There are no specific data about the percentage of African immigrants, refugees, and asylum seekers in the United States who have been involved in armed conflict, but it can be extrapolated from the data that most are coming from countries currently or recently involved in armed conflict (DHS, 2009a). The census data on the foreign-born population and ORR data provide information about the countries of origin for new arrivals. Looking specifically at those individuals emigrating from Africa, from 2000 to 2009, the 10 African countries with the greatest numbers of immigrants to the United States were Nigeria, Ethiopia, Egypt, Ghana, Somalia, Kenya, Morocco, Liberia, South Africa, and Sudan (see Table 1-2) (DHS, 2009a). All but two of these countries (Ghana and Morocco) were identified as having a current or recent armed conflict.[2] The 10 countries with the highest number of refugees arriving from Africa between 2000 and 2009 were Somalia, Liberia, Sudan, Ethiopia, Burundi, Sierra Leone, DRC, Eritrea, Rwanda, and Togo (see Table 1-3) (DHS, 2009b). Only Togo had not experienced a current or recent armed conflict but has had a recent history of political violence. The 10 African countries with the greatest number of asylum seekers arriving in the United States from 2000

[1]An *armed conflict* is a political conflict involving the armed forces of at least one state (or one or more armed factions seeking to gain control of all or part of the state), and in which at least 1,000 people have been killed by the fighting during the course of the conflict (Ploughshares, 2006)

[2]Ploughshares (2010) indicated the African countries currently experiencing armed conflicts as Algeria, Burundi, Chad, Central African Republic, Democratic Republic of the Congo, Ethiopia, Kenya, Nigeria, Somalia, Sudan, Sudan-Darfur, and Uganda. Countries with recently ended armed conflicts in Africa are Angola, Angola-Cabinda, Congo, Côte d'Ivoire, Egypt, Ethiopia/Eritrea, Guinea, Liberia, Rwanda, Senegal, Sierra Leone, and South Africa.

to 2009 were Ethiopia, Somalia, Cameroon, Liberia, Egypt, Sudan, Kenya, Eritrea, Togo, and Zimbabwe (see Table 1-4) (DHS, 2009c). Cameroon, Togo, and Zimbabwe were countries in this list without current or recent armed conflict. Clearly, most African immigrants, refugees, and asylum seekers are coming from countries with a recent experience of armed conflict.

In addition, other countries are almost always affected by current armed conflict on their borders. For example, Ghana is listed earlier as a country not affected by recent armed conflict; however, the recent political upheavals in Côte d'Ivoire were expected to cause instability in Ghana as civilians fleeing Côte d'Ivoire crossed into Ghana along the border of those two countries. Other African countries without a history of recent armed conflict are similarly affected by violence in neighboring countries. Children and families are often directly caught in the fighting in countries where there is armed conflict; in addition, the infrastructure of their societies, including the medical, educational, social, economic, political, communication, and transportation systems of the area are severely damaged, if not destroyed, as a consequence of the conflict. To emphasize this point, Collier (2007) studied the impact of civil wars on countries and determined that a war lasting an average of seven years in a country that was already economically and politically vulnerable leaves it 15 percent poorer than it would have been without such a war. Political instability, economic instability, and human rights abuses are often associated with these conflicts, which often result in mass displacement of populations. Such displacement of people from their countries of origin to neighboring countries, or elsewhere, poses huge challenges for human and social service resources at the local, national, regional, and international levels.

Resettlement Patterns in the United States

African immigrants arriving in the 1960s and 1970s seeking educational opportunities often remained in the areas in which they attended school, such as New York, Boston, Atlanta, Chicago, Detroit, Los Angeles, Houston, and the District of Columbia (Takougang & Tidjani, 2009). Since that time, more African immigrants have focused on establishing residences and employment in other places, such as South Dakota, Washington, and Ohio (Takougang & Tidjani, 2009). Takougang and Tidjani (2009) described the more recent African immigrants as economic refugees whose focus is on economic sustainability for themselves and their families and extended family networks in Africa.

The greatest numbers of African refugees have been settling in Minnesota, Texas, New York, Georgia, California, Arizona, Virginia, Pennsylvania, Maryland, Ohio, and Illinois (see Table 1-5) (ORR, 2009). Specific data exist on

TABLE 1-2: Immigrants from Africa 2000–2009

Country	2000	2001	2002	2003	2004	2005	2006	2007	2008	2009	Totals
Algeria	906	875	1,030	759	805	1,115	1,300	1,036	1,037	1,485	10,348
Angola	87	94	92	59	107	188	272	199	221	173	1,492
Benin	62	75	137	76	185	193	275	258	317	401	1,979
Botswana	13	24	30	27	34	54	53	49	41	55	380
Burkina Faso	48	68	64	60	103	128	221	238	238	416	1,584
Burundi	28	79	120	74	100	186	320	257	255	1,505	2,924
Cameroon	860	791	984	927	1,309	1,458	2,919	3,392	3,771	3,463	19,874
Cape Verde	1,079	868	871	745	1,015	1,225	1,780	2,048	1,916	2,238	13,785
Central African Republic	4	11	13	6	17	24	51	52	88	107	373
Chad	23	44	47	8	23	31	73	74	96	102	521
Democratic Republic of the Congo	123	145	178	110	155	260	738	1,129	1,261	2,122	6,221
Republic of the Congo	189	311	677	513	670	1,064	1,600	972	950	1,563	8,509
Cote d'Ivoire	439	596	629	483	666	930	2,067	1,193	1,645	2,159	10,807
Djibouti	14	22	30	16	37	50	34	23	39	54	319
Egypt	4,450	5,159	4,852	3,348	5,522	7,905	10,500	9,267	8,712	8,844	68,559
Equatorial Guinea	5	3	8	D	13	10	13	4	16	32	104
Eritrea	382	540	560	556	675	796	1,593	1,081	1,270	1,928	9,381
Ethiopia	4,053	5,092	7,565	6,635	8,286	10,571	16,152	12,786	12,917	15,462	99,519
Gabon	18	32	41	40	50	66	85	95	82	171	680
Gambia	231	390	343	263	422	581	897	826	739	978	5670
Ghana	4,339	4,023	4,248	4,410	5,337	6,491	9,367	7,610	8,195	8,401	62,421
Guinea	3	11	16	29	347	495	1,110	1,088	1,735	1,725	6,559
Guinea-Bissau	204	273	289	176	5	26	25	25	17	20	1,060
Kenya	2,197	2,501	3,199	3,209	5,335	5,347	8,779	7,030	6,998	9,880	54,475
Lesotho	9	6	13	5	14	12	18	14	16	14	121
Liberia	1,570	2,273	2,869	1,766	2,757	4,880	6,887	4,102	7,193	7,641	41,938

Libya	180	223	158	140	185	223	271	186	285	296	2,147
Madagascar	33	61	43	40	54	60	72	53	77	71	564
Malawi	61	70	56	62	83	131	131	123	133	164	1,014
Mali	109	119	105	124	163	277	408	412	523	576	2,816
Mauritania	88	117	124	131	170	275	720	651	844	597	3,717
Mauritius	54	84	83	57	65	99	108	88	83	110	831
Morocco	3,614	4,958	3,387	3,137	4,128	4,411	4,949	4,513	4,425	5,447	42,969
Mozambique	41	48	54	36	59	54	78	81	69	66	586
Namibia	30	54	46	40	40	63	56	57	46	53	485
Niger	30	1,330	1,263	808	62	126	116	97	107	183	4,122
Nigeria	7,831	8,253	8,105	7,872	9,374	10,597	13,459	12,448	12,475	15,253	105,667
Rwanda	73	148	217	109	163	276	502	357	378	952	3,175
Senegal	554	663	530	522	769	913	1,367	1,024	1,149	1,524	9,015
Seychelles	18	18	20	16	25	16	15	7	16	10	161
Sierra Leone	1,585	1,878	2,246	1,492	1,596	2,731	3,572	1,999	2,795	2,687	22,581
Somalia	2,393	3,007	4,535	2,444	3,929	5,829	9,462	6,251	10,745	13,390	61,985
South Africa	2,824	4,090	3,861	2,210	3,370	4,536	3,201	2,988	2,723	3,171	32,974
Sudan	1,531	1,650	2,921	1,883	3,211	5,231	5,504	2,930	3,598	3,577	32,036
Swaziland	12	18	12	23	15	16	11	13	18	42	180
Tanzania	480	476	577	554	747	829	949	832	838	2,773	9,055
Togo	386	487	935	1,187	2,041	1,523	1,720	1,565	1,661	1,680	13,185
Tunisia	307	438	540	353	457	495	510	417	410	416	4,343
Uganda	418	457	575	455	721	858	1,372	1,122	1,174	1,364	8,516
Zambia	211	295	308	280	359	499	672	576	613	704	4,517
Zimbabwe	322	475	484	358	628	923	1,049	1,057	953	983	7,232
Totals	44,534	53,731	60,101	48,642	66,422	85,098	117,422	94,711	105,915	127,050	

Note: Extracted from Table 3, U.S. Department of Homeland Security (2009a). D means that datum was withheld to limit disclosure.

TABLE 1-3: Refugees from Africa 2000–2009

Country	2000	2001	2002	2003	2004	2005	2006	2007	2008	2009	Totals
Algeria	57	31		4	D	D	D				92
Angola	D	34	16	21	20	21	13	4		8	137
Benin											
Botswana											
Burkina Faso											
Burundi	165	109	62	16	276	214	466	4545	2,889	762	9,504
Cameroon	7	5	6	6	D	6	29	5	D	4	68
Cape Verde											
Central African Republic		D		D	24		23	15	56	59	177
Chad	D	D	D	D	4		4	10	23	6	47
Democratic Republic of the Congo	1,354	260	107	251	569	424	405	848	727	1,135	6,080
Republic of the Congo	11	6	5	41	73	43	66	206	197	293	941
Cote d'Ivoire		D	3	4		5	23	11	30	9	85
Djibouti		12	D	D	6					3	21
Egypt											
Equatorial Guinea	12			D		25	11	14		9	71
Eritrea	94	109	13	23	128	327	538	963	251	1,571	4,017
Ethiopia	1,347	1,429	330	1,702	2,689	1,663	1,271	1,028	299	321	12,079
Gabon											
Gambia	13	5		9	3		6	13	6	10	65
Ghana											
Guinea											
Guinea-Bissau											
Kenya	11	13	24	3		D	5			D	56
Lesotho											
Liberia	2,620	3,429	560	2,957	7,140	4,289	2,346	1,606	992	385	26,324

Libya											
Madagascar											
Malawi											
Mali											
Mauritania		202	6			3	88	62	26	16	403
Mauritius											
Morocco											
Mozambique											
Namibia											
Niger											
Nigeria	50	85	28	57	34	11	15	20	76	3	379
Rwanda	345	94	47	47	176	183	112	202	108	111	1,425
Senegal											
Seychelles											
Sierra Leone	1,128	2,004	176	1,378	1,084	829	439	166	99	51	7,354
Somalia	6,026	4,951	237	1,994	13,331	10,405	10,357	6,969	2,523	4,189	60,982
South Africa											
Sudan	3,833	5,959	897	2,139	3,500	2,205	1,848	705	375	683	22,144
Swaziland											
Tanzania											
Togo	511	280	16	47	35	72	18	40	204	14	1,237
Tunisia	D	10									10
Uganda	18	12	D	D	8	10	20	38	42	8	156
Zambia											
Zimbabwe		6			D	D	13	D	3	10	32
Totals	17,624	19,070	2,551	10,719	29,108	20,746	18,129	17,486	8,949	9,678	

Source: Extracted from Table 14, United States Department of Homeland Security (2009b). D means that data were withheld to limit disclosure.

TABLE 1-4: Asylees from Africa 2000–2009

Country	2000	2001	2002	2003	2004	2005	2006	2007	2008	2009	Totals
Algeria	66	40	22	15	10	6	6	3	8	6	182
Angola	57	50	28	19	5	5	3	5	4	3	179
Benin											
Botswana											
Burkina Faso	9	4	3	7	7	9	13	31	17	21	121
Burundi	29	52	63	26	25	17	29	25	28	21	315
Cameroon	349	324	710	814	597	385	224	294	282	220	4,199
Cape Verde											
Central African Republic	D	5	23	22	7	17	5	6	12	15	112
Chad	16	11	13	24	20	12	19	31	35	38	219
Democratic Republic of the Congo	222	149	198	76	69	53	46	35	38	31	917
Republic of the Congo	258	247	255	119	92	55	51	71	54	42	1,244
Cote d'Ivoire	24	44	24	126	86	92	71	49	43	38	597
Djibouti											
Egypt	471	471	490	242	143	142	175	193	234	308	2,869
Equatorial Guinea											
Eritrea	204	143	167	124	132	142	112	152	181	234	1,591
Ethiopia	1,444	1,172	1,049	573	753	464	435	497	586	704	7,677
Gabon											
Gambia	24	31	21	29	31	28	37	43	50	49	343
Ghana	24	14	7	D	10	4	5	8	6	8	86
Guinea	95	160	184	122	155	127	94	121	117	117	1,292
Guinea-Bissau	5	D	D	D	11	D				3	19
Kenya	101	127	251	239	191	131	84	181	215	234	1,754
Lesotho											
Liberia	690	769	608	352	309	122	61	48	61	45	3,065

Libya	21	5	4	D	3		3		3	D	39
Madagascar											
Malawi											
Mali	5	3	9	9	18	25	28	51	36	52	236
Mauritania	96	98	91	60	58	44	13	11	4	13	488
Mauritius											
Morocco	7	8	15	3	5	6	3	D	D	4	51
Mozambique											
Namibia											
Niger	51	39	19	30	21	8	8	4	11	4	195
Nigeria	50	33	26	18	31	31	23	28	36	38	314
Rwanda	97	61	39	33	33	51	64	70	75	59	582
Senegal	17	15	18	15	18	10	7	11	9	22	142
Seychelles											
Sierra Leone	219	304	171	44	62	44	22	19	19	34	938
Somalia	1,994	1,279	431	142	146	74	48	71	69	87	4,341
South Africa	7	D	13	10	4	11	5	4	4	5	63
Sudan	512	520	446	110	84	56	52	84	86	75	2,025
Swaziland											
Tanzania	5	17	16	4	11	19	4	6	8	6	96
Togo	64	85	198	326	349	199	81	58	37	34	1,431
Tunisia											
Uganda	121	119	155	71	59	45	31	78	55	55	789
Zambia		8	14	7	14	13	6	9	6	D	77
Zimbabwe	8	42	94	192	238	202	141	156	193	153	1,419
Totals	7,362	6,466	5,891	4,017	3,819	2,665	2,016	2,473	2,635	2,805	

Source: Extracted from Table 17, United States Department of Homeland Security (2009c). D means that data were withheld to limit disclosure.

TABLE 1-5: States Receiving the Largest Number of African Refugees 2000–2009

	2000		2001		2002		2003		2004	
Total African Refugees entering United States	17,561		19,021		2,548		10,717		29,125	
	State	n	State	n	State	n	State	n	State	n
	Minnesota	2,593	Minnesota	2,489	Minnesota	286	Minnesota	1,452	Minnesota	3,412
	New York	1,490	New York	1,521	Texas	254	Texas	1,000	Texas	2,,579
	Texas	1,400	Texas	1,459	New York	166	New York	915	New York	1,771
	Georgia	1,096	Pennsylvania	1,125	Pennsylvania	164	Georgia	740	Georgia	1,749
	Virginia	1,080	Georgia	1,082	Arizona	142	Pennsylvania	652	Arizona	1,548
	California	992	California	969	Maryland	108	California	647	California	1,379
	Pennsylvania	875	Virginia	812	Georgia	106	Maryland	558	Ohio	1,185
	Arizona	684	Maryland	805	Illinois	106	Arizona	547	Virginia	1,079
	Ohio	642	Arizona	769	California	92	Virginia	517	Pennsylvania	959
	Maryland	516	Washington	648	Virginia	92	Illinois	444	Illinois	955
	2005		2006		2007		2008		2009	
Total African Refugees entering United States	20,709		18,155		17,476		8,935		9,690	
	Minnesota	3,039	Minnesota	3,999	Minnesota	2,310	Texas	1,067	Texas	1,133
	Texas	1,862	Ohio	1,632	Texas	1,735	Arizona	575	Arizona	797
	New York	1,265	Texas	1,315	Ohio	1,121	Minnesota	528	New York	718
	Ohio	1,230	New York	872	Illinois	804	New York	485	Georgia	655
	Georgia	1,066	Arizona	815	Arizona	770	Ohio	469	Colorado	388
	Arizona	1,000	California	785	New York	759	Pennsylvania	356	Ohio	347
	Illinois	808	Georgia	700	Georgia	701	Georgia	342	Tennessee	330
	California	749	Washington	670	Washington	684	Illinois	314	California	329
	Virginia	749	Illinois	605	California	590	Virginia	312	Washington	309
	Pennsylvania	674	Pennsylvania	538	Tennessee	576	Colorado	310	Utah	294

Source: State figures extracted from Office of Refugee Resettlement 2000–2009 data sets (Office of Refugee Resettlement, 2000–2009).

Somali and Ethiopian refugees, two of the largest African groups resettled in the United States. Approximately half of the Somali refugees have resettled in five urban areas: Minneapolis-St. Paul; Washington, DC; Atlanta; Chicago; and Seattle (Singer & Wilson, 2007). Approximately 38 percent of Ethiopian refugees have resettled in Washington, DC; Minneapolis-St. Paul; San Diego; Atlanta; and Dallas (Singer & Wilson, 2007).

The resettlement patterns for African new arrivals overlap to a small degree with the patterns for U.S. new arrivals overall. States such as California, New York, Texas, Florida, New Jersey, and Illinois have tended to receive the largest percentages of all immigrants (Fix & Passel, 1994; Urban Institute, 2006); however, beginning in the 1990s, immigrants started to move into other urban and rural areas including Nashville, Atlanta, Louisville, Minneapolis-St. Paul, Greensboro-Winston Salem, Charlotte, Memphis, Portland, Vancouver, Seattle, and Washington, DC (Morse, 2004).

Story Behind the Numbers

The demographics presented in the preceding section provide an overall picture of the population from Africa; however, these numbers do not provide an understanding of the individual stories connected to these numbers. Eugenie Mukeshimana, the author of chapter 3 describes her immigration experience from a context of armed conflict. Several of the issues outlined in her narrative illustrate the complexities of emigration from contexts of armed conflict. The first issue is that the label that is attached to the way individuals immigrate to the United States may not be an accurate signifier of their experiences. The term "refugee" connotes that someone is fleeing a condition of persecution or a well-founded fear of persecution in his or her country of origin. The conflict or violence-related experiences of individuals entering the United States on student visas or a family- or relative-sponsored visa, for example, may not be immediately apparent; however, these individuals may experience the emotional, social, and communal effects of armed conflict. The second issue is that the U.S. communities that receive new arrivals from conflict-affected communities very likely know little about the countries from which the individuals are coming. The nature of the conflict, the impact of conflict on everyday life, and the challenges of leaving one's country are important aspects of immigrants' lives. Helping professionals may be unaware of these specific circumstances. The third issue is the loss of connection that those emigrating from Africa may experience—the loss of family and community networks as well as the loss of an overarching culture of collectivism that orients individuals to social and cultural norms. The fourth issue is the challenge of starting life anew in the United States amid continuing concern about family remaining in the country of origin.

Efforts here to highlight of some of the factors underlying the experiences of individuals emigrating from African contexts of armed conflict may strengthen helping professionals' understanding of the human experience of immigrating to the United States from such situations.

Key Issues for New Arrivals from Africa

New arrivals from Africa come to the United States with particular worldviews, cultures, and histories that are distinct from the culture to which they are immigrating. Many come from traditional contexts in which collectivism is the predominant perspective, religion is central in everyday life, and cultural and traditional practices play a major part of their lives. The majority also come with some experience of armed conflict or political conflict.

Collectivism. The influence of the collectivist worldview on all aspects of life is an important cultural consideration when working with children and families from Africa. The defining characteristics of collectivism are as follows: the self is defined as interdependent; personal and communal goals are closely aligned; cognitions that focus on group norms, obligations, and duties guide social behavior; and relationships are maintained even when they are disadvantageous (Triandis, 1995). These characteristics can be quite different from those of an individualistic orientation in which the self is defined as independent; personal and communal goals are not necessarily closely aligned; social behavior is guided by attitudes, personal needs, rights, and contracts; and decisions about maintaining relationships can be evaluated on the basis of advantages and disadvantages (Triandis, 1995). Of course, not everyone from Africa will hold a collectivist orientation, but it is a prevailing perspective. It is also important to understand that these concepts are not mutually exclusive; many African individuals demonstrate aspects of collectivism in some spheres of their lives, for example, family, while displaying more individualist aspects in other areas, for example, work. Such a worldview permeates the social context of the individual and shapes the nature of the relationships in which one is embedded. Community identity is the basis on which individual identity has meaning in the African culture (Kamya, 1997).

It has been generally assumed that African cultures are collectivist; however, most of the research on collectivism has focused on Eastern cultures (Eaton & Louw, 2000). Eaton and Louw (2000) conducted one of the first studies to explore collectivism in Africa. They found that the African sample in South Africa demonstrated significantly higher dimensions of collectivism than the non-African comparison sample and concluded that theories about self, derived from collectivism, are useful and applicable in an African context. Certainly more research is needed to explore collectivism in other areas of Africa.

One's worldview influences understanding of self, self in relationship, definitions of health and mental health, and the interventions needed to address illness or psychological distress. Therefore, it is essential for social workers and other professional helpers to become informed about these critical perspectives. In writing about counseling in South Africa, Maree and van der Westhuizen (2011) noted that most of the counseling that occurs is informed by a Western worldview and is thus culturally incongruent; they recommended that indigenous practices and an understanding of the social and political context be included in counseling. I would add that it is also essential to consider how a collectivist orientation influences the issues that clients present in order to work with them in a culturally informed way.

Traditional Religion. Traditional beliefs of religion and spirituality are an important aspect of an African's life. One's entire life from before birth to beyond death is conceptualized as a religious experience, "The whole of existence is a religious phenomenon. . . . Both that world and practically all his activities in it, are seen and experienced through a religious understanding and meaning" (Mbiti, 1990, p. 15). The individual cannot be separated from religion or the religious connection within one's community. Names of people have religious meaning, as do features of nature, such as boulders, hills, and forests. Failure to recognize this integration of religion in all aspects of the African worldview leads to misunderstandings about fundamental aspects of African life by those with differing worldviews (Mbiti, 1990). Traditional religion has remained important even after the introduction of Christianity and Islam in Africa. For example, in Uganda, approximately 85 percent of the population is identified as Christian; however, most still participate in traditional religious ceremonies. Research conducted in northern Uganda found that those who were practicing Catholics retained traditional spiritual practices (Odoki, 1997). As a result of Vatican Two (1962–1965), the Catholic Church supports the use of traditional practices when they do not conflict with Catholic doctrine (Odoki, 1997).

Religion and spirituality remain important influences in the lives of Africans after immigration to the United States (Kamya, 1997). Kamya (1997) has found significant positive correlations between spiritual well-being and hardiness, spiritual well-being and coping resources, and spiritual well-being and self-esteem among African immigrants. Such data indicate the role of religion and spiritually in strengthening one's functioning. Formal religious connections in the lives of African immigrants have been important for maintaining and enhancing collective interactions and collective identity (Hume & Hardwick, 2005). Religious connections also have been the major source of support to new arrivals and providing them with social, cultural, economic, and political networks (Hume & Hardwick, 2005). Traditional African culture and the religious community have provided for the holistic needs of families; the church is not just a place to worship. "To be blessed implies having children and food, and to be healthy, but in this case only if the whole community shares in it. . . . most of the indigenous churches are simultaneously welfare organizations" (Oosthuizen, 1991, p. 41).

For immigrants from Africa, faith-based organizations in the United States are providing a role that the religious communities would have offered in their countries of origin. Faith-based organizations are especially important in areas with larger numbers of new immigrants. These new immigrants often rely on trusted religious leaders for advice, information, and support in adjusting to their new environment (Ochs & Payés, 2003). In addition to the religious groups and organizations in the United States, there are also continental organizations (for example, the African Immigrants and Refugees Foundation), national organizations (for example, Ugandan associations), and ethnic-based organizations that provide information, offer legal services, and provide support to individuals in times of need (Takougang & Tidjani, 2009).

Cultural and Traditional Practices. The African worldview is an important aspect of understanding the role and function of traditional practices and ceremonies for Africans. Culture shapes individuals' understanding of emotional, social, spiritual, and physical well-being. Concepts of health and illness are similarly shaped by one's cultural orientation. This understanding must be taken into consideration in the development of the interventions to address problems and illnesses. Traditional practices address this cultural understanding of illness and integrate the physical, psychological, and spiritual needs of an individual. For example, one ceremony used for cleansing an individual after exposure to an impure situation in northern Uganda is called Stepping on the Egg. This ceremony cleanses the individual who has been exposed to an impurity, repairs the disrupted relationship with the community and the spiritual world, and guides the individual and the community members to support one another in the future. (See chapter 4 for a more detailed explanation of Stepping on the Egg.) Similar ceremonies have been documented as occurring in other areas of Africa (Denov, 2010; Honwana, 2006). Such ceremonies have been meaningful for many African individuals who have been affected by armed conflict; they offer a culturally based way of making meaning of the experiences and provide for acceptance back into the community (Corbin, 2008; Honwana, 2006). Traditional cultural beliefs continue to be strongly held by Africans even after they have immigrated to Western cultures (Mbiti, 1990). Awareness of and acceptance by U.S. social workers of the concepts and practices that are part of traditional rituals can facilitate the process of assessment and diagnosis, establishment of supportive working relationships, and the design of interventions in their practice with African immigrants.

Impact of Armed Conflict. African immigrants coming from contexts of armed conflict may have been directly involved in the conflict as combatants, may have lived in the areas affected by the conflict, may have been displaced by the conflict, or may have resided in areas indirectly affected. Those involved as combatants may have been drawn into that role on a continuum from volunteering to being forced into the armed conflict. Those involved in combat have witnessed torture, beatings, and violent killings; had to torture or kill others; have been forced to engage in sexual acts; have destroyed homes and property, and have stolen from civilians. They have also often been seriously beaten or injured. Rape of women, men, girls, and boys has been increasingly documented as a weapon used in war in Africa and elsewhere.

Those residing in areas in which the conflict is occurring often suffer injuries, wounds, and death. There is little protection from armies responsible for protecting citizens, so individuals try their best to protect themselves and their families. Those who are displaced and living in internally displaced persons' camps or refugee camps have minimal protection from the combat experience and are often more vulnerable to attacks (Achvarina & Reich, 2006). Those residing in areas of armed conflict or in displaced contexts also witness and experience many of the atrocities of those involved in combat.

Those indirectly affected by the armed conflict and living at a distance frequently have family and friends who remain in the conflict area. Those indirectly affected must also deal with the breakdown in the government's ability to protect its citizens and depleted economic, medical, and educational resources. Those affected by the armed conflict directly or indirectly experience serious physical, psychological, social, cultural, and spiritual effects. To better comprehend the impact of armed conflict on their African clients, social workers can take advantage of the many sources of information on all African countries through the Internet. Connecting with the national groups that often exist in their communities can also provide greater depth of knowledge. Asking clients initially about their experiences in armed conflict may provide limited information, as it often takes time and the establishment of a trusting relationship for difficult experiences to be revealed. However, efforts to understand more about the actual context from which clients come can help social workers pay attention to the range of issues clients may be dealing with; such efforts are critical to forming strong relationships with clients.

Conclusion

The recent increase in the number of African immigrants, refugees, and asylum seekers settling in the United States offers a tremendous opportunity for U.S. social workers to expand their awareness, knowledge, and skills related to working with this population. Complex reasons and conditions affect the decision to immigrate to the United States, such as the consequences of armed conflict, concern about family left behind, and uncertainty about the future. In addition, issues of race, class, gender, ethnicity, language, and so forth can compound the challenges of immigration. Most African immigrants are coming from countries that are experiencing or have recently experienced armed conflict; thus, it is important for social workers to become familiar with these events. Services and interventions can be better developed for this population when practitioners understand the reasons that immigrants, refugees, and asylum seekers leave their home countries and the experiences they have had along the way.

In addition, social workers must expand their knowledge of cultural worldviews, religious values, and cultural practices of clients coming from African cultures, to avoid language, social, and behavioral misinterpretations. Increased awareness of cultural orientation will also increase practitioners' abilities to provide culturally grounded assessments and interventions. Generation of this type of practice knowledge is sorely needed. The following chapters are designed to provide such information for social workers and helping professionals so they can offer appropriate and effective assistance to the growing population of African immigrants, refugees, and asylum seekers.

References

Achvarina, V., & Reich, S. (2006). No place to hide: Refugees, displaced persons and the recruitment of child soldiers [Electronic version]. *International Security, 31*(1), 127–164.

Collier, P. (2007). *The bottom billion: Why the poorest countries are failing and what can be done about it.* New York: Oxford University Press.

Corbin, J. N. (2008). Returning home: Resettlement of formerly abducted children in northern Uganda. *Disasters, 32,* 316–335. doi:10.1111/j.0361-3666.2008.01042.x

Denov, M. (2010). *Child soldiers: Sierra Leone's Revolutionary United Front.* New York: Cambridge University Press.

Eaton, L., & Louw, J. (2000). Culture and self in South Africa: Individualism–collectivism predictions. *Journal of Social Psychology, 140,* 210–217.

Fix, M. E., & Passel, J. S. (1994). Setting the record straight [Electronic version]. *Public Welfare, 52*(2), 6–16.

Gibson, C., & Lennon, E. (1999). *Tech paper 29: Table 1. Nativity of the population and place of birth of the native population: 1850–1990.* Retrieved from http://www.census.gov/population/www/documentation/twps0029/tab01.html

Honwana, A. (2006). *Child soldiers in Africa.* Philadelphia: University of Pennsylvania Press.

Human Security Center. (2005). *Human security report: War and peace in the 21stcentury.* Retrieved from http://www.humansecurityreport.info/HSR2005_PDF/Part1.pdf

Hume, S. E., & Hardwick, S. W. (2005). The African, Russian and Ukrainian refugee resettlement in Portland, Oregon [Electronic version]. *Geographical Review,95*(2), 189–209.

Jefferys, K. (2007). *Annual flow report: U.S. legal permanent residents, 2006*. Washington, DC: U.S. Department of Homeland Security, Office of Immigration Statistics. Retrieved from http://www.dhs.gov/xlibrary/assets/statistics/publications/IS-4496_LPRFlowReport_04vaccessible.pdf

Kamya, H. (1997). African immigrants in the United States: The challenge for research-and practice [Electronic version]. *Social Work, 42*, 154–166.

Larsen, L. J. (2004). *The foreign-born population in the United States: 2003* (Current Population Reports, P20-551). Retrieved from http://www.census.gov/prod/2004pubs/p20-551.pdf

Maree, J. G., & van der Westhuizen, C. N. (2011). Professional counseling in South Africa: A landscape under construction. *Journal of Counseling and Development, 89*, 105–111.

Mbiti, J. S. (1990). *African religions and philosophy* (2nd ed.). Portsmouth, NH: Heinemann Educational Books.

Morse, A. (2004). *A quick look at U.S. immigrants: Demographics, workforce, and asset building*. Retrieved from http://www.ncsl.org/programs/immig/immigstatistics0604.htm

Ochs, M., & Payés, M. (2003). Immigrant organizing: Patterns, challenges & opportunities. *Social Policy, 33*(4), 19–24.

Odoki, S. O. (1997). *Death rituals among the Lwos of Uganda: Their significance for the theology of death*. Gulu, Uganda: Gulu Catholic Press.

Office of Health and Human Services-MA. (2011). *Refugee arrivals in Massachusetts by country of origin, 2006–2010, 2001–2005, 1996–2000*. Retrieved from http://www.mass.gov/?pageID=eohhs2terminal&L=4&L0=Home&L1=Researcher&L2=Specific+Populations&L3=Refugees+and+Asylees+in+Massachusetts&sid=Eeohhs2&b=terminalcontent&f=dph_cdc_r_refugee_arrivals&csid=Eeohhs2

Office of Refugee Resettlement. (2000). *Fiscal year 2000 refugee arrivals: By country of origin and state of initial resettlement for FY 2000*. Retrieved from http://www.acf.hhs.gov/programs/orr/data/fy2000RA.htm

Office of Refugee Resettlement. (2001). *Fiscal year 2001 refugee arrivals: By country of origin and state of initial resettlement for FY 2001*. Retrieved from http://www.acf.hhs.gov/programs/orr/data/fy2001RA.htm

Office of Refugee Resettlement. (2002). *Fiscal year 2002 refugee arrivals: By country of origin and state of initial resettlement for FY 2002*. Retrieved from http://www.acf.hhs.gov/programs/orr/data/fy2002RA.htm

Office of Refugee Resettlement. (2003). *Fiscal year 2003 refugee arrivals: By country of origin and state of initial resettlement for FY 2003*. Retrieved from http://www.acf.hhs.gov/programs/orr/data/fy2003RA.htm

Office of Refugee Resettlement. (2004a). *Annual ORR reports to Congress-2004*. Retrieved from http://www.acf.hhs.gov/programs/orr/data/04arc7.htm#2

Office of Refugee Resettlement. (2004b). *Fiscal year 2004 refugee arrivals: By country of origin and state of initial resettlement for FY 2004*. Retrieved from http://www.acf.hhs.gov/programs/orr/data/fy2004RA.htm

Office of Refugee Resettlement. (2005). *Fiscal year 2005 refugee arrivals: By country of origin and state of initial resettlement for FY 2005*. Retrieved from http://www.acf.hhs.gov/programs/orr/data/fy2005RA.htm

Office of Refugee Resettlement. (2006). *Fiscal year 2006 refugee arrivals: By country of origin and state of initial resettlement for FY 2006*. Retrieved from http://www.acf.hhs.gov/programs/orr/data/fy2006RA.htm

Office of Refugee Resettlement. (2007). *Fiscal year 2007 refugee arrivals: By country of origin and state of initial resettlement for FY 2007*. Retrieved from http://www.acf.hhs.gov/programs/orr/data/fy2007RA.htm

Office of Refugee Resettlement. (2008). *Fiscal year 2008 refugee arrivals: By country of origin and state of initial resettlement for FY 2008*. Retrieved from http://www.acf.hhs.gov/programs/orr/data/fy2008RA.htm

Office of Refugee Resettlement. (2009). *Fiscal year 2009 refugee arrivals: By country of origin and state of initial resettlement for FY 2009*. Retrieved from http://www.acf.hhs.gov/programs/orr/data/fy2009RA.htm

Oosthuizen, G. C. (1991). The place of traditional religion in contemporary South Africa. In J. K. Olupona (Ed.), *African traditional religions: In contemporary society* (pp. 35–50). St. Paul, MN: Paragon House.

Ploughshares. (2006). *Defining armed conflict*. Retrieved from http://www.ploughshares.ca/libraries/ACRText/ACR-DefinitionArmedConflict.htm

Ploughshares. (2010). *Armed conflicts report 2010 summary*. Retrieved from http://www.ploughshares.ca/libraries/ACRText/Summary2010.pdf

Singer, A., & Wilson, J. H. (2007). *Refugee resettlement in metropolitan America*. Retrieved from http://www.migrationinformation.org/Feature/display.cfm?id=585

Takougang, J., & Tidjani, B. (2009). Settlement patterns and organizations among African immigrants in the United States. *Journal of Third World Studies, 26*(1), 31–40.

Triandis, H. C. (1995). *Individualism & collectivism: New directions in social psychology*. Boulder, CO: Westview Press.

UN Security Council. (2005). *Report of the secretary-general on the protection of civilians in armed conflict*. Retrieved from http://daccessdds.un.org/doc/UNDOC/GEN/N05/610/43/PDF/N0561043.pdf?OpenElement

Urban Institute. (2006). *Recent findings. Immigration studies: A program of the Urban Institute*. Retrieved from http://www.urban.org/toolkit/issues/immigration.cfm

U.S. Census Bureau. (2002). *March 2000 Current Population Survey. Table 1-1 Nativity, place of birth of the native population, and region of birth of the foreign-born population: 2002*. Retrieved from http://www.census.gov/population/www/socdemo/foreign/ppl-145.html

U.S. Census Bureau. (2003). *United States: General demographic characteristics: 2003*. Retrieved from http://factfinder.census.gov/servlet/ADPTable?_bm=y&-geo_id=01000US&-qr_name=ACS_2003_EST_G00_DP1&-ds_name=ACS_2003_EST_G00_&-_lang=en&-redoLog=false&-format

U.S. Department of Homeland Security. (2008). *Yearbook of immigration statistics: 2007: Refugees and asylees*. Retrieved from http://www.dhs.gov/files/statistics/publications/YrBk07RA.shtm

U.S. Department of Homeland Security. (2009a). *Yearbook of immigration statistics (2009). Table 3: Persons obtaining legal permanent resident status by region and county of birth: Fiscal years 2000–2009*. Retrieved from http://www.dhs.gov/files/statistics/publications/LPR09.shtm

U.S. Department of Homeland Security. (2009b). *Yearbook of immigration statistics (2009). Table 14: Refugee arrivals by region and country of nationality: Fiscal years 2000 to 2009*. Retrieved from http://www.dhs.gov/files/statistics/publications/YrBk09RA.shtm

U.S. Department of Homeland Security. (2009c). *Yearbook of immigration statistics (2009). Table 17: Individuals granted asylum affirmatively by region and county of nationality: Fiscal years 2000 to 2009*. Retrieved from http://www.dhs.gov/files/statistics/publications/YrBk09RA.shtm

U.S. Department of Homeland Security. (n.d.). *The triennial comprehensive report on immigration*. Retrieved from http://www.uscis.gov/files/article/tri3fullreport.pdf

Wilson, J. H. (2009, March 24). *Trends in U.S. immigration*. Paper presented at the American Society of Public Administrators National Conference on "Public Administration in the Midst of Diversity: Social Equity and Immigration," Miami, FL.

2

The Nature of Children's Participation in Armed Conflict

Jo Becker

I'd like you to imagine that you are 11 years old. You've been visiting your aunt and on your way back home, you reach a checkpoint. A police officer asks you for your identification card. You don't have one, because you're too young to get one. But he tells you that you've broken the law. He gives you a choice—you can go to jail for six years, or you can join the army. He locks you in a cell for several hours to give you time to decide. You don't want to go to jail, so finally you tell them that you will join the army.

The police officer takes you to an army training camp, and when he hands you over, you see that he gets a bunch of money and a big bag of rice. Later, you find out that these kinds of payments are common in exchange for child recruits.

You are given a uniform and gun that is as tall as your shoulder. During training exercises, you fall behind the others because you are so small. You are often beaten. At night, you cry because you miss your family. You're not allowed to contact them, and you worry that they don't know where you are.

When you are 12 years old, you are sent into combat for the first time. You are scared. Your commander orders you to open fire, but you're too afraid to look, and instead fire your weapon up at the sky. You are afraid that if you don't fire your gun your commander will punish you. You are sent into battle more than 20 times. Once, 15 of your fellow soldiers are killed. The next day, you are forced to go back to the battlefield and carry back the bodies. Some you cannot find, because they have been literally blown apart.

When you are 13 years old, your company captures a group of 15 women and children, including three babies. Your leader gets orders from headquarters to kill them all. You see your fellow soldiers line them up and gun them down. When you are 14 years old, you finally have a chance to run away, and you escape across the border. But you don't dare to go home, because you might be arrested for desertion. You have little education and no real job skills. Your life has been changed forever.

This is the story of a boy from Burma named Aung. I interviewed him in 2002 while conducting an investigation on child soldiers along the Thai–Burma border. I picked this example deliberately, because many people think of child soldiering as an African phenomenon. Many people are surprised when I tell them that the country with the largest number of child soldiers in the world is actually found in Asia. Tens of thousands of children have been recruited into Burma's national army, and most of them, like Aung, have been taken by force or coercion (Human Rights Watch [HRW], 2002).

The recruitment and use of children as soldiers is a global problem. It includes children as young as eight years of age who are recruited into paramilitary groups in Colombia (HRW, 2003b), young girls kidnapped by the Lord's Resistance Army (LRA) in central Africa for use as soldiers and sex slaves (HRW, 2003a), and children used to carry out suicide attacks in Afghanistan (United Nations, 2011).

In total, there are approximately 15 countries in the world today where children are being actively used in conflict (United Nations, 2011). Child soldiers include both boys and girls. They serve in government armies, opposition groups, and government-linked militias on nearly every continent (Coalition to Stop the Use of Child Soldiers, 2008; Singer, 2005; United Nations, 2011).

Why Children Are Recruited

Many people wonder why a military force wants an 11-year-old, or in some extreme cases, even an eight-year-old child. There are a number of factors that help explain why children are recruited as soldiers.

1. Children are immature, vulnerable, and easy to manipulate. In Burma, for example, recruiters often prey on young boys because they are more vulnerable to threats and coercion than adults and, therefore, make easier targets (HRW, 2002, 2007b). Aung, you may remember, was told that if he didn't join the army he would go to jail. An adult is less likely to believe these threats and is more likely to have access to bribe money to use in escaping recruitment. So recruiters target young boys to more easily meet their recruitment quotas.

Some commanders seek children because they believe children follow orders more readily, especially if they do not realize the consequences of what they are being asked to do. They are gullible. For example, in some conflicts, children have been told that if they smear a particular oil on their body or wear an amulet around their neck they will be protected from bullets. So they put on the oil or the amulet and run off into battle, thinking they will be protected. But, of course, they are not protected.

When recruited, young children may be more easily indoctrinated into the group. They haven't had a chance to develop a real sense of right and wrong and may be more willing to commit atrocities.

Children may be valued for tasks that they can do more easily than adults. In Sri Lanka's civil war, children, particularly girls, were used by the Tamil Tigers as suicide bombers because they were more likely to get through army checkpoints undetected (HRW, 2004b). Similarly, children are often used as informants or messengers because commanders believe they are less likely to arouse suspicion than adults.

2. Children are considered dispensable. Compared with adult soldiers, who may have more training and experience, children are often considered expendable. As a result, they are often favored for particularly dangerous duties. They may be used as cannon fodder and sent into battle ahead of adult troops. In the Democratic Republic of the Congo (DRC), HRW researchers documented cases in which children were deliberately pushed into battle armed only with sticks. They were ordered to beat the sticks against trees to make noise and draw fire, while more experienced, older troops mounted an offensive from another direction. It is not surprising that many of the children were slaughtered. In other cases, children have been pushed into minefields ahead of adult soldiers because if they step on a mine and lose a limb or their life, it is considered less costly to the force than losing an adult soldier.

3. Warfare has changed. Wars today are more likely within countries than between them. The division between combatants and civilians is no longer clear, and combat zones are no longer well defined. In these situations, children are more likely to be drawn into conflict, both as victims and as perpetrators. Weapons technology has also changed. Automatic weapons with enormous firepower are easy for even a child to use, and thanks to the widespread proliferation of small arms, often cheap and readily available. For example, one girl who was recruited into the guerilla group in Colombia at 13 years of age said that she had used pistols, AK-47s, Galils, M-16s, R-15s, Uzi submachine guns, Ingrams, and a .357 Magnum. Another former child soldier from Colombia told HRW that he was only seven when he began handling an AK-47 (HRW, 2003b).

How Children Are Recruited

There are a wide range of practices and factors that explain how children become child soldiers. Some children, like Aung, are recruited by force or coercion. Others—their lives devastated by poverty or war—join armed groups out of desperation. As society breaks down during conflict, children are left with no access to school and are often driven from their homes or separated from their families. Many perceive armed groups as their best chance for survival—or simply a guarantee of at least one meal per day.

Some children join because they want to be part of a cause and believe they are fighting for their people. Some want revenge because of atrocities perpetrated against their families or communities. And some are motivated by the status or lure of a uniform, a gun, or financial incentives.

In northern Uganda, the LRA, a rebel group, waged war against the Ugandan government for 20 years. The group's leader claimed that he wanted to overthrow the government and reestablish it on the basis of the Ten Commandments. In reality, the group terrorized the civilian population and committed some of the worst atrocities imaginable. Lacking any popular support, the group literally kidnapped children to fill its ranks, taking children from their homes, schools, and displaced persons' camps. Some sources believe that 85 percent to 90 percent of the LRA's soldiers were abducted as children. The LRA used brutal tactics to demand obedience, forcing children to commit atrocities, to sever their ties with their home communities, and to kill others who disobeyed orders or tried to run away. Over a 20-year period, more than 30,000 children were abducted by the LRA. In 2003, recruitment was so widespread that thousands of parents sent their children to walk long distances each night to sleep in a more secure village or town rather than risk abduction during the LRA's nighttime raids. These children were locally known as "night commuters" (HRW, 2003a).

One poignant example about the prevalence of child recruitment in northern Uganda came from a study on war-affected children, which asked school children if they had ever been abducted. Among those that hadn't, instead of saying, "No," they said, "Not yet."

In some cases, abuses by government forces motivate children to join opposition armies. In Sri Lanka, a rebel force called the Liberation Tigers of Tamil Eelam (or Tamil Tigers) fought the government for about 25 years, seeking an independent state for the minority Tamil population. Many Tamil children witnessed human rights abuses by government forces against their own family members and joined the Tamil Tigers because they felt that it was their duty to protect their community.

In 2004, I interviewed a boy who joined the Tamil Tigers when he was 16. He told me that he joined because the army had burned his house and raped women in his neighborhood. "They tortured us," he said. But as we talked, it became clear that the events he described had taken place years before, when he was only two or three years old. Although he may not have remembered the events directly or understood their meaning at the time, they had become part of his family's narrative and heavily influenced his decision to join the Tamil Tigers a dozen years later.

Children are also recruited through indoctrination. When I was in Nepal in 2006, Maoist rebels and the government had been engaged in a 10-year civil war. Children told me that the Maoists often came to their schools to present cultural programs that included singing, dancing, and speeches. In the speeches, Maoists would tell the children that they were fighting for the people, fighting against corruption, and that everyone needed to support them. One 16-year-old boy told me that the Maoists started coming to his school when he was 13, in grade 6, and came nearly every day for three years. By the time he was in grade 9, he said that out of his 50 classmates, 45 had already joined the Maoists. He told me, "I decided to join too. I was very impressed with their speeches and very influenced by what they said about fighting for the people" (HRW, 2007a).

In Colombia, financial incentives influence many children to join armed groups. Paramilitary groups pay child recruits a monthly wage of $700, with bonuses for special missions. Most of the former paramilitary children HRW interviewed said that they joined primarily for the money. Many joined with friends or already had contacts within the group. Leonel, a boy who joined when he was 14, told us, "After school, I was a baker's assistant. It was hard work and paid badly. Then I went to work on a farm, but the work was hard too, so finally I joined the paramilitary. I had friends inside. It paid $100 a month. It seemed like an easier life" (HRW, 2003b).

These examples are illustrative, because in nearly every country, multiple factors influence child recruitment and often interact and overlap. Typically, the children most vulnerable to child recruitment are those who are poor, are displaced from their homes, are separated from their families, have experienced abusive homes, and are not attending school. In fact, the same factors that make children vulnerable to exploitation for child labor during peacetime make them vulnerable to military recruitment during wartime.

Reality of Child Soldiering

Leonel, the boy from Colombia who thought joining the paramilitary would lead to an easier life, soon found out that child soldiering was not so easy. Military training is often very difficult, with long hours of physical training, weapons instruction, and sometimes inadequate food and rest. Small and young children often find it difficult to keep up during exercises.

A girl in Sri Lanka told me, "The training was very difficult. They don't care if it's rainy or sunny. If you get too tired and can't continue, they will beat you. Once when I first joined, I was dizzy. I couldn't continue and asked for a rest. They said, 'We're the Tigers. You can't take a rest.' Then they beat me."

Children find out quickly that once they join, they cannot simply change their minds and leave. In most armies and armed groups, punishment for running away is brutal. In Burma, former child soldiers reported that boys who were captured while trying to escape from the government army were brought back to camp and forced to lie face down on the ground in front of their entire training company. Then, each member of the company—usually 250—was forced to line up and hit the victim one time each with a stick. Those that didn't hit hard enough were hit themselves. We heard of several instances in which children died after these punishments (HRW, 2002).

In Colombia, children who try to escape the Fuerzas Armadas Revolucionarias de Columbia may be executed, especially if they run away with a weapon. Children reported that those who were caught faced a "war council," in which all members of the company participated in a trial of one of the members. A decision was made by a show of hands whether the child should be executed or receive a lesser sentence. Other offenses that could result in death include being caught asleep while on guard duty, surrendering or losing a weapon, being an informer, and drug or alcohol abuse. In some cases, children who tried to come to the defense of the accused were then selected to pull the trigger (HRW, 2003b).

A child soldier's duties may vary considerably. Not every child soldier is a combatant. Some are sentries or guards, messengers, or spies. Some are used to carry supplies during troop movements or to help cook meals. Some are trained as medics or even for administrative posts. Most serve in multiple roles. Some begin as cooks or porters but are quickly given weapons and expected to fight.

In combat, children are exposed to all of the dangers of any other soldier and are put at even greater risk because their smaller size means that injuries are often more life threatening. No one knows how many child soldiers have died in war. During the 1990s, an assessment of Tamil Tiger soldiers killed in battle found that between 40 percent and 60 percent of the dead fighters were children under the age of 18 years. Many child soldiers who survive have witnessed the maiming or death of their fellow soldiers and have themselves been forced to kill. In some cases, children are forced to commit atrocities against members of their own family or community.

For girls, the burdens may be even greater than for boy soldiers. The stereotypical image of a child soldier is an African boy with an AK-47, but a significant number of child soldiers are girls. One study of conflicts between 1990 and 2003 found that girls were involved in armed conflict in 38 different countries and were active fighters in 34 of them (McKay & Mazurana, 2004).

In countries like Sierra Leone, Uganda, Colombia, Sri Lanka, and others, girls made up 30 percent to 40 percent of fighting forces.

Girls serve in all of the same capacities as boys and, in most countries, that includes bearing arms and fighting in combat. But many girls are also sexually exploited. In northern Uganda, girls abducted by the LRA were commonly forced to become "wives" to LRA commanders and were subjected to repeated rapes, exposure to sexually transmitted diseases, and unwanted pregnancies. According to some estimates, more than 3,000 babies have been born to girls who have been sexually enslaved by the LRA (Apio, 2007).

In Sierra Leone, where an estimated 12,000 child soldiers during the civil war were girls, one study found that all of the girls who said their primary role was a "fighter" were also forced to be wives. For example, a girl named Miata was captured by the Revolutionary United Front when she was 12. She was selected by one of the lower ranking commanders to be his captive "wife" and soon became pregnant. Even while she was pregnant, she was still required to fight; she went into battle up until her seventh month of pregnancy (McKay & Mazurana, 2004).

Children stop being child soldiers in a number of ways. Some who were forcibly recruited or find that being a soldier wasn't what they expected try to escape. They may be able to return home or surrender to the opposition. In northern Uganda, where abducted children were tightly controlled, children often waited for the confusion of battle and ran away while their commanders were distracted during fighting.

Other children may be arrested or captured during battle. Sometimes these children are immediately released or turned over to a rehabilitation program, but other times it begins another chapter of suffering. In Nepal in April 2006, I met a boy who joined the Maoist rebels when he was 15. He was only with the rebels for four months when he was captured by government security forces. He then spent more than a year in detention. The first three months he was blindfolded, handcuffed, interrogated, and beaten almost daily. For him, the experience of government detention was probably far more traumatic than his experience as a child soldier.

Children also leave armed forces when conflict comes to an end and a peace agreement is negotiated. During the last few years, tens of thousands of child soldiers have been demobilized as conflicts have ended in Sierra Leone, Liberia, and Angola.

Impact of Child Soldiering

The impact of being a child soldier can be profound. Child soldiers have often been separated from their families for long periods of time and lack the family- and community-based socialization that most children receive (Wessells, 2006). Their education has been interrupted, and they face great challenges getting back into school. In some countries, school fees place an education out of the financial reach for a child soldier. A 16-year-old who hasn't been to class for years is understandably reluctant to sit in a classroom with a bunch of eight-year-olds. Special education programs are often needed.

Without civilian job skills or an education, many child soldiers wonder how they can support themselves. This worry is compounded for girl soldiers who may return from armed groups with babies and young children. In Uganda, I met a young woman named Christine. She had been forced to become a wife to an LRA commander and, when she was released in 2002, had two young children fathered by the LRA commander. I spoke to her in a rehabilitation center, and she told me, "I'm not happy at all because they ruined me. I had to cut short my studies. I have no hope that I will one day be somebody. I gave birth to two children and was not prepared. I have two children and no means of survival. I worry about what will happen next."

Children also suffer emotionally and psychologically from their experiences. Counselors working with former child soldiers report that they "can't sleep at night. They have eating problems, anxiety, and fear about the future and about themselves." Many children may have recurrent nightmares about their experiences.

Rehabilitation and reintegration programs are sorely needed for these children. They need assistance locating their families, getting medical care, getting back into school or vocational training programs, finding a place to live, and being reaccepted in their home community. They need adults who will be their advocates. I asked one boy in Nepal who had been with the Maoists what was the most important thing that former child soldiers needed. He said, "we need to be provided with education and skills training and receive the protection of older people."

But too many children never have the chance to get this assistance. There are some excellent rehabilitation programs in Uganda, Colombia, Sierra Leone, and other countries, run by the United Nations Children's Fund and nongovernmental organizations (NGOs) like World Vision, Save the Children, International Rescue Committee, and Christian Children's Fund. But the majority of child soldiers do not get the help they need. Girls, for example, are often excluded from demobilization programs. In Sierra Leone, hundreds of girls were left out of the demobilization program and remained with their rebel captors. In the DRC, thousands of girls participated with various armed groups, but one demobilization program for 1,000 children included only nine girls. Girls may be overlooked because they may not serve in the most visible fighting roles, or they may be reluctant to seek help because of the stigma of being associated with fighting groups and the sexual exploitation that often accompanies them (McKay & Mazurana, 2004; Wessells, 2006).

Another problem is that the assistance is often too limited. But a failure to invest in rehabilitation and reintegration results in far greater costs to society later, as former child soldiers resort to crime or joining other armed groups. For example, in Liberia, where there has been recurrent conflict, a child soldier who fought in the 1990s went through an initial rehabilitation program, but he told us, "I received some assistance, but it soon ran out. For a while, I did some small jobs around Monrovia, but there was not much to do and I couldn't afford to go back to school. So two years ago, I decided to join the LURD [Liberians United for Reconciliation and Democracy], a rebel group in Liberia. I figured it was better to fight and try to get something, than hang around town doing nothing" (HRW, 2004a).

A stereotype we have to fight when it comes to child soldiering is that child soldiers are a lost generation and their experiences have left them so scarred that it is never possible for them to fully reintegrate into society. I wish people who believed this could meet my friend Ishmael Beah, who was recruited into the Sierra Leonean army when he was a child but later entered a rehabilitation program run by Save the Children. Later he was able to come to the United States. He graduated from Oberlin College a few years ago and sold his memoirs to a major publisher. His book, *A Long Way Gone: Memoirs of a Boy Soldier*, was on the New York Times bestseller list for over six months (Beah, 2007). He is now planning to go to law school and says that his experiences as a child soldier motivate him to want to return to Sierra Leone and help build a better, peaceful society.

No one knows how many former child soldiers are now in the United States or other Western countries as refugees, asylum seekers, or migrants. It is an elusive population, and many children do not reveal their history as soldiers for fear of jeopardizing their status. For example, a study in Germany found that 300 to 500 former child soldiers were living in the country as so-called separated children but that they were not eligible for asylum, as the law did not recognize the recruitment and use of child soldiers as persecution (Ludwig, 2004). Similarly, in the United States, child recruitment is not recognized as persecution under refugee law, and some of the groups that recruit children have been designated as terrorist organizations by the U.S. government, creating additional barriers for their claims.

Legal and Policy Initiatives

Since the late 1990s, there have been extraordinary efforts to establish new international laws, policies, and practices to prevent the recruitment of child soldiers and to aid their demobilization, rehabilitation, and reintegration.

International Law—In 1998 a network of NGOs came together to form the Coalition to Stop the Use of Child Soldiers (now known as Child Soldiers International). In part because of the coalition's campaigning, the UN adopted an international treaty in 2000 that prohibits the forced recruitment of children before the age of 18, or the use of children in combat. By early 2012, 143 countries had ratified the treaty, including the United States. One result is that it is now U.S. Defense Department policy not to deploy 17-year-old soldiers into combat situations.

As part of international labor law, the International Labor Organization (ILO) adopted a child labor convention in 1999 (ILO Convention 182 on the Worst Forms of Child Labor) that identified the forced recruitment of children for use in armed conflict as one of the worst forms of child labor. More than 170 governments have ratified the treaty and agreed to take immediate measures to address the problem. Both these treaties also oblige governments to provide rehabilitation and reintegration assistance to former child soldiers.

Criminal Law—The recruitment and use of child soldiers is also prohibited under international criminal law. In 1998, the Rome Statute was adopted to create an International Criminal Court, based in the Hague, to prosecute individuals for genocide, war crimes, and crimes against humanity. Because of lobbying by NGOs, the treaty defined the recruitment and use of children under the age of 15 as a war crime. The first person to be prosecuted before the Court, Thomas Lubanga Dyilo from the Democratic Republic of Congo, was charged with the war crime of recruiting and using child soldiers. Former Liberian president Charles Taylor has also been tried before the Special Court for Sierra Leone on charges of recruiting child soldiers. As recruiters are arrested and convicted and these cases become known, they will become a deterrent to others.

UN Security Council—The UN Security Council is also giving increasing attention to this issue and has requested several reports from the UN secretary-general that identify specifically which governments and armed groups are using child soldiers in violation of international law. The council has said that it will consider sanctions—including travel bans and arms embargoes—against groups on this list that do not stop their recruitment of child soldiers. The UN established a special mechanism to more closely monitor child recruitment and other war-related abuses in conflict countries, and the Security Council has formed a working group on children and armed conflict to consider countries in which child soldiers are being used on a case-by-case basis and recommend appropriate action to the council.

Disarmament, Demobilization, and Reintegration Programs—Growing attention to the child soldiers issue has also translated into growing numbers of programs to demobilize, rehabilitate, and reintegrate former child soldiers. Tens of thousands of children have been demobilized from armed forces and groups in countries including Afghanistan, Angola, Burundi, the Democratic Republic of Congo, Liberia, Sierra Leone and others.

These steps are very encouraging and reflect a new global commitment to end the use of child soldiers. But the process remains slow; it is taking time for these strategies to make an impact on the ground. The unfortunate reality is that tens of thousands of children continue to serve in government armies and armed groups.

This situation is not inevitable. We can change it. If governments, the UN, and local communities muster the will, we can make it clear that children have no place in war and that child recruitment cannot be tolerated. If we recognize the humanity, the rights, and the potential of former child soldiers, we will also be willing to make the investment needed to help them reenter civilian society, build new lives, and contribute positively to their communities.

References

Apio, E. (2007). Uganda's forgotten children of war. In C. Carpenter (Ed.), *Born of war: Protecting children of sexual violence survivors in conflict zones* (pp. 94–109). Bloomfield, CT: Kumarian Press.

Beah, I. (2007). *A long way gone: Memoirs of a boy soldier.* New York: Sarah Crichton Books.

Coalition to Stop the Use of Child Soldiers. (2008). *Child soldiers global report.* London: Author.

Human Rights Watch. (2002). *My gun was as tall as me: Child soldiers in Burma.* New York: Author.

Human Rights Watch. (2003a). *Stolen children: Abduction and recruitment in northern Uganda.* New York: Author.

Human Rights Watch. (2003b). *You'll learn not to cry: Child combatants in Columbia.* New York: Author.

Human Rights Watch. (2004a). *How to fight, how to kill: Child soldiers in Liberia.* New York: Author.

Human Rights Watch. (2004b). *Living in fear: Child soldiers and the Tamil Tigers in Sri Lanka.* New York: Author.

Human Rights Watch. (2007a). *Children in the ranks: The Maoists' use of child soldiers in Nepal.* New York: Author.

Human Rights Watch. (2007b). *Sold to be soldiers: The recruitment and use of child soldiers in Burma.* New York: Author.

Ludwig, M. (2004). *Former child soldiers as refugees in Germany.* Geneva: Quaker United Nations Office and Terre des Hommes Germany.

McKay, S., & Mazurana, D. (2004). *Child soldiers: Where are the girls?* Montreal: International Centre for Human Rights and Democratic Development.

Singer, P. W. (2005). *Children at war.* New York: Pantheon Books.

United Nations. (2011, April 23). *Report of the secretary-general to the UN Security Council on Children and Armed Conflict* (UN Doc. A/65/820-S/2011/250). New York: Author.

Wessells, M. (2006). *Child soldiers: From violence to protection.* Cambridge, MA: Harvard University Press.

3

Experiences of Refugee and Asylee Families Affected by Extreme Violence: *A Personal Narrative*

Eugenie Mukeshimana

In developing this chapter, I focused on what was important for helping professionals in the United States to understand about children and families coming from situations of armed conflict. Traditionally, helping professionals are trained to deal with crises in U.S. families such as homelessness, domestic violence, and mental and physical developmental disabilities. However, a rise in refugee and asylee populations in the United States, some fleeing persecution in their home countries, has intensified the need for professionals who are knowledgeable about the cultural practices of these groups.

My experiences as an immigrant asylee from Rwanda as well as my work with nongovernmental organizations in Rwanda in the aftermath of the genocide there serve as a foundation for this chapter; I also draw on narratives from others with similar backgrounds who candidly shared their experiences, some of which I have incorporated here. In addition, I worked in programs that provided services to refugees returning to Rwanda after months in refugee camps. Through my conversations with these refugees, I was able to gain insight into life in the camps and the hardships it presented to families, especially mothers and children. Further, as a BSW student and later as a professional in the United States, I worked with displaced U.S. families living in shelters and children caught in custody battles. These experiences challenged me because of cultural and language barriers, but they also provided me with an insight into the U.S. social welfare system. Finally, as an independent language interpreter for a global language services provider, each day I take calls from helping professionals who are providing services to refugees both in the United Kingdom and the United States. The majority of calls are related to medical and social services; the rest concern car insurance, utilities, immigration status, and legal services. This position gives me opportunities to observe the helping process between professional helpers and refugees seeking services from them; I also am able to gain knowledge of the policies and practice guidelines referenced in this process. Because I work with a nationwide clientele, I also have an overview of common problems at a national level. Thus, I have a broad perspective, both personally and professionally, on the problems that refugees and asylees confront in their transitions to a new country.

Experiences of Asylees and Refugees from Armed Conflict

Professional helpers cannot easily understand the full impact of the violence inflicted on refugees, and the disruptions and losses they endured along the way, without a fair understanding of who they were before they became refugees and asylees. Unlike those who immigrate voluntarily for educational and employment opportunities, refugees and asylum seekers are driven out of their homes for humanitarian and security reasons. As many countries continue to be ravaged by long-term wars, the number of people displaced from violent conflict zones is soaring (United Nations High Commissioner for Refugees, 2010). After many years in refugee camps, and with no sign of peace in their country of origin, refugees are relocated to any country willing to protect them from further harm. Because few countries open their borders to refugees, refugees in camps do not have many choices to consider for resettlement. Here, I will address the obstacles faced by refugees and asylee population during the first few years of their resettlement in the United States. In addition, I will discuss the practice challenges for professional helpers working with these groups during this critical period of adjustment and assimilation into the new culture.

Life in Rwanda before and after Genocide

This section presents my own experience in Rwanda and my decision to immigrate to the United States. I share my personal odyssey to bring to life the varied struggles and concerns confronted by refugees and asylees as they move from one society to another, often after living through extreme violence and loss. I was born in Rwanda, a country now famously known for the 1994 Rwandan genocide against Tutsis. I had a very good childhood, with many friends and plenty of time to play. As children, we were never bored and made our own toys, including marbles from clay and soccer balls from banana leaves and old plastic bags. We harvested wires from broken umbrellas and cut up old flip-flops to make toy cars. As a child, I felt loved and protected by my family and my neighbors. Every home was my home, and everyone in the community helped to raise me and the other children. Occasionally, I found it difficult that anyone older than I had the right to "correct" me if I was not meeting acceptable cultural standards. It happened often that reports of my misbehavior got home before I did, thanks to the large network of neighborhood mothers and other watchful eyes and ears. As a child, corporal punishment was normal. Shaming someone was another form of punishment. Some children preferred corporal to shaming punishment. My mother's success as a parent was based on how well her children behaved in the community. Any failure, on my part, to conform to community rules downgraded her in the eyes of others in the community and negatively affected the image of my whole family. She reminded me of this regularly.

My mother was a smart, self-confident woman who was well respected in our community. She demanded perfection of me and wished me to be a copy of herself. Never mind that I had a mind of my own, which kept me getting into minor troubles such as breaking gender code by playing soccer with boys. To some extent, all children were expected to run into some trouble for breaking the community behavior code; it was a normal part of growing up. Everyone in the community tried to teach you what was expected of you at every age level so that you always understood right from wrong; thus, any mistake was taken as a deliberate act to break the behavior code and, therefore, was punishable. In the West, the culture of individualism is the foundation on which individual rights, prosperity, and success are based, whereas people in my community put community needs above individual needs and pooled resources when necessary. They shared risks and success and supported one another during good and bad times. Overall, this system offered protection to children and allowed parents to perform their daily activities without worries or need to tend to their children all the time.

Community life also had a great impact on my views about freedom. Although the personal was collective, the trade-off was worth it. I did enjoy an abundance of love and caring from community members. I also greatly benefited from the freedom to explore my environment and safely feed my curiosity. Yes, my kind of freedom had limitations, but I was nevertheless free as long as I remained within the parameters of the community code of conduct.

Our daily routines hardly ever changed. The only relevant concept of time was daylight and nightfall. Because we did not have electricity, daily activities had to be finished before dark; however, there was no pressure to meet deadlines. Life was simple, there was no need to use a calendar, no events to confirm, no bills to pay, no monthly statements, no meetings to attend, no prescription to fill, and so forth. The time clock was based on the school day schedule. Most people did not have watches or wall clocks; a few had access to shortwave radio and could keep track of time from radio announcements.

My community offered a mentorship teaching style, which worked well considering the absence of written materials and limited access to any other teaching/learning methods. We learned from doing rather than from reading instructions. We also learned from watching others do what we wanted to learn how to do. Once at school, many children struggled with basic mathematical concepts because the European educational approach used by our teachers seemed abstract to us. Without pictures of objects to refer to, it became harder for students to understand simple arithmetic concepts. The absence of qualified teachers further derailed the learning process and led to an emphasis on memorization rather than critical thinking. As a result, adults rarely challenged any decision or statement made by a person of authority, such as a teacher, a government official, or a supervisor at work.

The community lifestyle made poverty more visible but at the same time protected poor families from discrimination and other unfair treatment by others. As a child, I was taught that poverty is not necessarily caused by laziness or people's inability to think right. My father, who was an educator, told me that poverty was caused by a lack of access to both intellectual and material resources. The main cause of poverty in my community was land scarcity and lack of alternative opportunities to earn income. What struck me most was how much the community was committed to maintaining dignity of people who had less than everybody else; those who offended the dignity of a poor person were sanctioned. The community held strict views that poverty was not a choice. The act of helping had to be well thought out to accommodate the feelings of the recipient.

Above all, the community was like a large family with many hands ready to help out in time of need. These hands carried the sick to the hospital, cultivated the field for weak and old members, celebrated a newborn baby, and got together to name the newest member of the community. These hands also helped neighbors build a home. Regrettably, these same hands later on brutally hacked neighbors with machetes and destroyed the same property they had helped to build.

Experiencing Genocide

My childhood was spared of disruptions and tragic events. It was not until after my 22nd birthday that my life changed. I was eight months pregnant with my first child when the genocide started in Rwanda in 1994. I was an ordinary citizen, living in a modest neighborhood in the city of Kigali. Many believed that only rich people and politicians were considered to be at risk if a conflict broke out, and I was neither.

The genocide targeted Tutsi families. The Hutu neighbors who had been living in the community like the one in which I grew up turned against their Tutsi neighbors and brutally killed them. For three months, extremist Hutus spent every day hunting down Tutsis to kill; women became the target for mass rapes. The perpetrators mentally and physically tortured them before killing them. Some were made to watch their daughters and infants gang-raped before the pack of rapists turned to them; they were raped in front of their own children and the entire community. Those not killed were left permanently emotionally stained by these experiences. Some of the women who survived also contracted sexually transmitted diseases (STDs), including HIV; others became pregnant and are now raising children from these rapes.

It is hard to describe the experiences of the genocide and how survivors felt after they realized they had survived. How can one explain what it feels like to spend three months without taking a shower or washing your clothes? Our main concern was not comfort but staying alive. If I attempted to take a shower, I could be discovered by family members who did not know that I was hiding in the house; in fact, children were often used as spies by Hutu neighbors and militiamen to inform about activities inside their homes.

The decision to eat depended on the likelihood of being able to safely use the restroom afterwards. I could only eat after the children went to play with the neighbors' children. Sometimes they refused to go. Other times, they went and came right back, and we (the adults and I) had to abort the feeding operation and I had to return to my hiding place underneath the bed, concealed by bags and household supplies. I was also sleep deprived for the duration of the genocide. Although nightfall usually provided relief to survivors hiding outside because the killers were asleep, I couldn't sleep because I was hiding inside, underneath the children's bed. For fear that I might sneeze, cough, or snore, I simply stayed awake. My body got used to this after a few nights. The most difficult part of all was that I could not talk to anybody. I hid alone, which made time extra long. The darkness underneath the bed made it very difficult to keep track of time, except when the children came to bed or got up in the morning.

A month into the genocide, I was discovered at the first house and taken to a different home, where I delivered my daughter by myself while still hiding from the militiamen who patrolled the neighborhood day and night. I had no clothes for her because I had fled the house with nothing. On my due date, I had planned to go to the hospital and certainly never anticipated that I would find myself forced to deliver my daughter alone without the support of my community; I also did not have the option to seek medical attention should there be complications with labor. I was very lucky that we both survived.

It was three months before the Rwanda Patriotic Front put an end to the genocide and rescued those few who had survived until then. After the genocide, I learned that my child's father, hiding in a separate house, did not survive. My neighbors had killed my father and other Tutsi neighbors. Those involved in his death were former elementary school classmates and childhood playmates. I also learned that my sister, my aunt, and my uncle had been killed. None of my mother's siblings survived. The loss was unimaginable. I became numb to the numbers of people my family had lost. At the same time, I had to raise a child alone. There was no community to help me out, no friends or neighbors to watch her for me. The community was no longer trustworthy. Love was a thing of the past. Fear had taken over everything; grief became the only true neighbor. Everything else seemed superficial.

After the Genocide

As survivors, our immediate concern after the genocide was to find our families, the ones who had survived and those who had perished. For a few years after the genocide, we spent most weekends finding and burying the remains of loved ones. Due to limited resources, I had to take my daughter with me to attend burial ceremonies for relatives whose bodies had been recovered from the marshes or pulled out of mass graves. Her very first childhood memories are about burial events. Like many other children in Rwanda, she has seen too much at such a young age. Survivors and their helping professionals still do not know the long-term impact of exposure to this level of violence on children and adults alike.

In an attempt to recreate a community and to make up for lost families and friends, a few friends of mine and I created an artificial family. Conversation with family members always led to the genocide and to remembering those who have died. Sometimes, we just needed to socialize without the pressure to talk about the genocide. We managed to move into the same neighborhood, which allowed us to spend more time together. We shared at least five meals a week. We spent most of our time joking and mutually supporting each other as much as we could. This small informal group significantly provided a safe place for us to talk about our loved ones lost to the genocide in a different way than we could with family. We made fun of some of them, made up ridiculous stories about what might have happened to relatives for whom the circumstances of their final moments were still unknown to us. This was the only way we could keep them alive and talk about them without shedding tears. We did cry, not from sadness though. We cried because we were laughing harder and harder as the stories got crazier and crazier. We also kept an eye on each other to prevent any of us from falling into loneliness.

We knew from our experience that loneliness and isolation could easily trigger a trauma crisis and that it would be much harder for the victim to regain the same level of energy, mental focus, and adequate productivity levels at work. Trauma triggers were everywhere around us on a daily basis. A little girl in a blue school uniform immediately reminds you of your little sister, cousin, niece, or simply a childhood friend, the same way the sight of an aging parent reminds you of your own parents or grandparents. A sound of a whistle, a song on the radio, a particular banging sound, the sight of a machete, all could plug you right back into the genocide moments. For us, the memories of the past were part of our present and future. We were very much aware that to survive, we all had to find a harmonious balance between the "before" and the "after" life. You could not think too far back in the past or too far ahead in the future. Traditionally, people invested in their own families the same way in which people in the West save for retirement and invest in the stock market. The larger the family, the better off economically everyone was, the greater the chances that more children would access higher education, and the fewer years aging parents would have to work before they retired. In a frightening way, losing your family was comparable to how the loss of one's retirement and social security would be for a Westerner. It was therefore important for us to forge a new family, not for economic reasons but to provide the mutual emotional support we needed to cope with the many losses of our family members. Without this social support system, it would have been impossible for most of us to rebuild our lives and move forward.

Leaving Rwanda

Despite such support, living in Rwanda became increasingly difficult. The cost of living went up while jobs became scarce due to the end of emergency relief programs. Aid agencies flooded the country after the genocide and created jobs for those able to work. They fueled the economy with U.S. dollars, thus rents skyrocketed and remained high after these organizations closed their offices. As jobs disappeared, so did our hopes. For a few years, we had not really thought hard about our future. We had taken comfort in aggressive government security policies. Those who had committed the genocide were being put behind bars. Emotionally, though, survivors were still struggling to come to terms with what had happened to them. Attending so many funeral ceremonies took a toll on most of us. We grew angrier as some began to testify about what had happened to them. Those raped and infected with HIV began to die. It became apparent to most of us that our pain was not over yet. The tragic deaths of survivors triggered trauma. The absence of qualified trauma counselors made it impossible for survivors to access treatment.

I finally got a chance to leave the country to attend a four-year college in the United States. Although the application process was long and difficult, I did everything required of me to meet the student visa requirements and submitted my application to the American Embassy in Kigali. To my surprise, my visa was denied. Apparently, my status as a "genocide survivor" led the Immigration and Naturalization Service officer at the American Embassy to deny me a visa because I had insufficient ties to return back home after graduation. There was no other option available to me at the embassy, so I had to wait until that officer's time in Rwanda was up to submit a visa application for the second time. The new officer granted our visas.

Securing the visa brought a whole new reality. I knew that it would be a minimum of four to five years until we would be able to return to Rwanda because my student visa did not allow me to work, and the cost of airplane tickets was prohibitive; I could not face my aging mother with this reality, so I said that I would return to visit after one year. Even that brought tears to her eyes. These were not just the tears of "I'll miss you both," it was the realization that she was also losing the emotional and financial support she had counted on her daughter to provide. From now on, she would not have anyone to call if she got sick or needed something she was not comfortable asking of my brothers. Girls have always been the caregivers in my culture; it was almost incomprehensible for her to picture her life after I was gone. Worse, my daughter who was almost eight years old was coming with me. It was customary that children of this age spend time with their grandparents to keep them company and help out with minor chores. This arrangement was also meant to initiate girls to gender roles such as housework. Most of the stories that grandparents shared were related to their own childhood and always had a moral lesson embedded in them. In an oral tradition like mine, this is crucial for nurturing your identity as a member of a family; this is how traditions were transmitted from one generation to another. Having lost so many relatives, friends, and neighbors to the genocide, any further loss, someone close to her, even for a few months, was especially painful for my mother to handle. It was a double blow to her fragile emotional state.

Fortunately, as sad as I was about leaving my friends and family behind, I was also excited about meeting my new host family. We had exchanged e-mails and had spoken on the phone a few times. They had rallied the Albany, New York, community behind their efforts to get me through college; the local paper had even written a long story about the struggle to get me the visa. The entire community was waiting for our arrival. My daughter and I were to arrive a day before New Year's Eve, December 30, 2001. As I prepared for my departure, I went shopping for the warmest coat I could find in Kigali. The weather in Rwanda never gets cold to the point where you would need a winter coat. There was no store to buy winter clothing, so I went to the largest secondhand market in the city. I told the market workers that I was looking for super warm jackets. In no time, they found me an overcoat and an oversize jacket for my daughter. They also brought me hats and mittens. When I walked out of this market, I was even more convinced that I was on my way to America.

When we finally got to the airport and got cleared to board the flight, my heart sank. I had a chance to hug everyone there goodbye at least twice, and still there was no sign of my mother and brother. I later learned that my brother, who was supposed to pick her up, did not get there on time. He and my mother hurried to the airport only to find the gate closed. My mother begged the security officers to let me know that she had finally arrived, but her pleas were met with indifference. As we walked on the tarmac to board the Kenya Airways flight, I tried hard to identify her among a large crowd of people waving from the balcony area of the airport but could not. I tried not to cry much, because my daughter was crying as well. You could hear other people crying on this flight; they too, perhaps, knew that it would be a long time before they could return home. The rest of the journey was less eventful. When I woke up the following morning at the airport in Amsterdam, my thoughts had shifted to America. I was only to take the next flight to Detroit and then another to Albany.

Our host family came with friends to meet us at the airport. They also brought warm coats for us. After a hot shower, we went to bed. The next morning, we noticed that trees had no leaves. There was no sign of life except for people. This was a shock because we were used to seeing green trees and blooming flowers and hearing bird songs every morning. Soon after, it started snowing. I had seen snow in the movies, and people seemed to enjoy playing in the snow. Excited, my daughter and I went out in our pajamas and flip-flops to touch it with our bare hands. It was then that I really understood what winter is. I was terrified inside but could not verbalize my fears. I had no idea how long winter might last or what comes after winter. It took a long time to get used to the idea of cold weather.

Experiences of Refugees

Refugee Camps

Looking back, my journey to America was far less complicated than that of refugees coming from refugee camps. At least I prepared for my departure, chose where I was going, and got a chance to say goodbye to family and friends. Most of all, I had someone waiting for me.

For many refugees, their journey started when their village was attacked, usually at night. There was no time to grab anything from home, and often families were separated as each member tried to flee for safety. The risks involved in these attacks vary, depending on age and gender. Young boys are abducted to become child soldiers, whereas young girls are abducted to serve as sex slaves and to perform other duties at the military/militia base.

Once at these bases, the boys are trained to kill and are often used as human demining tools in the areas feared to have antipersonnel mines. To prevent the boys from attempting to flee the military camp to return to their parents, military camp leaders often instruct them to carry out brutal acts against local civilians or other fellow abductees from the same region. The boys are then threatened that they will be killed by others in their former communities because of the brutal acts they committed if they try to return to their homes.

Female abductees serve as sexual slaves at the camps. Some of them become pregnant as a result of repeated gang rapes. If these girls are unable to escape, they are often killed because they can no longer carry out their sexual duties. Others develop severe infections from these repeated gang rapes and eventually die due to lack of medical care. Some of the girls also develop fistulas and are killed because they are no longer fit to serve as sexual slaves.

In recent years, rape has been used as a weapon of war indiscriminately on infants to grandmothers. Recent incidents in the Democratic Republic of the Congo in which women of an entire village were savagely mass raped are another example of this new war tactic. Research studies conducted about women who have suffered similar fates in Rwanda, Bosnia, Sudan, and other places warn about possibilities of long-term physical and psychological complications for women who survived them (Jansen, 2006).

The luckier community members end up in refugee camps, where they arrive with no personal possessions, often separated from other family members. Essential services are often slow to arrive at the camps because of logistical and security problems; as a result, the weakest refugees often die due to dehydration or an outbreak of illnesses such as cholera born out of poor sanitary conditions. Food is always a challenge in refugee camps. There may be insufficient provisions in camps, poorly managed distribution centers, a lack of means to prepare and cook food, and continuing logistical problems. Refugees still have to venture out in the dangerous bush to collect firewood to cook meals. This presents a challenge for women, who risk being caught and raped by militia/soldiers. In some areas, deforestation and scarcity of resources create tensions between refugees and the local population, leading to anti-refugee sentiments among the local population and mistreatment of refugees, such as solicitation of sex in exchange for money and other necessities. Another challenge for mothers in camps is the absence of community social support. At the village, mothers always had child care from a neighboring mother or could leave the children home alone because it was safe. At the camp, the community life is gone, it is no longer safe, and often family members are separated. All of these hardships have a significant impact on refugees already traumatized by the war.

Relocated Refugees

Refugees who are relocated have often spent many years in refugee camps and are unable to return home because of security concerns. The first step in the process of relocation requires that families fill out an application. Once a country accepts them, the refugees are given training to introduce them to the recipient country's culture. Refugees have reported that this training did not help to prepare them for the practical scenarios they encountered after they arrived. In addition, they were rarely given notice about when and where they would be going until a day before departure, apparently because of security concerns at the camp. It's also important to note that it is difficult to cover every aspect of life in these trainings, so most of the task was left to the resettlement agencies. At the airport, refugees were met by resettlement agency staff who were strangers and often did not speak their language. Some were fortunate to be met by an interpreter who helped to interpret the culture as well, which made the transition go fairly well; however, others had no such luck and found the first day in America highly stressful.

Employment

Refugees who immigrate to the United States come from diverse backgrounds. Some are well educated and have work experience; others may be illiterate. The most-educated refugees tend to be more dissatisfied with job placement programs run by resettlement agencies. As one of the refugees from Iraq who had been relocated to Baltimore put it: "The most frustrating issue for us is that nobody seem[s] to believe that we could have gone to school or lived a good life before we became refugees . . . our dignity was the only thing we thought we could keep but here, even that is no longer possible." Many of my clients and other refugees that I worked with felt that resettlement agencies paid little attention to their professional backgrounds. They were surprised and sometimes angry that employment services staff were not curious about the skills they brought into the country and rather tried to convince them to take low-end jobs. Many were disheartened that their previous experience could not get them a decent job.

However, resettlement agencies only had a four-month period of resettlement status to find jobs for these refugees. This four-month period of service provision rarely covers the range of needs that refugees have; career counseling services are not available postresettlement. Such a service could help refugees navigate the process of obtaining credits for their previous education and work experience through the Educational Testing Service, help them seek out training opportunities to get certified in their prior or related fields, or assist them with school applications.

Adjustment and Cultural Issues

Assisting refugees to adjust to their new lives is challenging for both the refugees and those assigned to help them. Agency and volunteer staff need to avoid making assumptions and carefully tailor their responses to the requests and preferences of the refugees; if not, they risk being seen as condescending to the refugees. As one refugee put it, they were "treated like little children being potty trained." Refugees have reported that they were never asked about their skills and knowledge. Rather, "everyone assumed that we have never lived in a house before, never made a bed, never mopped the floor, and could not possibly know the difference between a knife, a fork, and a spoon." It is, therefore, important for helping professionals to pay attention to body language and try to engage refugees during this initial contact with the family. It is also important to acknowledge the capacities and cultural experiences that refugees bring. If refugees are approached sensitively and with respect, differences in their experiences from those typical of American life can be explored jointly in a nonjudgmental way.

Although donations from members of the host community can be helpful, it takes a delicate process to make sure that donated items do not send the wrong message to the recipient family. Some refugees reported that they felt treated like destitute poor people who have never had anything nice of their own in their entire life. Resettlement agencies need to carefully assess the needs of a family before providing donations. Providers are often puzzled by the refusal of donations by refugees who clearly need them. The act of giving should always take the recipient's feelings into consideration. Some refugees might have been well off before they were forced to flee their homes and might have never accepted donations previously. In addition, it is always a good idea to check the state of items being donated. As a service provider, I have refused donations for homeless shelters because they were damaged or too old for anyone else to use. Another major problem reported by refugees is the resettlement location. Some refugees are resettled in small towns with limited job opportunities and limited services and supplies. In one case, I visited a family that has been resettled in a small town in New Jersey with one grocery store; there was no place for 45 miles to buy phone cards to call relatives left behind, nor could they find products appropriate for their type of hair and skin.

Refugees from temperate climates also were unfamiliar with the need to heat their homes and often did not have funds to cover these costs. This same family lived in a very large and drafty Victorian house. I visited them during the fall, when they were already finding the house too cold. On the basis of its size, it would cost at least $500/month to heat the entire house. The family was large and needed the space. They also had young children who might fall sick if heat is inadequate. When I called to check on them after the first winter storm, they reported being very cold but could not afford the cost of turning up the heat. Although some family members were working, the combined income was still not enough to keep them afloat.

In addition to living expenses, monies were deducted from paychecks to recoup the cost of expensive airfares to America. Refugee families agree to repay the International Organization for Migration the cost of the airfares to immigrate to the United States as soon as the family starts to receive an income. In this family, each person had to pay $35/month for the tickets, which added to $350/month for the entire family. All the children were minors and could not work. Even if both parents worked full-time earning a minimum wage, it would still be impossible to make ends meet.

On arrival in the United States, refugees are given assistance for four months during which they have to learn English and secure a permanent job. During the four-month period, refugees receive employment services, medical care, and food stamps benefits. In addition, they attend English as a Second Language (ESL) classes. Orientation classes largely focus on obtaining a job; the training staff may direct refugees to the businesses with whom they had established relationships or businesses that were willing to accept refugees, rather than matching the individual's skills and education to a more appropriate job.

I went through this program right after my graduation. During my training, I was told over and over that I could not find a job other than doing manual labor in a factory or in a warehouse. Although I clearly indicated on my resume that I had just graduated from a four-year college in the United States and had no language barriers, staff members were not interested in suggesting jobs in the field of human services as I requested. At the end of the training, I felt as if my experience could be summed up as follows: I was a refugee, and refugees are to work in places where limited language ability is expected and skills beyond manual labor are not needed. My brother had a similar experience; he was sent to work in the freezer department of a company that supplies food and beverages to airlines at Newark Airport. Only recent refugees and men on probation worked there, and the turnover rate was unusually high. The resettlement agency had made a deal with this company because it always seemed to have job openings. My brother became ill from the terrible working conditions and had to quit his job. By then he was also suffering from depression, and traumatic experiences were activated again. He spent days in bed and could hardly eat; gradually, he became better and able to look for another job. He was lucky. He was living with a relative who could take care of him until he found a new job. Another refugee asked, "How can you possibly be ready to take care of a family in just four months when you spend the first two months attending orientation and ESL classes?"

Impact of Social Welfare Policies

The social welfare policies and interactions with social agency workers are another major source of frustration for refugees. In some states, such as Kentucky, receipt of refugee cash assistance requires involvement in training or employment activity. I once came across a case of a refugee who was told by her caseworker to find a place to volunteer in the community to continue receiving cash assistance. The caseworker knew that the refugee was illiterate and had no English skills, yet she handed her a sheet of paper with names of places to call. When the refugee said that she was not familiar with the area, she was told to find a way to do volunteer work in the community if she wanted to receive the money. Fighting tears, the refugee mother calmly said thank you and left the office. In fact, the social worker could have done more in this case but did not. On learning that the refugee was illiterate, the worker could have reached out to the resettlement agency to inquire about literacy programs to help this woman and others in similar situations; participating in such a program would have allowed continued receipt of cash assistance. In a different case, a wife was told to abandon her career readiness class to stay home with her children because her husband had found a full-time job in a meat packing company making a minimum wage salary; therefore, day care benefits were no longer available for the family. Yet it should have been clear that the family could not survive financially without two incomes.

Refugees seeking health care services face an uphill battle due to the complexity of the health care system. They are unfamiliar with the paperwork that needs to be completed before they can be seen by a doctor and often do not understand why they need to sign so many documents. It is, therefore, important for health care and social workers to incorporate initial educational sessions about the process of getting medical care. For example, many refugees go to see a doctor unprepared and leave behind important documents that could have saved them a trip back to the hospital. Most refugees are unfamiliar with preventive medicine; they are used to seeing the doctor only when they are really sick. It is sometimes difficult for them to explain to the doctor how they feel, perhaps because some medical conditions do not always have names in their own culture and language. For instance, common medical conditions such as high blood pressure or high cholesterol may not have a name in the country of origin. Insufficient knowledge about the anatomy of the body may make it difficult for refugees to effectively communicate with health care workers. Refugee patients may find it difficult to interpret test results and may have a hard time understanding explanations about their diagnosis.

Professionals also need to attend to problems that arise with obtaining access to medications for refugee clients. Although they may be familiar with going to a pharmacy to get the medicine they need, co-payment is a new concept for most of them. As an interpreter, I noticed that many patients did not go to the pharmacy to fill their prescriptions because they feared that they would be unable to pay for the medicines. They know that medicines are costly and do not understand that insurance pays for a large portion of the cost and their co-payment may be affordable. They may not be aware that they can use their health insurance at the pharmacy. Moreover, when patients require medication refills, they often do not understand this process of refilling medication. In their countries of origin, they were given all the medicine they needed for their condition by a pharmacist at the first visit, and there was no need to return for a refill. In addition, there are some illnesses that are rarely diagnosed in their countries, such as high cholesterol, that require medication over a prolonged period of time. Refugees are not used to taking medication for a prolonged period of time, especially if symptoms are not obvious. Health care workers should inform refugee patients about the refill process and make a note to the pharmacy to remind the patient to return for a refill. Patient education about chronic conditions should be incorporated into work with refugee populations as well.

In addition, poor or disrespectful communication by providers can add to mistrust and avoidance of care. For example, a refugee parent seeking medical attention in a different state was told by her doctor that she was sick because she was not taking her medication. The patient argued that she indeed took all her medications as prescribed, but the doctor continued to say that she was telling lies. Frustrated, the sick patient went back home and brought all the medications she was taking and explained to the doctor how she was taking them. The doctor realized that she had wrongly accused this patient but never apologized for the unnecessary comments and overall mistreatment of this patient. These examples of possible misunderstandings around health care point to the necessity for helping professionals to consider all aspects of daily living that might affect health when working with refugees and asylum seekers, because their experiences in their countries of origin can often be very different than their experiences in the United States for things that U.S. practitioners may take for granted.

Mental health care is another area of service that poses challenges to both the refugees and the professionals working with them. Most refugees come from cultures that have not been exposed to professional mental health diagnoses and treatments. In some communities, an individual with severe mental health issues is defined as crazy, and there is no cure for "craziness." Once crazy, always crazy, even if the person's "crazy behavior" is no longer present. The origin of mental problems is subject to debate, depending on belief systems. It is very important for mental health professionals to educate refugee families about the origins/causes of mental health conditions. It is also important to keep in mind that some families may not feel comfortable fully disclosing mental health symptoms, either because of shame, because of unfamiliarity with mental health professional treatment, or because traditionally they are not used to providing personal information to people outside of their immediate family. It is important for mental health professionals to build trust with refugee families and acknowledge their belief system before presenting their professional point of view.

Concern about confidentiality is yet another barrier that might prevent refugee families from seeking professional help for mental health or STD treatment. Some refugees fear that their immigration status, job status, or education will be jeopardized should the information get out. All providers need to assert their professional commitment to confidentiality and help refugees understand that there are legal protections as well. It is also important for providers to ask refugees about the ways that mental health crises are handled traditionally in their cultures. Most refugees are happy to share such information if they believe that the worker inquiring is sincerely interested in learning about where they came from. Sincerity and trust are the most important ingredients to make the relationship between mental health therapists and refugees work.

Refugee abuses are also a common challenge to newly arrived refugees. Some refugees only get a small portion of their entitled benefits. In one case, a refugee family was supposed to have housing for eight months but was evicted after five months without any prior written notice, likely because the landlord wished to pocket the remaining months of rent money. Refugees have been advised by insurance agents to buy car insurance policies that cost more than the car is worth. Because refugees lack a long credit history, they are often offered higher than average rates for loans and insurance. In addition to unfair practices from financial institutions, con artists have made fortunes from unsuspecting refugees who make verbal rather than written financial transactions or may not keep written evidence because financial transactions in their country of origin might not have relied on written evidence. Scams have also occurred around enrolling new arrivals in education programs that do not exist. These refugees are new to the United States, have no English language skills, and are unfamiliar with the law, making them easy targets for victimization.

The U.S. higher education system is another place where refugees may receive confusing information. Refugees attending community colleges need to complete an English language requirement before taking other classes; this may take several years, and the individual may not be able to access courses in the field of her or his area of interest. At a four-year college, a refugee may not need to take an English language required course and can complete her or his degree in four years. It is important that refugees are informed and have access to resources that can guide them in the best choices for their educational needs.

Legal and illegal discrimination against refugees is yet another challenge for many refugees who were granted protection in the United States. For example, in 2010, the state of New Jersey enacted a law to deny Medicaid to any adult parent who has held a green card for less than five years, citing severe budget shortfalls. Among these immigrants are refugees who are less likely to hold jobs that offer benefits and who still have severe trauma treatment needs. Or refugees may encounter hostility or harassment from other low-income groups who feel refugees are getting priority for jobs and services that they also need.

Other barriers include U.S. government practices around obtaining travel documents allowing refugees to travel out of the country. These travel documents are valid for one year and cost approximately $400 each. The barrier is that the application processing time is 45 days or longer, which means that an individual wishing to travel might lose the opportunity to attend a scheduled event, such as a conference, or miss an emergency event, such as a funeral.

Dealing with the School System

At schools, refugee children face challenges of their own. One week after our arrival, my daughter started school. As far as I know, nothing was done to prepare her classmates for her arrival. It would have been helpful if the school had told her classmates about her and where she was coming from. During the registration process, the school did not ask for information about her education background or whether she had any learning disabilities. Because she had no English language skills, the school lowered her from third to second grade; I still do not understand how that determination was made. The school offered her ESL classes, which took place during her regular English class period. The class combined beginner and advanced students who were already doing well in regular English classes even if not quite ready to test out of ESL. After a few years, my daughter became bored with the ESL classes; I had to advocate for moving her into regular English classes. I finally made a case by using the state test results, which showed that her proficiency in the English language was good. My daughter was lucky that I could fight for her. I can only imagine what happens to other immigrant children whose parents are not as forceful, do not speak English, and are perhaps far less familiar with the education system. There is no handbook for immigrant parents and students to educate themselves about how school systems work, how to read a report card, why state tests are important, and how to interpret results from these tests. Professional helpers need to educate refugees about how their children are being evaluated and the implications of such evaluations for the future, for example, the impact that grades will have on access to higher education, grants, and scholarships. Refugee families clearly need professional assistance in navigating the school system.

Parental involvement in their children's education is another area that challenges refugees. Because of cultural and language barriers, many refugee parents are often not involved with their children's schools. Interpretation services are rarely available to facilitate communication between parents and school services. Often, in the country of origin, the school–parent relationship is different from what it is in the United States. In some cultures, parents give the school total control over the education of their children. They are not invited to school unless the child is in difficulty. There are no parent–teacher conferences, and the communication between school and home is almost nonexistent. There are no parent–teacher associations or extracurricular activities that engage students and parents. It is, therefore, critical for schools to inform parents about different expectations as to their involvement with the school and to encourage them to participate as much as they can.

However, communicating with refugee parents is not always easy for schools. In some cases, schools have had to rely on refugee children to assume the role of interpreters between their parents and school officials. Under these circumstances, many parents feel ashamed that they have to depend on their children. They also feel helpless because they cannot help their children with homework or properly advocate on their behalf when necessary. For instance, in cases of school teasing, bullying, and other forms of harassment, the victim's parent is often the one to report these incidents to school officials. For immigrant children, especially those coming from conflict zones, these incidents are often not reported because their families have been exposed to much more dangerous circumstances in their home countries. Also, culturally, they may fear that reporting these incidents could endanger their children even more. In addition, in the country of origin, harassment and teasing may be accepted in the culture. For instance in Rwanda, it is acceptable to tell someone that she or he is "fat" or "too skinny." Traditionally, the recipient of such comments is expected to hit back with a comment about the physical appearance of those who teased first. This becomes a game of challenging participants' humor skills, and nobody is expected to feel offended. In U.S. culture though, such comments are insensitive and can lead to severe ramifications. It is also important to note that being "fat" in other cultures may equate with good health. As immigrant children are prepared to enter U.S. schools, the issues they may encounter in the school hallways and playgrounds need to be anticipated and discussed with both parents and students. Unfortunately, because schools may not be aware of what refugee students have experienced, they may not be able to protect them against unpleasant experiences that could trigger trauma.

Issues for Professionals Working with Refugees

It is important for helping professionals working with African refugees to be aware that repeated interviews about traumatic incidents may retraumatize refugees. Support groups may work for some but not for everyone. It is common for refugees to use work as a coping mechanism. Staying home doing nothing creates opportunities for their thoughts to focus on the traumatic experiences. Finding ways to engage refugees in productive and meaningful activities can be a useful coping strategy. Helping professionals should always remember that grieving will go on for a long time and may take different shapes along the way. Personal success is usually the most efficient coping mechanism for refugees and the best means to right the wrongs done to them. As long as they feel that they are accomplishing and gradually recreating a sustainable life for themselves and their families, the grieving process becomes easier.

Refugees attending adult schools find it difficult because they are unfamiliar with the teaching methods used. Human service providers should explore how people learn in their culture of origin because in most cultures, preferred methods of learning may vary from the Western system. Because demonstration is often a teaching tool in refugee home countries, refugees may learn better that way than by reading from instructions; demonstration methods take limitations in English into account as well. For example, when giving directions to refugees, it might be better to sketch a map and mention any specific visual markings such as a yellow church at the corner, a gas station on the right hand side of the road, and so forth. Handing out a map alone will not be helpful to most refugees, who likely have never used a map before.

Another common challenge to refugees is time management. Some refugees come from cultures that place less emphasis on being sensitive to time than on creating and maintaining relationships. This inattention to time can affect refugees' personal and professional lives. It is important for service providers to recognize this different approach to time management and make sure that they highlight and fully explain the importance and consequences of missing an appointment or being late. Appointment reminders and education in the use of a calendar may be necessary to help refugees adapt to the importance of time in Western culture.

Along with time management, productivity measurement for refugees in the workplace is yet another area that deserves attention. When working with refugees, it is important to recognize that many of them may be unfamiliar with measurement mechanisms that evaluate individual productivity outcomes. Therefore, it is important for professionals to work with refugees and, possibly, their bosses, to assist them in understanding the individual tasks and expected productivity results so that the workers can adjust their productivity speed accordingly.

Working relationships between African refugees and professional helpers can sometimes be challenging on both sides. Some professionals who are used to being addressed by their last names may feel offended when refugees refer to them by first name. Many refugees may have grown up known by their nicknames only; also, they will typically introduce themselves by their first name rather than their last name. Some African cultures do not use family names or surnames. Helping professionals should be aware of this cultural difference and recognize that just as it might be difficult for them to pronounce the names of refugees, refugees may have the same difficulty with Western names. It is not out of disrespect that refugees may prefer to use the professional helper's first name instead of last name; it may be a difference in cultural orientation about names and may take time to change.

Depending on gender and circumstances, and the person with whom they are interacting, a refugee may change his or her demeanor. Some women may not look a professional helper in the eyes when speaking or may not answer all the questions asked. This is because some cultures encourage women to be quiet when they have no good answer to offer. Also, the presence of a husband may affect how much the wife can express. For example, if a wife goes to the social welfare office with her husband, she may check with her husband on answers before she responds to the service provider. Wives may not know what the household income is and will have to consult their husbands before responding on such issues. Many refugees are coming from countries in which the power dynamics between men and women are different; service providers may need to take the time to make sure that both husband and wife are informed and brought into the decision-making process. Regarding African refugees and health care, it is usually better for women to work with a female doctor, especially around obstetrics and gynecological issues. In some African cultures it is not appropriate for women and men to discuss these issues or talk about sexual or intimacy issues; therefore, African women may be more at ease with female doctors. African men may also be more at ease with a male doctor.

Despite the challenges that refugees encounter after resettlement, refugees pursue education. Education is regarded by refugees as the only ticket out of poverty. Often deprived of educational opportunities in their home countries either because of poverty, discrimination, or even corruption, the majority do not take an educational opportunity for granted. Because of the financial hardships many families face, the children are encouraged to study even harder so that they can obtain scholarships and grants. Refugee families also provide mutual encouragement and support to each other as well as friendly competitiveness that makes every member guilty of not making as much progress as everyone else. Parents constantly remind the children that everyone started from nothing and that everyone has faced hardship; therefore, if one of them can achieve, so can everyone else.

Parenting is an area where there are likely to be differences in practices between African refugees and asylees and the U.S. culture. Nutrition may be an area in which helping professionals need to support new parents of infants. In the country of origin, there is usually nothing like the baby foods that are found in U.S. supermarkets. Babies are usually fed on breast milk and then later on some of the typical foods for that region, such as porridge. Helping professionals will have to find out from parents what they are used to feeding their children and then try to find comparable foods here.

Verbal and behavioral signs of affection between African parents and children may be different than those familiar to helping professionals in the United States. African parents may not tell their children that they love them, but it is clear there is a strong bond between the parent and the child. Obedience is an important factor between parents and children, and parents expect children to obey their instructions. These expectations may appear very different than the more permissive or flexible parenting styles in the United States. Helping professionals also need to keep in mind that refugee parents come from a culture in which corporal punishment is still in practice and, thus, may have a hard time finding other ways to discipline their children. Refugee parents will need education about the severe sanctions for endangering the welfare of a child that can occur if they use corporal punishment or leave children unsupervised in the United States. Parents who have used corporal punishment may find it hard to stop this practice if they are not provided another strategy of discipline. The recommendation is to work with parents to develop alternative strategies. It is very important to discuss alternative disciplinary methods with parents and their children so that communication lines can be opened to reduce conflicts among family members, refugees, and other immigrants. Refugee parents were used to getting assistance from the community to raise children; with large families, many refugees find it challenging to entertain and care for such a large family without an alternative support system. Some immigrant mothers coming from areas of conflict may bring orphans who lost parents to the conflict in addition to their own children. In most cases, they have no idea what it costs to raise a child in the United States and do not initially realize that they will have to do without the financial and emotional support they used to have in their countries. This is one of the main reasons why immigrant families wish to move close to each other.

Conclusion

Psychosocial adjustment is challenging for refugees and asylees. We are called to assimilate into the new culture, which often requires giving up our own culture. Although every refugee's experience is different, most of our stories are similar. Our conversations tend to focus on our early days in America. The common denominator is that we were not fully prepared for the kind of realities we found in America. The weather in some parts of the United States is the biggest challenge for refugees from warm climates. Winter is brutally cold, especially when you do not own a car. We also had to learn to use public transportation, use the library, figure out different coins and bills, and use maps for directions. We had to learn how to order food in a restaurant and how to read bills and school report cards. We had to learn the names of hundreds of items in stores and how to read prices. This learning process goes on and on; there is always more to learn about ourselves and the environment in which we live.

It is very important for professional helpers to understand the nature of the violence that refugee families survived, for the purpose of accurately evaluating its short- and long-term impact on their physical and psychological well-being. Besides the trauma that refugees suffered during the conflict, refugees seeking services from professionals are also struggling with multiple involuntary relocations, loss of identity, constant anxieties about relatives left behind in camps, isolation, language and cultural barriers, a competitive work environment, reactions to trauma such posttraumatic stress disorder, the high cost of living, unfamiliar weather, and a complex lifestyle, among other things.

Living in America so far away from our families is not easy. Yes, America is a great country, yet home was once good too. We did not have much, but we were, for the most part, happy. Life can be too complicated here, as reported by many refugees with whom I have spoken. The stress that refugees face here is almost nonexistent in home countries. We miss the food, the people, the land, and the laid-back lifestyle we used to have before the war took all that away. Refugees whose families remain in refugee camps are emotionally stressed by not being able to help them. All refugees come with a dream that if they work hard they will be able to help their relatives left behind, only to realize that they can barely meet their own needs, yet their relatives in refugee camps are waiting for the help that will not come. "Every phone call is hard on our family," said one mother of five. "I have had to take from my own children to pay for medical care for my parents, whose lives are deteriorating in the camp. I always took care of them before I came to the USA. So it is hard to stop now, especially when I know how hard life is in those camps. I am exhausted, and I don't know what to do."

Because most refugees come from a more collectively oriented culture than is common in the United States, resettlement agencies and other providers working with recent immigrant families should help families locate and connect with a local community, remotely if necessary. The emotional and social support offered through these informal communities is priceless to families dispersed by wars. The opportunity to communicate with someone who speaks their language is rare, especially when the threat of children losing their cultural heritage, including the language, is a reality.

For parents, losing one's heritage is devastating. My daughter was seven and a half years old when we came to the United States. She was fluent in Kinyarwanda and French. After one year in America, her Kinyarwanda and French language skills were gone. I was hurt that she could not communicate with my mother, who blamed me for it. Had I had a community to converse with on a regular basis, she would have retained at least some of her language skills. Furthermore, most conversations among refugee families focus on their experiences in the new country; therefore, connecting with other immigrants helps them to freely express their feelings, fears, and concerns. It is also through these connections that immigrant families are able to find out where they can find food from the region they come from, beauty products, cheap phone cards to call relatives overseas, and get news about relatives and friends left behind. Moreover, these informal sources of information also provide the opportunity for those who have been around for a while to share their own experiences, warn newcomers about any mistakes to avoid, and encourage them to rise above the challenges.

Grieving is a long and slow process. Because refugees have been through a lot, they often only begin to grieve when they finally feel safe and are slowly recovering. This process is personal but occasionally communal depending on where the refugee lives and the community around her or him. Many refugees struggle to memorialize their loved ones who were victims of the war. There are no pictures, no gravesite, nothing to hold on to. Closure is hard to come by. We often try to reconnect to friends who knew the victim with the hope that they may provide fresh memories.

Working with refugees and asylees can be demanding at times, especially when adequate resources are not available to professionals assigned to help them. Despite good intentions, helping professionals cannot fully assist refugees without a clear understanding of the psychosocial background of those they wish to help. Cultural differences will always pose difficulties for both professional helpers and refugees; yet cultural awareness and sensitivity will ease the challenges faced. Finally, it is imperative that helping professionals understand the multiple challenges that refugees face after they arrive in the host country and strive to eliminate shortcomings both in social work education as well as in social work practice with immigrants who have experienced extreme violence.

References

Jansen, G. G. (2006). Gender and war: The effects of armed conflict on women's health and mental health. *Affilia, 21,* 134–145. doi: 10.1177/0886109905285760

United Nations High Commissioner for Refugees. (2010, June 15). *Number of forcibly displaced rises to 43.3 million last year, the highest level since mid-1990s.* Retrieved from http://www.unhcr.org/4c176c969.html

SECTION 2

African Experiences and Responses

Interventions developed in Africa to address the needs of communities affected by armed conflict and multiple adversities are described in this section. The destruction of the social, health, and education structures and systems from armed conflict compounds the challenges that helping professionals face during conflict and postconflict. All interventions in this section highlight the importance of the holistic and interconnected nature of African culture. All interventions include significant involvement of community members, community leaders, and local mental health professionals.

Chapter 4 describes the individual and communal life prior to armed conflict in northern Uganda. The explanation of the concepts of spiritual nature of life and interconnectedness provides an understanding of the depth of the social and communal disruption caused by the armed conflict. This description and the resulting peace-building intervention calls attention to the issues that must be addressed to restore peace and well-being to all aspects of life postconflict. Chapter 5 explicates the development of a child-based psychosocial intervention to support reintegration of formerly abducted children in northern Uganda. This intervention also addressed the concerns and needs of the families and communities receiving these individuals. Chapter 6 describes a culturally informed, family-based intervention, developed through qualitative methodology, to strengthen the functioning of families that have been severely affected by genocide and the AIDS epidemic in Rwanda.

4

Peace Building

Reverend Father Remigio C. Obol

Northern Uganda experienced more than 20 years of armed conflict beginning in 1986. Principle actors in this conflict were the Lord's Resistance Army (LRA) and the Ugandan Army, but citizens were caught in the ensuing violence and many, including children, were abducted to fill the ranks of the LRA. Life as people knew it was forever changed; people were killed, families displaced, and villages broken apart. People were not able to farm, get water, or attend school due to the threat of attack from the LRA. Violence destroyed interpersonal relationships, means of livelihood, and personal and communal safety. This chapter explores the many aspects of life that were destroyed as a result of the armed conflict, and the steps needed to re-establish peace in this area including the reintegration of children and adults involved in the conflict into society.

On the basis of my work in northern Uganda, I will conceptualize peace building holistically in this chapter; the political, economic, social, and cultural issues are important and interconnected factors in any armed conflict and must also be considered as key factors in the resolution of armed conflicts. As a result of this holistic conceptualization, peace building involves the creation of interventions, activities, a social climate, and a mind-set that allows for individuals to be able to care for self and family, to live in harmony with those around them, and live in harmony with their environment. First, the impact of armed conflict on the political, economic, social, and cultural aspects of life will be explored. Second, the peace-building interventions will be presented with a focus on one program, Education for Peace and Prevention of Violence HIV/AIDS (EPPOVHA). Finally, the role of traditional practices in rebuilding relationships among family members, within and beyond communities, will be discussed.

Helping professionals in the United States working with individuals from areas of armed conflict will gain an understanding of the experiences of those living through such conditions and the importance of a multifaceted concept of peace building. Peace building involves a person's relationships with others and the environment; this is important in African society, where the individual is recognized because he or she is part of a community not in isolation. The work of peace building involves repairing and restoring relationships that have been damaged in the conflict. Helping professionals may be able to draw on these ideas by recognizing and possibly including other members of the client's system in their work with individuals and families in the United States.

Introduction

Uganda, a country baptized the "Pearl of Africa" by Winston Churchill in 1908, is endowed with some of the finest natural resources in sub-Saharan Africa. Uganda gained its independence from Britain peacefully in 1962. At that time, it was one of the most prosperous countries in the continent, with an average economic growth rate of 3 percent per annum, derived from an agricultural export economy introduced and promoted by the British Colonial Administration from 1890 to 1962 (Bibangamabah, 2001). The new nation began its independence with a progressively healthy economy and respect of human rights, especially regarding children and women.

This prosperity was shattered by a series of armed conflicts; periods of political unrest; and coup d'états, with destruction of human lives and physical and institutional infrastructures. These circumstances gradually retarded the economic development and eroded the moral standard of the people by promoting violent behavior in the society. The Acholi subregion in northern Uganda was engulfed in armed conflict beginning in 1986 when the Uganda People's Democratic Army (UPDA), a rebel force, fought the Uganda government. The UPDA was a loose coalition force, made up of factions with widely varying motives and histories united only by their opposition to President Museveni. In early November 1986, Alice Lakwena, a priestess, took over command of the UPDA, which later became known as the Holy Spirit Mobile Forces. This force proved briefly to be a serious military threat to government forces, known at that time as the National Resistance Army and later known as the Ugandan

People's Defence Forces (UPDF). Although the military potency of the Holy Spirit Mobile Forces was short lived, it ultimately evolved into the LRA led by self-styled General Joseph Kony (Behrend, 1999; Lamwaka, 1998). The LRA continued to fight against the UPDF, causing much bloodshed, looting, and the abduction of children to fill its ranks (Human Rights Watch Children's Rights Project, 1997). This conflict continued until 2007; a peace agreement was being negotiated but was not completed. After this unsuccessful negotiation, remaining members of the LRA moved into neighboring countries such as the Democratic Republic of the Congo and the Central African Republic, where they continue to enact violence.

This violent rebellion resulted in the mass displacement of families in rural communities into Internally Displaced Persons (IDP) camps to improve their safety. Because the UPDF is widely regarded in the Acholi subregion as unable to protect the people and the IDP camps from the LRA, and they themselves have been accused of harassing and abusing civilians (Refugee Law Project, 2004), security remained a key issue in the camps. Staff members of government institutions, such as health units, schools and government administrative units; and religious and social services, such as parishes, convents and nurseries were also displaced. Some of the staff members of these institutions are returning now that the violence has diminished.

The violence and brutality of the armed conflict destroyed the possibility of economic development, human development, and respect for human rights and led to the spread of violent behavior and conflict in schools, workplaces, families, and communities.

To understand the peace building that will be needed in the area, it is important to first gain a sense of the peace that existed for individuals, families, communities, and society before the conflict. Background information about the Acholi population, the region in which they live, and their cultural beliefs will be presented. These issues are useful for understanding the real risk for the everyday lives and livelihood of the people, especially the children in northern Uganda. This in-depth description of the Acholi is not only important for understanding how the group lived before the conflict, but also important for understanding the aspects that many will re-establish during postconflict. This information is passed down orally through the generations so that all members understand this history, and it remains a history that shapes current experiences. What may be salient for individuals and families that have experienced armed conflict may be the way of life before the conflict that they are hoping to regain, rather than the conflict itself. Helping professionals must understand the historical and cultural context to place an individual's concerns in context.

Who Are the Acholi?

Region and Population Affected by the Armed Conflict

The northern Uganda armed conflict encompassed the Acholi, Teso, and Lango subregions. These regions are located to the extreme of northern Uganda, bordering the Islamic Republic of the Sudan. This chapter focuses only on the Acholi subregion. The Acholi subregion is occupied mainly by the Nilotic people of Lwo ethnic group known as the Acholi. The population of this region in 2002 was 1.2 million (Uganda Bureau of Statistics, 2006a). English is the official language, and the indigenous language of the Acholi is Lwo. Kiswahili is another East African language spoken in this region. The literacy rate among the rural population is 67 percent (Uganda Bureau of Statistics, n.d.). The majority of the population practices Christianity, and a minority practice the Islamic faith; many practice traditional Acholi spiritual practices along with Christianity and Islam.

The social structure of the Acholi subregion is based on the family unit. A number of family-related houses form a village, a number of villages form a subclan, a number of subclans form a clan, and a number of clans form the Acholi tribe.[1] By the end of the 19th century, there were approximately 350 clans in the region (Atkinson, cited by Harlacher, Okot, Obonyo, Balthazard, & Atkinson, 2006). Each clan lives in specific geographic areas and has its own royal family. The clans are linked fraternally with each other and with the royal houses of the traditional kingdoms in southern Uganda, specifically, Bunyoro, Toro, Buganda, and Busoga. The royal families of these kingdoms originally came from the Lwo of Acholi peoples. Subclans do not have royal families but have respected elders who are *heads of the subclans*. Family units are independent, with every Acholi man being a "king in his own house" (Pain, 1997, p. 75). Such authority with the family unit limits the authority of the traditional chiefs to rule by consensus; chiefs cannot force decisions upon the community (Pain, 1997).[2]

The influence of the traditional chiefs has eroded over time as a result of historical political and economic influences beginning with colonialism. Their authority has been further eroded by the specific influences of the LRA conflict, such as mass displacement of the population; the national politics, which is based on elected leadership versus traditional leadership; and the breakdown of the social and cultural institutions. Today their roles are reduced to performing traditional rites of reconciliation, paying of compensation for

[1]The Acholi is one of the tribes within the Lwo ethnic group. The Lwo ethnic group also includes the Alur and Lwo (from Uganda, Sudan, and Kenya).

[2]The author was an unpublished source of this information for Pain, 1997.

murder, and cleansing the individuals who were forced into armed conflict and are now returning to their families.

Occupation and Livelihood

Before the war and mass displacement into IDP camps, the Acholi people lived a communal life in their own land. In their communal worldview, there was interdependence among all members of the group. An individual took action for the sake of the family, community, or tribe. An individual's possessions were generally owned by the family, community, and tribe. This understanding of interdependence is a part of the active traditional norms that ruled the ownership and use of things. Everyone lives in attachment to others in all aspects of life and activities.

Although a significant number of people were involved in business or the civil service, and many young men were employed by the military, police, or prison services, the majority of the population were peasant farmers. The livelihood of many households depended on cultivating food and cash crops and rearing animals and poultry. The major cash crops were cotton, tobacco, rice, groundnuts, simsim (sesame seeds), and sunflowers. The resulting income was used to pay school fees; arrange marriages; build permanent houses and shops; and purchase bicycles, motorcycles, cars, and other household properties. Crops grown for household consumption included, but were not limited to, sorghum, beans, cassava, sweet potatoes, peas, cowpeas, and finger millet. These crops were also sold to purchase domestic items that were needed, pay the graduated tax (a direct tax on all individuals over 18 years of age), and obtain medicines. Every family kept animals, such as cows, goats, and sheep, which they could sell if the need arose. Funds were maintained by individual households. The conflict and mass displacement of people to the IDP camps have prevented the population from engaging in these activities and left them in abject poverty.

Cultural Beliefs of the Acholi

There are many cultural beliefs in Acholi, but they are not formulated into a set of dogmas that a person is expected to accept. These beliefs pertain to the meaning of land, the spiritual world, traditional religion, and death.

Land, Mountains, and Trees

The biggest and most important asset of Acholi people is their homeland. The homeland sustains their livelihood and spiritual beliefs. The land has great diversity in its forests, plains, dry lands, and rivers. It was known as the breadbasket of Uganda. The land had supported farming, hunting, and fishing. Wood from the forests supplied timber for building homes and furniture and for fuel. These activities stopped during the war due to the violence. The Acholi practice of communal ownership of the land meant that resources of the land, such as forests, water, and land for cultivation, were reasonably distributed among the clans. Some mountains and hills, which are owned and named by those inhabiting these areas, are regarded as sacred and are given religious meaning because it is believed there is a *Jok* ("Spirit," including ancestral spirits and others; plural *Jogi*) that takes care of the people who own it. People pray and make sacrifices to this Jok, who is believed to be active in their livelihoods. Some of the biggest trees were not cut down because they were believed to be the dwelling places of Jogi who cared for children and grandchildren. The inhabitants often offered sacrifices to their ancestral spirits under those honorable trees. Today, the elders are very angry because the soldiers have cut down many trees for use as timber. The land is not only an asset to the Acholi, but also their pride, unity, wealth, peace, and life. One of the most painful and traumatizing parts of the armed conflict for this population is living in the IDP camps, as if they have no land. One fear of many Acholi is that the government will try to take away their land and give it to foreign investors because they have been away from their land for so long (Rugadya, 2007).

Spiritual Beliefs

Jogi are the ultimate explanation of the genesis and sustenance of both human beings and all things. Each clan has its own Jogi to which they pray and offer sacrifices; there is no connection to the Jogi of other clans. In each clan there is a supreme Jok that deals with big matters of the clan, and there are other Jogi that deal with lesser matters. All these Jogi have different functions in the community. The Jogi comprise supernatural beings and spirits of men and women who died long ago. The Jogi provide reassurance to the clan about the well-being of its future. They are also believed to play a great role in pacifying the land, providing prosperity, assuring fertility of women, bringing good health for children, good harvests, and good luck in general. They are the protectors of the clan, bringing good fortune for farming, hunting, traveling, bearing children, and bringing well-being and good health.

Each sacred mountain has a special day during the year for its celebration, when sacrifices are made to it. However, the influence of Christianity and other religions has decreased the significance of the roles of these sacred mountains among the population. Most young people are not familiar with these practices. In addition to religious influence, the armed conflict has also prevented people from being able to go to these places for over 20 years due to risk of abduction.

Religion Is Life

In the Acholi tradition, to be human is to belong to the whole community that involves participating in the beliefs, ceremonies, rituals, and festivals of that community; participation in religious practices is not optional or negotiable. Everyone is part of this traditional religious community from conception and even after death. A person cannot detach herself or himself from the religion of her or his group, for to do so is to be severed from his or her roots, foundation, context of security, kinship, and the ethnic group of those who make an individual aware of his or her own existence. To be without a religion in the traditional Acholi culture amounts to self-excommunication from the entire life of the society and clan, resulting in cultural death (Mbiti, 1990).

Traditional religion is infused in all aspects of Acholi life, and every moment of a person's life is spent faithfully in the presence of his or her Jok. There is no moment that one is free from it. It begins in the morning and goes until evening and from evening to morning. Jok is present during all aspects of daily life and activities, like farming, hunting, relationships with the others, traveling, cooking, eating, and collecting water and firewood. These traditional religious beliefs are also found in many who practice Christianity and Islam.

Traditional beliefs are found in many activities of daily life and bring meaning to a variety of daily events. For example, the day can begin in a pleasant and optimistic way, known as *oru ma dako,* "day breaks woman," or in a rough and unfortunate way, known as *oru ma laco,* "day breaks man." Other signs that can signal bad or good luck are the gender of the person one meets as one starts a journey and the songs of birds.

Beliefs about Death

There are also beliefs surrounding death. The Acholi believe that when people die, they have actually been killed by something. This leads to finding the causes of the death for each person. Often, they find that the death was caused by a person or a bad spirit, or that the dead person did something wrong that was not known to others. Due to the pain and loss caused by death, the Acholi people try to fight death at all cost. Evidence of the belief in fighting death is seen in the war dance performed at the funeral rites and the war songs used to fight death. Children prepare themselves to fight death in the form of games, play, and mock fights.

Another important belief is the continuation of life after death. This belief does not constitute hope for a future and better life after death. To live well here and now is the most important concern; on earth, one must live well and in peace with others, without theft, quarrel, anger, jealousy, and hatred. When a person dies, he or she must die with peace in his or her heart, with a good and clean name, and without anger or debt in relation to anyone left behind on earth. This is because of the belief that life on earth takes a person to a place either of peace or of suffering.

Leaving a good name behind on earth is important for the individual, the family, and the clan. Spirits of the dead are not in any way separated from their living community, as they continue to be members of these communities by joining the communion of the dead of that clan and family; however, the dead continue to be spiritually present in all activities of the community. The dead go on to live in trees, in mountains, or by the banks of rivers as spirits; through this transformation, the individual becomes more powerful than the living person. Spirits are even approached and consulted, and they may speak through people serving as mediums. If the living learn that the spirits are hungry—through evidence of sickness, misfortunes, dreams, failures of crops, and failures in hunting—they will provide food. Spirits are also invited to give their blessing in ceremonies such as praying for the healing of those who are sick, cleansing of those returning from captivity with the LRA, and conducting reconciliation practices and funeral rites.

This brief description of the Acholi and the land in which they lived before the war provides a context for understanding the nature of the lives and culture of the population most affected by this violence. This description also gives an understanding of the gravity and amount of loss in many areas that the Acholi suffered during the war. Next, the war and its impact on the people and community are explored so that helping professionals will have knowledge about the experiences that children and families from this area were exposed to.

Experiences of Children, Families, and Communities

Although the extent of the casualties is not easily available or known, it was the civilians, especially children, who bore the brunt of the protracted LRA conflict in southern Sudan and northern Uganda. In Uganda alone, almost 1.6 million people (approximately 90 percent of the population) were displaced by the ongoing armed conflict (Women's Commission for Refugee Women and Children, 2007). Many people resorted to spending sleepless nights in the bush away from their homes and villages to avoid the attacks and abductions occurring in villages and IDP camps. Children caught in the midst of this conflict in northern Uganda were constantly vulnerable to sudden attacks, violations of their basic rights, abuse, and displacement. Many witnessed the destruction of their homes and villages, as well as massive killing and the abduction of others, sometimes their own sisters, brothers, mothers, and fathers.

One of the most tragic aspects of this war was the abduction of children by the LRA. Lacking a base of popular support, the LRA depended on abducting adults and children from their homes, villages, IDP camps, and schools to carry out its operations. Children were targeted because they were fearful and easy to indoctrinate and, therefore, often would not escape (Becker, 2012; de Silva, Hobbs, & Hanks, 2001). Children also did not know the geography of the land very well and were not confident about escaping into unfamiliar rural areas. Parents, teachers—basically all adults—were helpless to stop these attacks and abductions. Approximately 71 percent of those abducted were taken from their homes. Estimates of the number of youths under the age of 30 who were abducted vary from 25,000 to as many as 66,000 (Annan & Blattman, 2006; Human Security Center, 2005). One sample of children in northern Uganda revealed that one-third of male and one-sixth of female children had been abducted (Annan & Blattman, 2006).

Children and adults were generally used as porters for short periods and were then either allowed to return home or killed. Those children kept by the LRA were forced to march for days to the Sudan, with little, if any, food and water. Some ate tree leaves and drank their own urine to survive. In Sudan, they received military training, were given automatic weapons, and then were thrown into active combat the LRA was involved with in Sudan before being taken back to Uganda to attack the local civilian population. Some girls were trained as combatants, but most were forced to become "wives" to LRA commanders based in southern Sudan (Williams, Aloyo, & Annan, 2001).

The initiation period into the LRA for those abducted could be very brutal. Most were made to burn houses and granaries or were forced to loot, rob, lay ambushes, and witness brutal murders (Annan & Blattman, 2006). Many were made to rape and kill (Annan & Blattman, 2006). Some were forced to drink the blood of the victims in the name of giving courage so that they can kill by themselves. Many formerly abducted individuals have reported that they were made not only to witness gruesome tortures, but also to participate in acts such as chopping off buttocks, noses, ears, lips, and limbs and skinning the heads of victims (Lamwaka, 1998).

Those who were abducted and returned, either because they were lucky enough to have escaped (80 percent of those returned), were rescued by the UPDF (15 percent), or were released (5 percent), were offered various forms of support through local authorities, nongovernmental organizations, and their own communities (Annan & Blattman, 2006). Some returnees were taken to the Child Protection Unit of the UPDF (Ugandan Army-Uganda People's Defence Force) for debriefing and then taken to a psychosocial rehabilitation center for assessment and treatment.

Effects of the War

The diverse and often violent experiences of armed conflict had profound effects on the physical, psychological, social, and cultural lives of those affected. Children coming from LRA captivity have had knee joint fractures, limb fractures, gunshot injuries, eye problems, malnutrition, and various other types of physical injuries and disabilities. Many young girls came back with children born in captivity. These medical and health issues were largely untreated during the individuals' time in captivity. Even when individuals returned to their town or camps, they were not likely to receive medical treatment because of the destruction of health centers and dispensaries, reduced services, and lack of medicines.

Beyond the children's physical wounds, children and adolescents struggle daily to cope with the psychological effects of 20 years of armed conflict. Those returning from captivity are frequently haunted by, and feel deeply ashamed of, their experiences. Although most communities are now committed to receiving their formerly abducted children, many individuals within these communities initially feared them, making their reintegration into the community very difficult. Formerly abducted children endured constant fear of reabduction and almost certain death as retribution by the LRA for escape. Yet most formerly abducted children have readjusted well to their communities with the help of family, friends, and agencies that worked to reunite them with their families and to address their medical and psychological concerns. Some find relief in traditional and spiritual cleansing practices. However, many also display challenging or negative behaviors, such as aggressiveness, physical attacks on others, disrespectful behaviors toward elders or teachers, staying apart from the community, learning and memory problems, and low tolerance for frustration.

The violence that many children experienced in captivity has left a deep scar not only in the lives of the children, but also on the community. In addition, wide rifts have developed between the families of individuals who committed violence while abducted and the aggrieved families. Traditionally, Acholi people believe that the ancestral spirits of vengeance take revenge not only on the person who committed that act, but also on his or her family and relatives. The result may be misfortunes, death, insanity, or bad luck. Therefore, the person who committed the violence and his or her family remain worried and fearful of the consequences of the behaviors.

Socially, relationships have been altered due to death, separation from family members, estrangements, family and community breakdown, and damaged social values and practices. Approximately 15 percent of children in Uganda are orphans, largely because of the AIDS epidemic (Uganda Bureau of Statistics, 2006b). However, in northern Uganda, this issue has been compounded by loss of and separation from family members and communities due to the armed conflict. Children as young as five years of age have become heads of families, and they are especially vulnerable to all types of abuses.

The breakdown of traditional customs that protected children and adolescents has given rise to increased domestic violence, including child abuse and sexual gender-based violence (Okello & Hovil, 2007). Young people report that this violence has worsened due to the increase of alcoholism among the male adults, adolescent boys, and others. The girls, particularly in the IDP camps, say that they are being raped, sexually assaulted, and exploited principally by soldiers of UPDF, but also by adult men and adolescent boys.

Many individuals and families became destitute as a result of the loss of their homes, farmland, villages, livestock, and birds. People also lost their social status and place in traditional social networks as a result of the economic devastation. The food production capacity of the region was destroyed, and people became dependent on handouts from the World Food Program and other organizations (Cox & Pawar, 2006; Women's Commission for Refugee Women and Children, 2007).

The long-term impact of this economic devastation will be felt by a generation of children who have had little to no education. All children who were abducted had their education interrupted. Those abducted for a number of years may have felt too old to go back to regular school. Often these young adults have become involved in some type of skills training. Many primary and secondary schools were burned or destroyed by the rebels, making it difficult and unsafe for children to continue their education. Temporary schools were established within the IDP camps; however, these schools are overcrowded, lack sufficient chairs and desks, and have poor sanitation. During this period of economic strain, many families cannot afford to send children to school.

There is a growing realization that care and protection are required not only for children who have experienced the terrorization of rebel captivity, but also for the children and adults who remained with their communities and also faced perilous circumstances. The whole community in the affected area is traumatized and stigmatized by continuous experience of violence; lack of food, shelter, sanitation, and clean and safe drinking water; and fear of death and threat from the rebels. People have experienced resignation and despondency in response to this unrelenting situation (Mirembe, 2003). Support then is needed for families who have either lost loved ones or are suffering from chronic effects of the prolonged conflict. Each and every person has been affected directly or indirectly by the war; every family has lost two or three members in this conflict.

The war in this area has ended; the LRA moved to neighboring countries, such as the Democratic Republic of the Congo and the Central African Republic after the peace talks in Uganda did not reach a conclusion. All in northern Uganda are now turning their attention to restoring relationships and promoting peace among all levels of the social system—individuals, families, subclans, clans, villages, workplaces, schools, and religious institutions.

Peace Building

What Is Peace?

In Acholi culture, a person is said to be at peace when he or she is one with the rest of the family, community, tribe, and society. Thus, the notion of peace is more comprehensive in this culture than just an absence of war or formal conflict; it includes notions of harmony, tolerance, calmness, enjoyment in being a part of the community, knowing and accepting the social roles, respect for the rights of others, and the ability to meet basic needs. I find that a Hebrew word meaning peace—shalom—represents another aspect of peace that is important for the Acholi; it "signifies in general a completeness, perfection—perhaps most precisely, a condition in which nothing is lacking" (McKenzie, 1965, p. 651).

Prior to the 20-year period of war, peace in the land and in society was manifested by harmonious relationships, respect for children's rights, adequate resources and provisions, education, freedom and protection of rights, and greater unity. However, armed conflict has systematically destroyed all these domains. The war disrupted everyone's normal existence and feelings of safety, acceptance, and contentment. The psychological and spiritual quality of well-being, including respect for dead ancestors according to traditional norms, was disturbed. The social structure that made up the Acholi social network—family, village, subclan, clan, and ethnic group—was broken through attacks, abductions, and displacement to IDP camps. The peace of being in one's homeland and having the necessities for a peaceful existence, such as the ability to engage in livelihood activities, access water, raise livestock, farm, and enjoy good health, was destroyed. The conflict interrupted the social orderliness important for public safety, specifically, trust in the law and the ability to have harmonious relationships within the framework of the Acholi culture.

Peace Building

Peace building consists of reconnecting individuals to their communities and to a supportive social structure, teaching the necessary skills to live without violence, and addressing the underlying conditions that promote violence to help them regain a sense of trust and contentment in their ability to restore relationships and promote a peaceful existence (Tuyizere, 2003). A major peace-building goal is to rebuild a sense of trust in relationships and the hope for a peaceful existence, which requires a culture of tolerance and respect for each other in the population; this must include intolerance by citizens of the use of war and other forms of force to resolve disputes (Ekundayo, 1997). Another key peace-building goal addresses the prevention of violent behaviors by teaching prosocial skills and values to all community members, particularly the youth (Wessells & Monteiro, 2006). A third goal of peace building is to ameliorate the conditions that underlie the violence, by re-establishing the economic, political, and social stability of a community (Fellowship of Reconciliation [Uganda], n.d.; Mehta, 1997; Van Soest, 1997). Therefore, the work of peace building necessarily includes the development of human and economic resources so that food, supplies, and services can be available to those who have not had these resources due to war (Obol, 2001). In essence, it means improving the standard of living for those affected. This multidimensional approach cuts through the differences in religions, cultures, tribes, interests, and opinions that may often lead to violence (Obol, 2001).

Education for Peace and Prevention of Violence and HIV/AIDS

One local program involved in peace building is Education for Peace and Prevention of Violence and HIV/AIDS (EPPOVHA). EPPOVHA supports the ability of communities to restore relationships, rebuild communities, and promote peace; the hope is that new bridges can be built despite the broken and distorted past. The program holistically addresses the underlying context and attitudes that give rise to different types, forms, and categories of violence, such as unequal access to employment, discrimination, unacknowledged and unforgiven responsibility for past crimes, prejudice, mistrust, fear, abuses of rights, corruption, and hostility between groups that are detrimental to re-establishing relationships and restoring peace. Peace-building activities strengthen social cohesion by promoting understanding and dialogue among people (Cox & Pawar, 2006). Individuals are trained in peace-building strategies to give them tools they can use to prevent and stop violence and conflict; in addition, it is hoped that such strategies will allow them to foster constructive relationships and engage in useful work in the community (Deutsch, 1973; Ekundayo, 1997). The organization has created a full array of peace-building programs for implementation at various levels of the community to meet its objectives. The activities can be categorized as peace educational services, income-generating activities, financial support for education, and peace promoting/recreational activities. The organization also supports the use of Acholi traditional cleansing and reconciliation practices that further the efforts of restoring interpersonal bonds broken by the war.

Peace Education Services. Violence and conflict became entrenched in workplaces, families, schools, IDP camps, communities, and the media because of the duration and intensity of the war. Therefore, peace-building educational programs are designed and planned with the purpose of imparting and disseminating knowledge and skills to manage violence and conflict. It is a participatory process that changes the way individuals think, act, and behave (Obol, 2001).

EPPOVHA has developed a "training-of-trainers" program in peace education, seminars, and a range of other initiatives to counteract and reverse this multifaceted trend of violence and conflict. It has coordinated its efforts with other peace initiatives in the district to minimize duplication and fragmentation of services and trained others in peace-building skills; in addition, EPPOVHA has aided peace negotiations between the government and the LRA.

The content of the training-of-trainers programs includes knowledge and skill development in conflict resolution, peer mediation, anger management, impulse control, problem solving, children's rights, and social justice. The training occurs in three phases over a period of 12 weeks. The program operates in primary and secondary schools, teachers' colleges, and a university. A team of 24 well-trained teachers, who are certified by the Gulu District Education Office, facilitates the program. The facilitators also manage refresher courses, seminars, and workshops organized every term by the organization. For example, one seminar that the teachers organized brought children and military personnel together to dialogue about adequate protection of children and create mentoring relationships with children experiencing grievances. Dialogues were also planned between the great cultural leaders of the Acholi; the district, county, and subcounty leaders; and the members of parliament. These dialogues, seminars, and workshops can be held both within schools and in the larger community.

EPPOVHA is based principally on education or training of the mind and heart on different social skills and techniques that can be used to "encourage the values, attitudes, and knowledge that foster constructive rather than destructive relations among people" (Deutsch, n.d.). Peace-building education teaches people to actively and productively use their time, energies, and resources in the development of peace rather than violence (Bilubyeka, 2001).

Community Initiatives. The workplace, the family, and the IDP camps are all contexts in which the traditional social interactions have broken down. Because conflict and poor interactions in the workplace prevent organizations from carrying out their work, it is important to provide training for administrators, employees, and customers to reduce and prevent violence, conflict, and poor service delivery. The EPPOVHA training helps those in workplaces deal effectively with difficult interpersonal interactions by providing practical techniques to manage workplace violence and conflict to help managers, program coordinators, officers, and parish priests to deal effectively, peacefully, and responsibly with their coworkers and subordinates. EPPOHVA also recognizes the influence that the leaders of workplaces and places of worship hold over the culture. Without their participation, the attitudes of the organizations in which they work are unlikely to change, resulting in the continuation of conditions that promote violence and disrupt healthy interactions (McCaffrey, 2005).

Peace workers in Acholi are also aware that the influence of the family is the earliest and most profound factor in children's development of social skills. The situation of war has eroded the protective and educational functions of the family. The increase in domestic violence among families in the camps, in villages, and in town is thought to result in part from the families' inability to fulfill traditional functions (Okello & Hovil, 2007). EPPOVHA's training on parental skills and the use of peace-building activities in families can restore a family's dignity and its function of protecting the children and their rights. Similarly, related social skills are taught to camp leaders and camp residents who participate in the peace-building programs that prepare them to be qualified trainers-of-trainers in their own communities.

Training in peace-building skills is available to members of the larger community so that they will be able to address community-based violence and conflict in a more effective and timely manner. Because the community is often linked through the media, especially the newspapers and radio stations in the area, EPPOVHA works with media members in the district and provides short courses, workshops, and meetings to encourage reporters and journalists to adopt more responsible, nonoffensive, and less violent news reporting and programming; they are encouraged to avoid presenting stereotyped or prejudiced positions about cultures, religions, gender, or age groups. Media programs can be a tool to promote personal responsibility and accountability by modelling objective reporting and developing characters on shows that are resilient and are able to think critically, plan their actions, and avoid violence. The media holds great responsibility to educate the public about social responsibility, civic virtue, community service, justice, fairness, and, most important, the necessity to balance individual freedom with social responsibility. This responsibility is shared, as well, by the schools.

School Initiatives. Although the family is key to development in children, subsequent experiences in schools can strengthen that foundation by supporting the development of prosocial skills and peaceful interactions, even if such support is absent in the home. EPPOVHA trains teachers, lecturers, and student leaders from nursery school to university in peace building. Peace education in the schools can provide children with the attitude, understanding, and skills to live in peace with others regardless of differing political beliefs, religious practices, backgrounds, or ethnic groups (Tuyizere, 2003).

It is critical that peace education in schools address human rights violations in general and, specifically, gender inequity and gender-based violence. Children can be taught to recognize behavior within themselves that promotes these types of abuses and to offer support to one another in changing these oppressive behaviors. More important, peace education can provide children with skillful ways of dealing with situations that undermine their self-esteem and dignity—situations such as living in an IDP camp or being dependent on food programs (Tuyizere, 2003). For example, EPPOVHA established peace clubs in 10 primary schools and 10 secondary schools. One teacher in each school has been trained to be the "school peace club coordinator." These teachers coordinate and manage the affairs of the peace club in their respective schools. Peace education programs are broadcast over the radio, and the organization provides a radio for each peace club so that they can listen to the broadcasts of peace education programs and prepare and broadcast their own. The clubs also help to take care of the community by working on homes for elderly people and people with disabilities. Such specific actions put children in an active role in repairing the damage done to their communities and community relationships as a result of the armed conflict. In addition, they engage in music, drama, dance, drawing, and writing. The content of these activities often relates to their encounters with armed conflict, postconflict experiences, and visions of peace.

One peace club coordinator, Lanyero Grace P'Lajok of Bungatira Primary School, discussed the importance of teaching students about the root causes of conflict and the effects of conflict on individuals, families, communities, and schools. P'Lajok explained that the peace programs use various tools to help children understand difficult and painful concepts involved in peace building, such as an individual being both a victim of violence and a perpetrator of violence. Body mapping is one such tool that is used to help individuals see how at times they had to enact violence and at other times they were victims of violence, as explained in the example below.

> We look at the person as an individual, in this case what the arms were doing and what was done to the arms. All the parts of the body in that way—what has been done to the arms and what the arms were doing. So, for example, we see that our legs were used for walking long distances, our arms were used for cutting people into pieces using pangas [machetes], shooting people with bombs. Our shoulders were also used for carrying the dead bodies. So we look at the body parts, part by part,

> what they have been doing during the war. (personal communication with L. G. P'Lajok, peace club coordinator, Awac, Uganda, March 2008)

Another tool, the Balloon Tool, developed by Save the Children (2008), uses the image of a hot air balloon to help children understand peace building and the multiple factors that affect the process. P'Lajok explained how she uses it to explore the factors that interfere with progress toward peace. The balloon is labeled peace, and factors that hinder the peace process are indicated by the nails that keep the balloon anchored to the ground. Other obstacles that can prevent peace from moving are indicated by dark clouds in the sky (see Figure 4-1).

> [The balloon tool] is in the form of [a] balloon, whereby, it is designed in the middle, it is written *Peace*, we need peace, and then we look at the obstacles from [holding it] down which are known as the nails. And in the nails we are looking at these people who are preventing the balloon to flow up. So these people, they [are] still angry; the army men, the government, religious leaders, the local leaders, the parents, the community, all the stakeholders who are involved in peace building. They were seen as people who were now—they were the obstacles to peace [their anger at one another or at government groups was a barrier to peace]. On the other side, from above, when we look at the clouds, the clouds can also bounce back the balloon [keep balloon from rising]. And these clouds we were looking at this as another obstacle. (personal communication with L. G. P'Lajok, Awac, Uganda, March 2008)

In these examples the balloon tool and body mapping tool have been used to depict the negative effects of armed conflict on the individual or the factors that limit peace building. Both tools can be adapted to focus on the positive ways the body is used to rebuild in the aftermath of armed conflict or positive factors that support peace building.

A final example provided by P'Lajok is that the students in the peace clubs wanted to express their opinion to political leaders about ending the violence. They wanted the leaders involved in the peace negotiations to have the International Criminal Court (ICC) charges against the leaders of the LRA withdrawn. The students believed this, rather than a protracted ICC hearing, would lead to a quicker resolution of peace. The peace clubs developed a memorandum for the peace talks and traveled hundreds of miles to take the document to the peace negotiators. P'Lajok said that the obstacles the children encountered, such as walking long distances, experiencing hunger,

FIGURE 4-1: The Balloon Tool

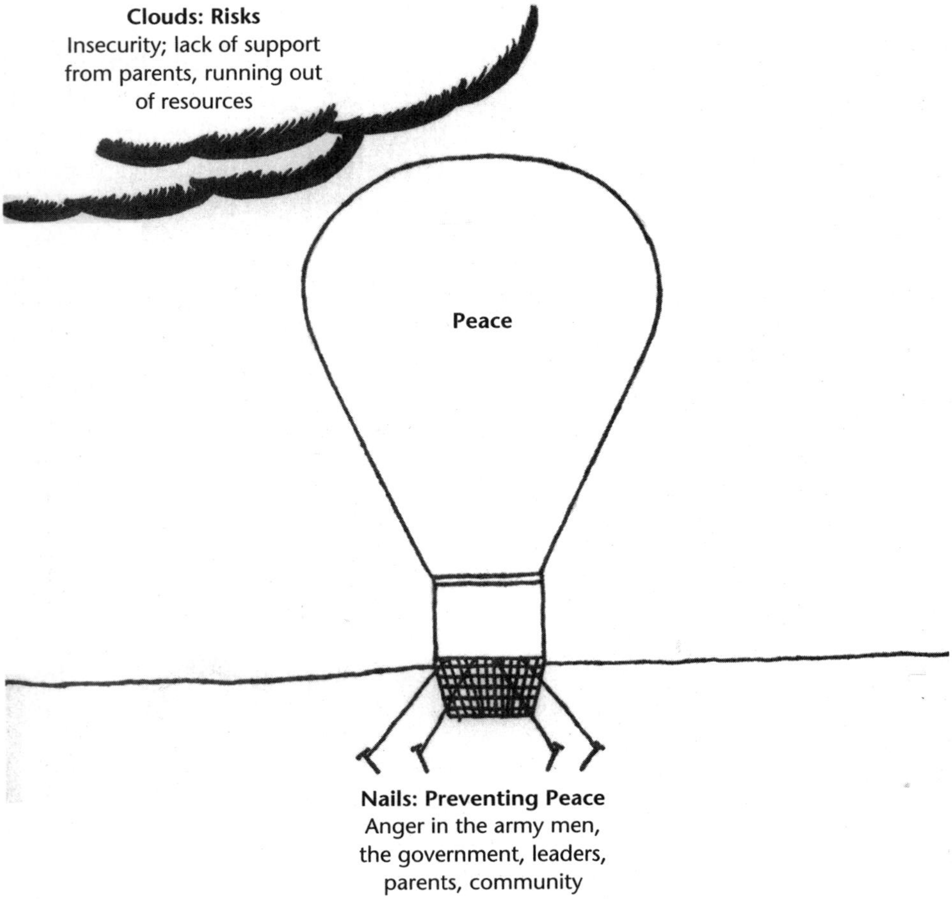

receiving little support from others, and so forth during the journey to the negotiation city were like the clouds in the balloon tool—factors that hampered their peace-building efforts.

Income-Generating Activities. EPPOVHA is involved in promoting small income-generating activities in 10 primary and 10 secondary schools through the peace clubs. Income-generating activities help the children reduce the stress of their economic deprivation. It also trains the children in the qualities of self-reliance, sharing, and cooperation. The peace clubs are involved in horticulture cultivation and tree planting, and they provide seeds, hoes, water cans, and pesticides to the children. The peace clubs also raise poultry; the organization provides seed money to buy chicks, feed, medicines, water containers, lamps, fuel, and housing. The schools involved sell the products to raise funds to support other activities and use part of the profits to buy scholastic materials needed in the schools.

Promoting Education of War Affected Children

Hundreds of thousands of children are out of school due to financial difficulties (Save the Children, 2010). Education is recognized as a means to re-establish structure in the lives of children whose lives have been disorganized by conflict, provide hope for a better future, and teach skills to prepare for the future (Save the Children, 2010). Therefore, support for children's education will achieve the goal of developing peaceful and self-sustaining communities by transforming the underlying political, economic, and social conditions that provide the context for conflicts to take hold (Mehta, 1997).

EPPOVHA looks for financial support from local and national organizations to pay for the tuition, school fees, uniforms, scholastic materials, and so forth needed for war-affected children to continue their education. With funding from Missio, a German organization, EPPOVHA is building four classrooms onto an existing IDP camp primary school. In 2006, the organization bought 10 wheelchairs, school bags, uniforms, and scholastic materials for children with disabilities who could not go to school because of their disability. In the future, the program will also look for ways to promote adult continuing education to transform the untapped human, economic, and political potential within communities (McCaffrey, 2005).

Peace Promoting/Recreational Activities

The organization uses games, sports, drama, and dance as means of developing, promoting, and actualizing what has been taught in the peace education seminars and workshops. These activities also allow for the appropriate release of stress, anger, and emotional effects of trauma and are organized to express peace, reconciliation, unity, and love among the participating children in ways that no ordinary language can do. The activities occur in both the schools and the IDP camps in the area. The organization has established football, traditional dancing, and drama teams in all the camps in its area of operation. Friendly competition is arranged between different children in different schools, camps, and communities. Uniforms, footballs, and netballs and baskets are provided for every sports team; costumes, drums, and other items are provided for the dance and drama groups.

EPPOVHA also collaborates with the Masters of Scouts and Girl Guides in the primary and secondary schools to enhance the peace-building programs (Hassell, 2006; Scout Association, 2006). The rules of the scout and guide programs already encourage collaborative activities among children and young people, so EPPOVHA teaches these groups specific peace-building skills to increase participants' capacities for understanding, reconciliation, forgiveness, and togetherness.

Reconstruction of Relationships: Traditional Cleansing and Reconciliation Practices

Acholi traditional practices of cleansing and reconciliation are critical strategies toward restoring damaged relationships among community members, used historically in this area long before the LRA conflict. EPPOVHA supports the use of traditional practices in its work with communities. The maintenance of harmonious relationships among individuals, groups, communities, and clans is very important for the Acholi, and anything that destroys this harmony must be addressed; the rites of traditional reconciliation are deeply rooted and, thus, provide a culturally compatible form of restorative justice. Groups in conflict and their supporters must be involved in the process of restoring the original relationship. These practices are often used with youths returning to communities after abduction by the LRA because they have been exposed to a range of violence toward one another and the community.

For those abducted individuals who return to families and communities after escape or rescue from the LRA, there are three phases that they may participate in to restore damaged relationships: reception by family and community members, a precleansing ceremony, and other rites administered dependent on the experiences of the returnee. The emphasis through all of the phases is on assessment of the problem, necessary psychological and social support, and social reintegration of the returning person.

Phase 1: Reception of the Returnees. As described earlier, formerly abducted children often stay for a period of time at a psychosocial rehabilitation center. Before they return to their home, arrangements for the transfer of the individual to their IDP camp or village is arranged and the family is informed so that they can begin to make arrangements for the ceremony. When the returnee arrives at home, he or she stops at the threshold of the family's compound so that the appropriate initial ritual ceremonies can be performed. Traditional cleansing rites are used in purification of the formerly abducted individuals who committed atrocities against others. Family members arrange this ceremony, and the elders, wise men, parents, and neighbors participate in the ceremonies. This cleansing ceremony, *stepping on the egg*, is performed on all those who have been away for a long period of time.

The parents or any family member brings an *opobo* plant (a plant with slippery sap or liquid substance in the bark). Also used is the *layibi* (a long stick used for opening the roof of the granary in which families store their grain harvest). These two objects are placed across the path for the returnee to walk over; the returnee goes a few more steps and then crushes an egg placed just immediately after the two objects. Only then can the returnee enter the compound of his or her home and rejoin the family with a joyous welcome. The opobo plant symbolizes cleansing, the layibi represents the community caring for the individual's well-being, and stepping on the egg symbolizes purification.[3] The person does not yet enter the house; he or she remains in the compound until another ritual is performed. This time, a calabash full of water is brought, often prepared in advance, and the returnee is then beckoned to come forward and stand at his or her mother's door. The parents then make a brief potent recitation known as *lamu dog*. This is a prayer of innocence [for the returning child] to the God of ancestors for receiving the misfortune of their child's long absence; the God is thanked for keeping the child alive and returning the child home:

> This child has taken too long outside. Our ancestors, we cherish your blessing and guardianship that allowed our child to return back home safely. Here is my water, let the child enter and dwell in the home and let there be no more trouble upon her/him.

Then the water is splashed over the front roof at the entrance door and drips on the child as the child goes into and comes out of the home. This movement "in and out of the house" is repeated three times for a male returnee and four for a female returnee. Each time the child enters the house, water is poured over the door. After entering the house for the last time, the child can sit and relax inside the house and can come out at a later time. The water that is dripped on the child as he or she enters the house symbolically represents cleansing. The remaining water in the calabash is then poured away while the family prays, "Pour away any misfortune. Water, go with it. Let the sun take it away." The calabash used in this ritual is left overnight fixed on the grass-thatched roof over the entrance door. It is removed the next day.

Phase 2: Assessment or Pre-cleansing Ceremony. Moyo kum (a major precleansing ceremony) means searching for what is wrong on the victim (health and mental health are conceptualized holistically; therefore, the parents and elders will look for signs of physical, psychological, social, and spiritual distress). After two or three days from the reception of the returnee, the parents get a goat for the ceremony known as *moyo kum*, which literally means cleansing of the body. The parents invite the elders. When the elders arrive and are seated in the compound of the returnee, one of the parents says, "We have called you—our child left home long ago—we have actually thought he/she was

[3]Elaboration on the meaning of this ceremony can be found in chapter 8.

dead or would not return home alive again. But now that he/she has returned back, we hand over this goat to you to help us perform the *moyo kum* exercise on him/her."

The goat is slaughtered, cooked, and eaten by everybody to accomplish the *moyo kum* exercise. After eating the goat, the people wash their hands in water, which is then collected in one container from the various groups who have eaten the goat. The elders bless and give well wishes to the victim. The elders then dip their hands in the water and sprinkle it on the returnee. The remaining water in a container is then poured to the western direction of the home while the elders say, "*Marace wang wang ceng oter,*" which means "let the sun set with all the bad fortunes or misfortunes."

Many of the returnees who have had this ritual indicate better functioning with family and peers and improved feelings about their mental health. The exercise is believed to build a defense against misfortunes. The ceremony provides comfort to the returnee from the community. It also provides comfort to the family who has experienced a long period of sorrow as a result of the absence of and separation from their child.

As the elders leave, *buku tyen ludito,* meaning cleansing the feet of the elder, is conducted. In this brief, concluding ceremony, the participatory elders line up. A chicken of a required color and nature is brought and held by the legs by one of the family members and swung around the elders' feet. The chicken flaps its wings and cries, and this is the cleansing of the legs exercise. After this, the people present retire in peace. The used chicken is set free.

Phase 3: Additional Rites. Other cleansing practices may follow after a thorough assessment of the returnee's health and behavior by community elders and those close to the returnee now that he or she is living in the community. If there are concerns, those elders or close family members or neighbors will counsel the returnee to disclose what transpired with him or her while in captivity, diagnose the returnee's problem, and then perform the appropriate ritual ceremonies required for the problem; on most occasions, such ceremonies help to relieve the situation.

Many of the returnees have been exposed to death, witnessed death, or participated in killing during their period of abduction. In Acholi culture, the traditional chiefs court and the elders examine the issue of murder frequently, because they believe that most returnees from LRA captivity are likely to have been involved in murder more than any other act. They are also concerned that the intensity of the act of killing causes most of the psychological, spiritual, and social problems of returning abducted children. These issues are dealt with using traditional rituals of cleansing and reconciliation. Compensation is also required to be paid to the family of the person who was killed if the identity of that person is known.

Three specific rituals that may be performed are the ritual practice for forced murder of a known person such as a family member or someone close, for forced murder of an unknown person, and for murder of an enemy. The ceremony for an enemy is the most practiced ceremony at this time as most abducted individuals had to kill people during battles. These rituals serve to restore the relationships among individuals, families, villages, subclans, clans, and ancestors that were broken through the act of murder. Acknowledging the killings and associated violence to the community, reconciling with involved parties if known, and compensating for the loss are vital to recreating harmonious relationships within the region.

Conclusion

The process of peace building in communities affected by armed conflict must address conflicted relationships between individuals and among family members, villages, subclans, clans, and the larger social system networks. Although attention is paid to the actions and words that fuel violent and negative interactions, the peace-building efforts described in this chapter also address the underlying political, economic, and social inequalities that create the conditions for violence to take hold. The peace-building efforts in northern Uganda are further complicated by the experience of reestablishment of communities and village networks after two decades of displacement.

EPPOVHA's peace-building efforts are geared toward teaching individuals how to build supportive relationships with others. Various approaches are used to teach community members at all levels and in varying positions of responsibility about peaceful and prosocial skills needed to establish and sustain peace. As a result, more people are able to share peace-building knowledge and skills with ever-widening circles in the community. Peace clubs in local schools provide children with the skills for recognizing and changing beliefs and actions that promote violence. Youths are also engaged in activities such as repairing homes and schools damaged during the conflict, thereby helping to rebuild the community and reconnect themselves with community members. EPPOVHA also has focused on supporting children to complete their education as an important means to improve the community's standard of living and alleviate the underlying conditions of violence.

Traditional cultural practices of cleansing and restoring relationships in which killing has occurred continue to be very important in this work. These practices repair the relationships broken through long absences of family members who were abducted or through horrific acts of violence and killing during captivity. Conducting these practices may also provide a form of safety for many—an important social norm is once again being observed.

Although this chapter describes peace building in a country where the violence occurred, understanding these processes may help professionals working with individuals affected by armed conflict who are no longer living in their home country. New arrivals may encounter, once again, underlying conditions of violence, such as political and economic injustice; they may be placed in neighborhoods that are isolating or unwelcoming to them. New arrivals who cannot find meaningful work or daily activities are reminded of the economic, political, and social injustice they experienced in their country of origin. This chapter raises the importance of exploring the peace-building activities that individuals may have been involved in prior to arrival in their resettlement country to better understand the strategies that may be useful in their current environment. Lastly, the chapter presents the role and meaning of traditional cultural practices in restoring relationships damaged as a result of the consequences of armed conflict. Refugees, immigrants, and asylum seekers who have experienced the violence of war and are living away from their country of origin may have a need to connect with some aspect of their traditional cultural beliefs and practices as a way of restoring peace within themselves and with family—no matter the distance—and ancestors. Helping professionals must find ways to increase and explore their knowledge of the importance of these cultural practices to their clients.

References

Annan, J., & Blattman, C. (2006). *SWAY research brief 1: The abduction and return experiences of youth.* Uganda: Survey of War Affected Youth.

Becker, J. (2012). The nature of children's participation in armed conflict. In J. Corbin (Ed.), *Children and families affected by armed conflicts in Africa: Implications and strategies for helping professionals in the United States.* Washington, DC: NASW Press.

Behrend, H. (1999). *Alice Lakwena & the holy spirits: War in northern Uganda 1985–1997.* Oxford: James Currey, Ltd.

Bibangamabah, J. R. (2001). *Ending the scourge of hunger and poverty in Uganda* (Discussion Paper 4, p. 4). Kampala: Uganda Debt Network.

Bilubyeka, E. (2001). *Peace education coming to schools.* Kampala, Uganda: New Vision Printing Press.

Cox, D., & Pawar, M. (2006). *International social work: Issues, strategies and programs.* Thousand Oaks, CA: Sage Publications.

de Silva, H., Hobbs, C., & Hanks, H. (2001). Conscription of children in armed conflict—A form of child abuse. A study of 19 former child soldiers [Electronic version]. *Child Abuse Review, 10,* 125–134.

Deutsch, M. (1973). *The resolution of conflict: Constructive and destructive processes.* New Haven, CT: Yale University Press.

Deutsch, M. (n.d.). *Education for peaceful world.* Unpublished manuscript.

Ekundayo, T.J.D. (1997). *Governance and civil education.* Nairobi, Kenya: Ruaraka Printing Press.

Fellowship of Reconciliation (Uganda). (n.d.). *Pertinent issues on peace building.* Arua, Uganda: Education Programme for Sudanese Refugee and Displaced People Printing Press.

Harlacher, T., Okot, F. Z., Obonyo, C. A., Balthazard, M., & Atkinson, R. (2006). *Traditional ways of coping in Acholi: Cultural provisions for reconciliation and healing from war.* Kampala, Uganda: Intersoft Business Services, Ltd.

Hassell, S. (2006). *Girlguilding UK: An introduction to international guiding.* Retrieved from http://www.girlguiding.org.uk/xq/asp/sID.279/qx/whoweare/article.asp

Human Rights Watch Children's Rights Project. (1997). *The scars of death: Children abducted by the Lord's Resistance Army in Uganda.* New York: Human Rights Watch.

Human Security Center. (2005). *Human security report: War and peace in the 21st century.* Retrieved from http://www.humansecurityreportinfo/HSR2005_ PDF/Part1.pdf

Lamwaka, C.C.H. (1998). Civil war and the peace process in Uganda, 1986–1997. *East African Journal of Peace and Human Rights, 4*(2), 139–169.

Mbiti, J. S. (1990). *African religions and philosophy.* Portsmith, NH: Heinemann.

McCaffrey, J. (2005). Using transformative models of adult literacy in conflict resolution and peacebuilding processes at community: Guinea, Sierra Leone, Sudan. *Compare, 35,* 443–462.

McKenzie, J. L. (1965). *Dictionary of the Bible.* Milwaukee: Bruce Publishing.

Mehta, V. (1997). Ethnic conflict and violence in the modern world: Social work's role in building peace. In M. C. Hokenstad & J. Midgley (Eds.), *Issues in international social work: Global challenges for a new century* (pp. 92–109). Washington, DC: NASW Press.

Mirembe, M. N. (2003). Children in the war zone of Africa. In N.R.K. Deusdedit & M. Levis (Eds.), *Developing a culture of peace and human rights in Africa: Africa peace series* (Vol. 1, pp. 85–92). Kampala, Uganda: Konrad Adnauer Stiftung.

Obol, R. C. (2001). *The importance of peace education in development: Case study Gulu District 1980–2000* (Unpublished postgraduate dissertation). Kampala: Uganda Martyrs University, Ethics and Development Studies.

Okello, M. C., & Hovil, L. (2007). Confronting the reality of gender-based violence in northern Uganda. *International Journal of Transitional Justice, 1,* 433–443. doi:10.1093/ijtj/ijm036

Pain, D. (1997). *The bending of the spears: Producing consensus for peace & development in northern Uganda* [Report commissioned by International Alert in partnership with Kacoke Madit]. London: International Alert and Kacoke Madit.

Refugee Law Project. (2004). Behind the violence: Causes, consequences and the search for solutions to the war in Northern Uganda (Working Paper No. 11). Kampala, Uganda: Author.

Rugadya, M. (2007, January 1). Allay land grabbing concerns in Acholi. *The New Vision.* Kampala, Uganda, p. 8.

Save the Children. (2008). *I painted peace: Handbook on peace building with and for children and young people.* Oslo: Save the Children Norway.

Save the Children. (2010). *Rewrite the future: Education for children in conflict affected countries.* Retrieved from http://www.savethechildren.org.uk/en/docs/The_Future_is_Now_low_res.pdf

Scout Association. (2006). *International scouting.* Retrieved from http://www.scouts.org.uk/aboutus/international.htm

Tuyizere, A. (2003). Introduction of peace education in secondary schools: A strategy for promotion of peace in Uganda. In N.R.K. Deusdedit & M. Levis (Eds.), *Developing a culture of peace and human rights in Africa: Africa peace series, volume one* (pp. 73–84). Kampala, Uganda: Konrad Adnauer Stiftung.

Uganda Bureau of Statistics. (2006a). *The 2002 Uganda population and housing census, population size and distribution*. Retrieved from http://www.ubos.org/

Uganda Bureau of Statistics. (2006b). *Uganda National Household Survey 2005/2006: Report on the socio-economic module*. Retrieved from http://www.ubos.org/onlinefiles/uploads/ubos/pdf%20documents/UNHSReport20052006.pdf

Uganda Bureau of Statistics. (n.d.). *2002 census analytical report executive summary*. Retrieved from http://www.ubos.org/2002%20CensusAnalytical ReportESummary.pdf

Van Soest, D. (1997). *The global crisis of violence: Common problems, universal causes, shared solutions*. Washington, DC: NASW Press.

Wessells, M., & Monteiro, C. (2006). Psychosocial assistance for youth: Towards reconstruction for peace. *Journal of Social Issues, 62*(1), 121–139. doi: 10.1111/j.1540-4560.2006.00442.x

Williams, G., Aloyo, C., & Annan, J. (2001). *Resilience in conflict: A community-based approach to psychosocial support in Northern Uganda*. Kampala, Uganda: AVSI and UNICEF.

Women's Commission for Refugee Women and Children. (2007). *Listening to youth: The experiences of young people in northern Uganda*. Retrieved from http://www.womenscommission.org/pdf/ug_machel.pdf

5

Psychosocial Approaches to Addressing the Needs of Children Affected by Armed Conflict in Northern Uganda

Stella Ojera

The purpose of this chapter is to describe the psychosocial approaches to working with children affected by armed conflict in northern Uganda. The content of this chapter is largely based on my work as a former regional director with Save the Children, one of the main sponsors of interventions for war-affected children in northern Uganda; in particular, I will draw on my experiences in Gulu District. First, I will provide a brief recent historical context of Uganda, with primary focus on northern Uganda. (A fuller description of the historical and cultural history of this area is presented in chapter 4.) I will then discuss the types of violence that children were exposed to, the effects of this exposure, and the evolution of the psychosocial programming that developed to address the needs of the children and community. Lastly, I will identify the challenges and lessons learned.

Background

Uganda is a landlocked country; it is bordered by Kenya, Rwanda, Democratic Republic of the Congo, and Sudan. (The region between northern Uganda and southern Sudan was the region affected by the 22-year LRA armed conflict.) The country is divided into four main geographical regions: northern, western, eastern, and southern. The total population is approximately 33 million (Index Mundi, 2010), with 1.2 million people living in the north; half of these are children. English is the official language spoken throughout the country; however, there are over 27 ethnic groups living in Uganda speaking different languages but bonded by their culture, traditions, beliefs, and norms. The population is highly religious, with the majority being Protestant (42 percent) and Catholic (42 percent) and a smaller percentage being Muslim (12 percent) (Index Mundi, 2010). Traditional religion and practices still exist in some communities.

Of the four regions of the country, the northern part is most economically underdeveloped. The people of northern Uganda speak Luo and live a communal life; their major economic activities are agriculture, subsistence farming, and livestock rearing. However, their section of the country has been affected by war for over 20 years; as a result of the war, traditional chiefdoms and structures of cultural political leadership have been weakened.

The war in northern Uganda started in 1986 when the current president, Yoweri Kaguta Museveni, who had been fighting a very long bush war, overthrew the elected government of Dr. Apollo Milton Obote. Museveni's leadership met with resistance from some people from the North; those who wanted to overthrow the government voluntarily joined rebellion groups with the hope of recapturing power. These opposition efforts were defeated, and people deserted these groups. Some of these rebellion leaders reorganized as the Lord's Resistance Army (LRA) and took revenge against the deserters by killing them and their family members. The LRA began abducting children and forcing them to fight in the armed group. Since that time, over 24,000 children have been abducted by the LRA. Approximately 10,000 children have returned and resettled into the community, but the rest remain unaccounted for.

The intensity of the violence and abductions increased over the years, and in 1996, the government established Internally Displaced Persons (IDP) camps as a way to provide the population with protection from the violence. During the war, children and families were displaced to these camps that hosted between 12,000 to 40,000 people living in small huts and congested areas. Many children lost opportunities for education. Nearly all children had been exposed to some kind of atrocity and violence. Many children were orphaned by HIV/AIDS and by the war itself. Several children were labeled *night commuters*—children who commuted daily from areas outside the town that were isolated and less safe into the safer areas of town to spend the night on verandas, in churches, in schools, in search of protection. Many children under age 5 were malnourished and died in great numbers as parents were not able to provide food through farming due to the violence. Parents were not able to support or provide for their children; they were powerless. But the worst experience was the abduction of the children.

Many children and adults were abducted during the LRA attacks on villages during the night, but abductions also occurred in the normal course of daily routines. Children were abducted as they walked to school, attended classes or churches, or cultivated the farms with the parents; they were abducted from anywhere, a clear indication that they were not—could not be—protected in any way, by the community structures, by the institutions, or by the duty bearers.[1]

During the course of the abductions, some children were commanded by the LRA to kill family members and community members as a way to force the children into submission and to create fear so that they would not escape from the LRA. After abduction, these children were given rudimentary training, such as assembling and dismantling of guns, and then ordered into combat. They were involved in marauding villages, looting, stealing, and destroying properties, crops, and infrastructures. Children were also directed to lay land mines, ambush vehicles or people, abduct other children, and kill. They had to nurse wounded combatants and bury the dead. Children were exposed to many frightening and life-threatening events, such as being fired on by helicopter gunships, harsh weather, bush fires, crossing large bodies of water, attacks by wild animals, thirst, and starvation.

Children ended their involvement with the LRA in various ways. Hundreds of abducted children managed to escape on their own and return to their communities/IDP camps. Others were captured by government troops during combat with the LRA and brought back into the communities. Many children were reluctant to return to the communities because of the violence they had committed, some on their own communities. A high percentage of the children returned with illnesses, malnutrition, disabilities, and physical injuries such as gunshot wounds and maiming, for which they had received no medical attention during their time in captivity. Both boys and girls experienced rape, and some became infected with HIV/AIDS; girls were used as sex slaves, some were married to commanders. Many girls returned from the LRA with children fathered by the LRA commanders. Some girls who were not in good health, possibly infected by HIV/AIDS, or were not considered attractive in some way were discarded by the LRA. Girls who lost their "husbands" in battle were considered cursed, and another LRA commander did not want to risk inheriting them. Girls and boys were exposed to the traumatic experiences of war and returned to communities also coping with the psychological and social effects of war and child abduction. Many of these children lost their identities and their childhoods; some bonded with their captors and identified more with being part of an armed group, thus developing militarized

[1]The primary duty bearer is the state, which has the main responsibility for bringing about realization of children's rights and is accountable to both the international community and to all people living within its borders. Secondary duty bearers, such as, teachers, social workers, and parents have clear moral and/or legal responsibilities toward children. They help the state to secure children's rights (Save the Children, n.d.).

habits. Many changed their names because of the fear that they would be traced by the LRA and reabducted after they returned to their families. All of these children have missed out on the normal opportunities of education, socialization, and development that occur during childhood and adolescence.

This war gradually diminished in intensity in the mid-2000s, and by 2007, those living in the IDP camps were urged to leave the camps and return to former villages. There was no definitive *ending* of this war; therefore, it is important to understand that many of the escapes or rescues of children from the LRA occurred during the ongoing conflict, which added to the fear of reabduction by the LRA. The development of the psychosocial programming that will be discussed next occurred during the ongoing conflict. In other armed conflicts, the psychosocial programming associated with disarmament, demobilization, reintegration, and rehabilitation (DDRR) interventions occurs after the conflict has officially ended.

Common Psychosocial Reactions

Formerly abducted children (FACs) reacted to these extreme events differently, depending on individual characteristics and environmental factors. Having been exposed to traumatic events beyond the normal boundaries of human experiences, they have shown varied stress reactions in their day-to-day lives. Many continued to live in states of extreme fear after their return to their families because of the possibility of reabduction by the LRA. Returning children also feared rejection by family members, peers, and community members as well as stigmatization due to their experiences and actions while abducted.

Common behaviors and symptoms that children exhibited included loss of speech, loss of bladder and bowel control, flashbacks, daydreaming, hallucinations, nightmares and night terrors, regression to developmentally younger forms of behavior, preoccupation with their roles in past experiences, excessive clinging to familiar people, and militarized habits (authoritative and commanding behavior). Other manifestations included headaches and other physical pain, sleep disturbance, eating disturbance, sudden mood changes, crying easily, irritability, anxiety, sadness and depression, suicide and suicidal feelings, feelings of guilt, separation anxiety, lack of interest and energy, restlessness, deviant behavior, poor school performance, withdrawal from relationships, disturbed relations with peers and adults, mistrust and suspicion, lack of interest in education, and irregularity of school attendance. Some children expressed their increased anxiety or arousal through increased aggressiveness, destructiveness, restlessness, disobedience, poor concentration, dizziness, absent-mindedness, and poor memory.

The Acholi people are the primary ethnic group in the Gulu area of northern Uganda; some aspects of Acholi culture had a significant impact on the reentry of child soldiers to the community. In particular, children involved in armed conflict were seen to have violated three key Acholi taboos: they had likely been involved in killing, they had walked or slept in the bush, and they had taken shelter under big trees. The bush, forests, and trees are areas that have been viewed as sacred places where Acholi spirits reside. Such cultural and spiritual violations are believed to unsettle a person psychologically and spiritually. It is believed that most children who returned from the armed conflict were affected by these spiritual transgressions; the Acholi culture would say that they have been "possessed by the evil spirits." If children speak in tongues—talk in a language that they cannot understand—they are characterized as being possessed.

Development of Psychosocial Approaches

Psychosocial work with former child soldiers began in 1993 with an increase in the number of children escaping and returning to communities. The programs evolved over time. Initially, when children escaped, they were brought by the Ugandan military into the military installation. After reporting to the army barracks and being interrogated, the children would be displayed in a big public rally, where parents and relatives would be asked to identify and *claim* them. Some children were never claimed; they were rejected outright because they had killed people and were possessed by the evil spirits. Killing is taboo among the Acholi people. Some of the children, on return to the military installation, committed suicide because they were not accepted by their own people. When children were returning to communities, the community members did not understand their behaviors; some were called names such as "rebel," and others were attacked. This situation was unique and the community as a whole did not know how to address it, but it was clear that the current approach was not working.

A group of female politicians sympathized with the children and called on other members of the community to support these children. They were able to collect food items, clothes, and other basic requirements and delivered them to the children who remained within the military installation; these efforts were considered psychosocial support but did not adequately meet the psychosocial needs of the children. So what was lacking? Many discussions were generated among the military and the local leaders to identify better approaches. Eventually, a breakthrough was made; a reception center supported by Save the Children–Denmark and run by the Gulu Support the

Children Organization, a local nongovernmental organization (NGO), was created for the children that provided clothes, food, and shelter. However, the workers feared interacting with the children and left them on their own, sleeping in a dorm. The older boys became very aggressive, and many of them verbally and physically attacked the staff. Recreational activities were introduced and were successful in engaging the children. Contacts were made with families, and families began to see that these children were not totally lost. They still had certain values that could be built on. At that point, many more people started seeing the need to welcome the children, be close to them, and support them in coming back home. The work of the center helped to reduce the stigmatization of these children.

Agencies interested in developing an approach to support these former child soldiers worked to develop a clear definition of psychosocial support as a guide to the provision of services to them. This was followed, in Gulu, by wide consultation with the affected people to obtain their perspectives and identify their needs; a process of community resource mapping also was useful in identifying gaps in services. A Core Team for psychosocial support was formed to comprehensively look at the issues of children affected by conflict. The term "psychosocial" denotes a dynamic relationship between psychological and social experiences in which the effects of each continually influence the other. It was also important to demystify the concept of psychology, because it was something new in the Ugandan context. *Psychology,* refers to someone's emotions, behaviors, thoughts, beliefs, attitudes, perceptions, and understanding of themselves. *Social* was defined as the relationships between individuals, families, and communities and their environment. The psychosocial approaches developed thus focused on helping individuals regain lost capacity, restore relationships and functioning, and acquire skills to build resilience. They also focused on strengthening family and community structure to respond to the needs of war-affected children and resettled FACs. The two broadly categorized approaches to psychosocial support are center-based approaches and community-based approaches. The definition of psychosocial support and the following nine principles, developed in 1990 by the National Core Team for psychosocial support, were used to help design programs and deliver services for the war-affected children in northern Uganda.

Principles and Practice in Working with Formerly Abducted and War-affected Children

1. Family reunification of formerly abducted and other separated children is the priority of all psychosocial programming.
2. The overall determinant for all programming is the best interest of the child.

3. Center-based care should be used as a last resort, for the shortest possible time, and should take place within the context of the child's cultural and familial environment.
4. When nonfamily care arrangements are necessary, they should be community based and appropriate to the child's age, gender, and culture.
5. The aim of reintegration efforts is to enable FACs and other vulnerable children to access the same range of services available to all children in the community.
6. Some children may be particularly vulnerable and require additional support to promote reintegration and healing.
7. Psychosocial interventions aim at promoting well-being and emphasize children's capacities and resilience.
8. Involvement of children in the armed groups is never in the best interest of the child.
9. The rights on dignity of formerly abducted and other vulnerable children must always be promoted and protected.

Center–based Psychosocial Approach

There are two main components of the center-based approach, the Child Protection Unit (CPU) and the reception center. The CPU is located just outside of the military barracks or detaches. Children who have escaped from the LRA or been rescued by the military are first brought to the CPU. The CPU serves as a transit center, where the process to promote reconciliation and trust between the former child soldiers and the military begins; this is challenging because the children consider the military to be their enemy. Activities designed to assist children in the CPU to reintegrate into their communities include a briefing about the next phase of their reintegration, engagement in confidence-building activities, emphasis on activities that promote reconciliation, and re-establishment of a sense of safety for these children. Only military staff who received training on psychosocial support worked directly with the children; in addition, some family members were allowed to visit the children. Staff working with the children wore normal civilian clothing instead of military uniforms, which would have been more stressful for these children.

There were distinct differences between the objectives of the military and the objectives of the psychosocial support team. The military was interested in interrogating the returning children to get information from them about the movements of the LRA. The psychosocial support team was focused on support, healing, and recovery. An agreement was reached that children would be moved to a reception center within a week of arriving at the CPU to begin the support, healing, and recovery aspects of reintegration, after a military debriefing.

The reception centers were in a relatively safe environment, and there were no sign posts or guards as there were in the CPU. The term "reception center" was used to avoid the stigma of a rehabilitation center. The first phase of settling in to the reception center took one to two weeks. During this time there was the initial briefing, including the welcome, introductions, and exposure to the center facilities. This was often a difficult time because some of the children had been the victimizers of others. These former child soldiers were expected to dine together and see one another as brothers and sisters. Despite the strain, staff used the potential for conflict as an opportunity. The social workers would recognize the children's anger, bitterness, feelings of revenge, and resentment and support them to reflect on their past bush life and experiences as well as their futures after leaving the center. The social workers used the forum to begin the process of reconciliation and taught the former captives about love, forgiveness, and peaceful coexistence; they stressed that the children would need one another upon resettlement in the community. After the welcome at the reception center, children were engaged in activities that included the following: registration, health screening, rituals symbolizing breaking connections with the past, and efforts at tracing and locating family. Staff also stressed socialization and re-establishment of daily routines.

Rituals symbolizing a break with the past and a step back into normal society took on great importance at the reception centers. In Acholi culture, there are still traditional rituals that are believed to help in healing and cleansing people of the evils in the society. These ceremonies were done for many children, and all children participated in a burning of the uniforms and military equipment they had brought back from war. The burning symbolized the development of a new identity and prepared the children to go back into the society. Tracing their families allowed for interaction with visiting family members/relatives at the reception centers or at home. Because the health of many children had been affected by their experiences, initial first aid was given, then referrals for medical examination and treatment were made where needed. Therapeutic feeding—the provision of supplementary food to those who were highly malnourished—was also provided at this point.

During this initial time, children became refamiliarized with the acceptable norms of the society. Often, a group of children was guided by adult or elder staff members to learn about Acholi cultural taboos and to understand which behaviors are not acceptable in the Acholi culture. This guidance helped to socialize children to expectations regarding how they should live when they return to their families. Children who were healthy enough were encouraged to get involved in the daily routine activities. The approaches used at the reception centers were vital to helping the children to re-establish the trust, hope, and sense of safety necessary for development of a nonmilitary identity, which was essential to a successful reintegration process.

Two Traditional Ceremonies

Two traditional ceremonies often performed in the reception centers are (1) stepping on the egg (Nyono Tong Gweno) and (2) the Moyo Kum cleansing ceremony. The stepping-on-the-egg ceremony involved the returnee and his close extended family members. An unbroken egg is placed next to a branch of a slender slippery tree (leaves removed) called *opobo* and a traditional strong dry stick used for opening an Acholi granary. The stick has a forked end. The materials are placed across the road leading to home, just before stepping onto the family compound. The person being received home steps on the egg with one foot, breaks it, and proceeds straight into the house. The stepping-on-the-egg ceremony is performed to welcome home a member of the family who has been away for a long time and to facilitate the reintegration process for the returning person. The stick signifies that the door to the house has been opened, the slippery stem signifies that a person "*Tyeni obed ma pwot*" (should always come back home regular in event of future travel), and the egg signifies good health during the stay at home. Many of the FACs had committed atrocities against their family members and had very strong feelings of guilt about this; they also had been repeatedly told by the rebels that they would not be welcomed or accepted at home and would never belong again to their family and community. The stepping-on-the-egg ceremony mediated many of these concerns and contributed to sustainable reintegration into the family and community.

The Moyo Kom cleansing ceremony is performed to appease the spirits and cleanse the hearts of those who have passed through unknown areas. The Acholi believe that a person's passing through unknown areas or areas exposed to violence will affect that individual's psychosocial well-being. This ceremony is performed by the elders and a few trusted members of the family. A discussion occurs between the person and those who are concerned about the person's well-being. The person must reveal everything that has happened to him or her during his or her time in this spiritually unknown/unclean place. After this discussion and resolution process, a goat is slaughtered and other activities are performed with the community to signal that this person can resume his or her normal activities with the community.

The next stage at the reception center (four to five weeks) focused on building/rebuilding relationships. Staff focused on building relationships between one child and another child, a child and a staff member, a child and the caregivers, and a child and the community. This stage began with a thorough assessment of the physical, psychological, social, and educational status of the child by a social worker, a teacher, and a nurse. Another assessment was done on the child's return to the family. To some extent, the child's family supportive environment was also assessed. Structured interviews using forms were conducted to get responses from the child and family members in combination with direct observation.

The relationship-building activities included religious programs and services. This region is highly religious, and most people believe in spirituality, so it is an important aspect of healing. The children were actively involved in the processes. For children who were interested, there were weekly Sunday prayers/masses led by religious leaders and evening prayers led by children. There were family talks about peace, love, forgiveness, and reconciliation for all the children. These talks helped to decrease the feelings of revenge, because there were groups that wanted to hurt another group, yet they were living together. The important thing was that adults were physically present at all times at this stage, when the relationships were being created. Just the physical presence of others made a difference in the life of a child, even if the adult/staff member was not talking with the child.

Interactions between children during indoor and outdoor games involving children of the center and children from the neighborhood were encouraged and supervised. Another important aspect in the reception center was the participation of children in cultural activities. Cultural activities are one of the richest aspects of Acholi culture, and their impact could not be underestimated as a key intervention. There is the *wang oo*, the family fireplace, around which children are typically gathered and informally educated about the society, the relationships that exist, and appropriate interactions among children and between children and elders. Cultural practices also include traditional dances, songs, riddles, folk tales, and storytelling.

Because many families came to the center to visit with their children, family support was provided. Families were gathered and provided an explanation of the experiences of the children during combat, what was being done to help, and what was expected of the families once the children returned home. Meetings with families were helpful to ascertain other factual information or assess the attitude of the families and the children toward each other. Class therapy also was provided to help children re-establish the school routine. They were taken through basic literacy, writing, and simple drawing; this basic introduction helped to motivate some to regain interest in returning to school. In addition, children attained skill training while at the reception center, such as tailoring, weaving, and knitting, that allowed them to earn a living once they returned to the camps. Support and guidance was provided around the first visit to home, a friend, or a close relative with permission.

Counseling occurred at both individual and group levels on a case-by-case basis. There was also a critical incident debriefing process, specifically for groups of children with similar experiences or reactions; these debriefings could include groups for those who experienced trauma, groups for returnees who may be aggressive, groups for those who may have been extremely fearful, and those who were not willing to go back home and resettle. Critical incident debriefing is an approach developed to help people exposed to disasters to reduce severe stress and mitigate psychological trauma; specific instructions are outlined for the process (Gordon, Farberow, & Maida, 1999). These critical incident debriefing groups helped children to express their fears and concerns, problem solve, and develop positive coping strategies.

Recommendations were developed to support children on return to their families. There may have been recommendations for specialist services such as psychiatric help, HIV/AIDS treatment, family planning, religious support, or traditional cleansing or healing rituals. The returning children were assessed once again and categorized into two major groups, high risk and low risk. This assessment helped to ensure that appropriate help and support were available. Once this was done, children were prepared to be resettled with their families, usually in the sixth week. Preparation for return involved signing a letter of understanding with the parents, getting clearance from the resident district commission, and acquiring an Amnesty Commission certificate. Amnesty certificates provide legal immunity from persecution or punishment for acts committed when the child was with the LRA (United Nations, 2006). The child and family met with the staff to discuss how a child should be treated and resettled at home, and they were given a resettlement package, consisting of a mattress, scholastic materials, utensils, and a hand hoe for cultivation, dependent on the individual child's need and the family need. Follow-up was provided through the community-based approach.

Community-based Approach

The focus of community-based approaches was on strengthening the capacity of the family and community structures, including the government structures, to respond appropriately to the psychosocial needs of children. The community-based approach was designed to provide continuity of services to those who were transferred from the center-based programs. Community-based approaches had nine areas to attend to: (1) follow-up of resettled former child soldiers; (2) development of mutual support groups; (3) community empowerment; (4) community activities; (5) economic development activities; (6) education and vocational skills training; (7) improvement and maintenance of health and nutrition; (8) capacity building of community structures and the performance of duty bearers (police, military, educators, civil society organizations); and (9) development of a child protection committee.

Follow-up of Resettled Former Child Soldiers. Follow-up of resettled children into the community was conducted to see how the children were adapting. The reception center staff conducted the follow-up for the high-risk category and community volunteer counselors who were trained in basic psychosocial healing conducted follow-up visits for those in the low-risk category. Follow-ups were normally done at three-, six-, and 12-month intervals; the staff or volunteers also completed the assessment at each visit. The health and nutrition status, educational needs, and psychological status of the children were assessed. Appropriate cultural supports were also determined and provided.

Development of Mutual Support Groups. Mutual support groups provided support to peer groups for children who were not in school, and peace clubs were developed in schools and in the community; there were also support groups for young mothers who had returned with children fathered by the LRA commanders. The goal of all children's mutual support groups was to foster positive reintegration into the community, especially peer groups. A second type of mutual support group was for parents, to support their psychosocial and advocacy activities. These groups formed to meet the needs of some parents whose children had not returned. These parents needed help to deal with the loss of their children and the emotional distress they felt on seeing other children return. They were provided with psychosocial support, training to facilitate their groups, and advocacy skills. They became active in advocating for unconditional release of abducted children by the rebels.

Community Empowerment. Community empowerment involved training of local leaders to address psychosocial issues so they could better support children and families to cope more positively. Community dialogues were conducted to address the challenges of reintegration of the children, children's rights, and child protection issues. A large part of the work was to involve the duty bearers (police, military, educators, civil society organizations) within the community in the dialogues to be able to improve the reintegration efforts. Community empowerment approaches also involved promoting traditional ceremonies and parish-level reconciliation activities for psychosocial healing.

Community Activities. Community recreational activities were structured activities that organized children, youths, and their family members in small groups that engaged in cultural activities, games, sports, drama, and traditional/cultural dances. Such activities supported a more harmonious reintegration experience between FACs and war-affected children and community members.

These types of activities worked so well in the communities that the staff realized that economic development activities would also likely be effective.

Economic Development Activities. Small groups of children, youths, and families were supported with a "revolving fund," or seed money, to start a viable and sustainable livelihood option. Examples of these economic activities included ox plowing, poultry keeping, piggery tending, carpentry, and tailoring.

Education and Vocational Skills Training. There was a large need in this area because the educational infrastructures were destroyed in the conflict; thus, most children were not able to continue with their education. A large part of NGO support was to form learning centers in a relatively safe area comprising a cluster of four to five schools that were relocated from the unsafe rural areas. The rehabilitation of schools and building of semipermanent structures, classroom blocks; and provision of scholastic materials, furniture, and sanitary facilities helped to maintain the children in schools, particularly girls. Teachers also needed to be retrained regarding psychosocial support, children's rights, and issues of effective classroom management. Many teachers had lost their teaching ethics, and many were just as affected by the violence as the children, so effective learning was not taking place. Increasing the standard of education was and continues to be a major issue and will require much effort to address. Children who were away from classes for a number of years may have felt that they could not return to school, and "catch-up classes," or remedial education classes, were created to support such children. Some of these children were then able to reenter the formal education system. Pre-existing vocational schools were also destroyed, so apprenticeship programs, using local resources, were designed for children who were not attending school so they would have a vocation to sustain themselves. They were trained in a specific income-generating activity, such as tailoring or carpentry, and then provided with basic hand tools and start-up materials to establish their own workshops. Many children formed collaboratives with others who had the same training. Through this strategy, children became self-reliant and able to support their families.

Improvement and Maintenance of Health and Nutrition. Nine therapeutic feeding centers were established in the IDP camps to address the needs of moderately malnourished children five years of age and younger. The program trained community volunteers to work with the mothers and the children to follow their progress. Through this program, staff recognized a serious consequence of the war: A significant number of children were born to mothers as a result of rapes during warfare; such rapes were an instrument of warfare against girls and boys. The staff encountered some mothers with children conceived of rape who did not follow the feeding program because they wanted the children to die; staff members were able to intervene in such situations to protect the children. A related issue is the exposure to HIV/

AIDS for these rape victims. Currently, there are many HIV/AIDS orphans among the orphans whose parents have been killed by the LRA and the other armed groups. An integrated HIV/AIDS and psychosocial project to respond to the needs of these children was developed. The program solicits support to enable these children to access HIV/AIDS treatment drugs and continue with their education.

Capacity Building of Community Structures and the Performance of Duty Bearers. Building the capacity of community structures to support the needs of returning children in the community meant conducting training and dialogues with various official and informal groups within the area. For example, it was not easy to work with the military, especially when they initially saw these child soldiers as their enemies. A lot of training occurred to develop an appreciation of the problems of the children and also to mainstream children's rights issues into the groups' systems and structures at different levels. Training was provided to various groups, such as the district offices, government implementation teams, health workers, reception center staff, and community volunteers. This training developed more of a prevention focus over time.

Development of a Child Protection Committee. Concern about prevention was the catalyst for the development of a "child protection committee model" to strengthen child protection, rehabilitation, and reintegration of war-affected children at the grassroots level. Community-based referral units were established with selected communities. The committee was composed of nine to 15 members, including field-based workers, who were employed to work with government social workers and community members, some of whom were children 15 to 18 years of age. It is an interagency strategy that was implemented through community structures. A training module was developed for the training of the Child Protection Committee and was used by all agencies. The role of the committees was to monitor children's rights violations, report the violations to local authorities and other agencies established through the referral system, follow-up on the management of cases, and properly identify the most vulnerable children and refer them for specialized services. These committees also supported the development and implementation of child friendly, community action plans with host communities.

There are advantages and disadvantages of community-based approaches. Advantages are as follows: More people are involved in the support of children; a community base encourages and builds on a natural healing process; it tends to be less stigmatizing; it reduces dependency and is cost-effective; and, perhaps most important, it is community owned and thus easier to sustain. One challenge was the difficulty in accessing and following up with the children. Because of the stigma of their identities as formerly abducted children, some children preferred not to have a follow-up visit from the reception center after they returned to their communities; they preferred to go into town for their follow-up visits. During the time of the active LRA conflict, community-based children could also be exposed to reabduction.

In the aftermath of the LRA conflict, much of the funding for the programs has ended and the follow-up of those children who had been in the reception centers has ended. There is minimal information about the current experiences of these youths.

Challenges and Lessons

During the development of the psychosocial approach, we learned several lessons such as attending to the importance of context, using familiar concepts, and developing interventions that are culturally and contextually relevant. Gathering information about the contextual issues before a crisis occurs is important to effectively develop programs; it is also important for planning for future needs. For example, in northern Uganda it would be essential for program developers to first understand how the family and community support the individual. Although during a time of crisis the community may appear to be fragmented, knowing the strengths of a group, such as the traditions and values, can be useful in developing effective interventions. This type of understanding is certainly important for helping professionals working in this area, but it is just as important for helping professionals working with those who have emigrated from these communities.

Psychosocial support remains a gray area in northern Uganda because understanding the concept was a big challenge, and pronunciation of the word "psychosocial" was a bigger challenge. During the initial psychosocial support trainings, many being trained could not pronounce the word, which was an obstacle to understanding its meaning and its importance. We needed to demystify this essentially Western concept. We decided to engage the children and parents and to draw on their past experiences. For example, it was helpful for parents to understand that their efforts to support good development in their children was a form of psychosocial support; however, it was important to find words and descriptions that people could relate to and not simply use the word *psychosocial,* which had little meaning to them.

Another challenge is that there are very limited resources to deal with the mental health needs of the area. There is only one psychiatrist and two psychiatric nurses in an area with such overwhelming needs. Because of this underresourced situation, we have had to develop ways to support the needs of children that did not depend on formally trained mental health personnel. Our challenge when trying to implement these approaches was whether to adopt a purely Western way of healing trauma or a balanced approach of traditional and Western approaches. The question of adopting a purely Western counseling approach or a traditional way of "counseling"—supportive talk and keeping physical presence with the children—is yet to be explored. Currently, the traditional approach to counseling is used more often.

Counseling has been one of the best things, practiced along with entertainment like cultural dances and other activities that interest the children. In the African context, especially in northern Uganda, traditional counseling teaches behavioral skills and provides for positive coping mechanisms among the children. Also, in developing psychosocial programming, it is important to integrate some kind of tangible outcome, such as an income-generating component in addition, to addressing the relational (community) and mental health aspects. But to a larger extent, the existing counseling does not address traumatic stress, especially posttraumatic stress disorders (PTSD). More specialized mental health services are needed to address PTSD.

As psychosocial programs are being developed in northern Uganda, many groups are looking at the challenges of what psychosocial is and how it should be implemented. Programs are coming from other countries and being presented as the right program for the children, and often with a large investment. Some programs have been rejected. For example, if the programs involve play, the children will say, "We don't need play, we need protection by the military, we need to go to school." Another example of the importance of assumptions and imported ideology that may conflict with the current context is that the DDRR for children involved with armed groups worked in Sierra Leone after the peace agreement and the end of war, but it may not be successful if replicated in totality in northern Uganda, where there is ongoing armed conflict and conflicting parties are not ready to compromise. These were lessons that helped us to reshape our program; we began to conduct situational analyses before intervening and regularly conduct evaluations to review the progress of these interventions.

When FACs returned to camps and communities, they naturally formed peer support groups and gained enormous strength and support from each other. We have built follow-up visits to these groups into our schedule, to be familiar with the issues that are arising in these meetings. Critical debriefing meetings or community dialogues may be needed to prevent individuals from being isolated or retraumatized by each other's experiences. This can be very important to monitor if the group comprises perpetrators and victims. Helping professionals in the United States working with war-affected children and families may need to pay attention to similar dynamics or issues that may arise in support groups.

Another implication for social work is that lobbying and advocacy are an important part of any psychosocial program and should be integrated as part of the ongoing work. There are structural issues that affect the well-being of individuals and communities that will not be solved through mental health services, physical health services, or services that improve relationships. Without advocacy and lobbying efforts social work services will be less likely to succeed.

There remain huge knowledge gaps around the issues of reintegration in northern Uganda. Little is known about the large number of people who return from captivity straight back into the community. Access to the IDP camps and provisions of supportive follow-up visits were not possible during the active conflict because of the insecurity. Understanding the needs and challenges of this group of formerly abducted children would help to inform intervention. Such knowledge would also inform the work of helping professionals in other countries working with this population.

One of the biggest questions for service providers in northern Uganda is whether it is possible to reintegrate children into communities that have been disintegrated. This will be the focus of their future work: How can service providers improve this situation for children?

References

Gordon, N. S., Farberow, N. L., & Maida, C. A. (1999). *Children & disasters*. Philadelphia: Brunner/Mazel.

Index Mundi. (2010). *Uganda demographics profile*. Retrieved from http://www.indexmundi.com/uganda/demographics_profile.html

Save the Children. (n.d.). *Save the Children on: Accountability*. Retrieved from http://resourcecentre.savethechildren.se/node/2137

United Nations. (2006). *Country profile: Uganda*. Retrieved from http://www.unddr.org/countryprogrammes.php?c=37

6

Global Mental Health Programs for Children and Families Facing Adversity:

Development of the Family Strengthening Intervention in Rwanda

Theresa S. Betancourt, Sarah E. Meyers-Ohki,
Sara N. Stulac, Christine Mushashi,
Felix R. Cyamatare, and William R. Beardslee

This chapter discusses an ongoing research collaboration between the Harvard School of Public Health and Partners In Health (PIH) to design and evaluate a mental health intervention to assist families facing multiple adversities in Rwanda. Using a mixed-methods approach, this research invites local input and engagement at all levels of program assessment, design, implementation, and evaluation and represents a service model that is complementary to the community-based PIH system of care in Rwanda and to efforts by the Rwandan government to scale up mental health care, including family-based preventive interventions. Qualitative methods were used to gain knowledge of the cultural-specific problems, resources, and contextual dynamics present among HIV/AIDS-affected families, many of them led by caregivers who are also genocide survivors. In particular, our focus on protective processes and resilience revealed that an initial set of individual and family strengths may be leveraged by interventions to prevent the onset of mental health problems among children. Given these results, and the existing literature on mental health interventions, we found that a prevention-oriented, family-strengthening intervention would best leverage the protective mechanisms operating in Rwandan children, families, and communities. Our qualitative data were also used to guide the selection and adaptation of mental health measures for assessing family dynamics and mental and behavioral health of children participating in the intervention, which will initially be implemented by PIH social workers. To ensure the cultural relevance and acceptability of the intervention and assessments, community advisory boards (CABs) were established to provide routine feedback and guidance to the project.

Although the example presented here comes from Rwanda, the lessons learned and implications of this research have relevance to other settings. The approach presented in this chapter offers a model for planning and evaluating mental health services in low-resource settings, where systems to address the mental health consequences of compounded adversity may be lacking.

Rwinkwavu, a poor, rural area in the southern Kayonza district where this project is based, represents a site where multiple forms of adversity have converged: The area was hit hard by the 1994 Rwandan genocide and by the HIV/AIDS epidemic. Although the Rwandan Ministry of Health and PIH have responded to the region's dire need for HIV/AIDS treatment (Stulac, 2006; Stulac et al., 2006), the mental health of residents in this area has, until recently, been largely understudied and services have been severely limited. In particular, there has been very little information on the mental health needs of children and adolescents. We sought to gain a thorough understanding of how mental health problems in children and adolescents were seen locally and to investigate protective constructs that were described as mitigating the risk of mental health problems in children and families. By integrating this information into intervention development, the locally informed approach presented here proposes a strategy for combating negative outcomes among children and families in situations of extreme adversity. The Family Strengthening Intervention-Rwanda (FSI-R) intervention is aimed at strengthening family communication, parenting skills, and problem solving and promoting families' knowledge of and access to formal resources. Along with formal medical care and antiretroviral therapy (ART), this is seen as a first step in helping families to better navigate the challenges they face in coping with day-to-day stressors. This same approach allows for an integration of cultural perspectives that may be applied to other settings beset by multiple forms of adversity to develop both assessments and targeted intervention models.

The Rwandan Context

Families Affected by Genocide and HIV/AIDS

In Rwanda, HIV/AIDS and the legacy of the 1994 genocide have had devastating and continuing consequences for children and families. The genocide resulted in the death of more than 800,000 Rwandans and the displacement of 4 million; in addition, the conflict ravaged the country's health infrastructure, including programs established in the 1980s to monitor and treat HIV/AIDS (Kayirangwa, Hanson, Munyakazi, & Kabeja, 2006). Although the Rwandan Ministry of Health has made significant strides over the past 15 years in rebuilding and developing programs to combat the spread of HIV, little programming has addressed the ways in which present-day child rearing and mental health have been disrupted and undermined by the compounded adversities of genocide and HIV/AIDS.

The social implications of these adversities have been vast, especially as they relate to family functioning, caregiving, and child development in Rwanda. Studies on genocide survivors from other countries have shown that war-affected individuals are at increased risk for mental health problems such as depression and posttraumatic stress disorder (PTSD) (Barenbaum, Ruchkin, & Schwab-Stone, 2004; Dyregrov, Gupta, Gjestad, & Mukanoheli, 2000). In Rwanda, where many genocide survivors are now parents or caregivers, these lingering effects on adult mental health may impair parental functioning and threaten children's healthy development (Karen & Joy, 2003; Lyons-Ruth, Wolfe, & Lyubchik, 2000). In addition, the genocide and HIV/AIDS epidemic have abraded many of the social supports previously used by Rwandan caregivers, including extended family networks that traditionally offered help and guidance to parents (Obura, 2003; Tikly et al., 2003). In our CAB meetings, the Rwandan cultural worldview was described as a "continuum" represented by a large spiral from the self to the cosmos, reflected in traditional Rwandan dung paintings or *Imigongo.* This continuum of life linked the individual in a continuous fashion to family, community, and the larger societal and spiritual world. In fact, in the Rwandan culture, the word for family and community, *umuryango,* is the same. As described in our CAB meetings, the genocide and, later, the HIV/AIDS epidemic, led to rifts in this seamless spiral. This was described as severe "damage" to the rich fabric that once bonded all Rwandans together and has led to severe societal rifts along both ethnic and class lines.

In modern Rwanda, social breakdown presents a challenge for many aspects of family life. Available research documents that war survivors are at increased risk for mental health problems such as depression and PTSD (Stulac, 2006; Stulac et al., 2006). However, little research has examined the ways in which present-day child rearing has been undermined by intergenerational trauma and by interruptions in social networks that have traditionally supported healthy adult functioning and parenting. High rates of familial conflict are often compounded in the postwar environment by poor educational attainment and poverty, which pose additional challenges to healthy child rearing. Studies have shown elevated rates of intimate partner violence among war-affected populations (Barenbaum et al., 2004), and evidence exists for the intergenerational transmission of trauma in other war-affected populations such as genocide survivors (Danieli, 2007). In terms of HIV/AIDS and its social and cultural consequences, several studies have underscored the social ostracism and stigma experienced by HIV/AIDS-affected people in sub-Saharan Africa (Spaar et al., 2010), including South Africa (Simbayi et al., 2007), Zimbabwe (Duffy, 2005), and Rwanda (Feldman, Friedman, & Des Jarlais, 1987; Keogh, Allen, Almedal, & Temahagili, 1994). These negative effects have interrupted the social processes that normally allow an extended community network to provide support for families facing adversity.

In the postgenocide environment, parental impairment and damaged family networks can lead to a dramatic shift of responsibilities between caregivers and children, especially in HIV/AIDS-affected households, where children may be forced to assume adult responsibilities such as taking care of ill family members or contributing to household income (Bachmann & Booysen, 2003; Bauman, Foster, Silver, Berman, Gamble, & Muchaneta, 2006; Stein, Riedel, & Rotheram-Borus, 1999). Studies of youths struggling with such compounded adversities have shown heightened levels of depressive symptoms, social isolation, and emotional distress in these children, as well as increased risk of family conflict, community stigma, and compromised educational achievement in the family (Bachmann & Booysen, 2003; Bauman et al., 2006; Boris, Thurman, Snider, Spencer, & Brown, 2006; Brouwer, Lok, Wolffers, & Sebagalls, 2000; Doku, 2009; Lester et al., 2006; Murphy, Greenwell, Mouttapa, Brecht, & Schuster, 2006; Nampanya-Serpell, 2000). However, the mental health needs of children often receive little attention as families focus on addressing the immediate economic and social consequences wrought by civil conflict and HIV/AIDS (Bachmann & Booysen, 2003; Barenbaum et al., 2004; Bauman et al., 2006; Brouwer et al., 2000; Doku, 2009; Lester et al., 2006; Murphy et al., 2006; Nampanya-Serpell, 2000; Seeley & Russell, 2010).

Implications for Policy

Despite known risks, few programs exist to prevent mental health problems in children whose families face multiple forms of adversity, and mental health care remains out of reach for many in low- and middle-income countries (Earls, Raviola, & Carlson, 2008). Although an emerging literature argues for mental health to be integrated into health care systems as a necessary component of overall well-being, mental health services remain a low priority for stakeholders and service providers, who often view these programs as separate or additional treatments that demand supplementary budgetary funds (Jacob et al., 2007; Lancet Global Mental Health Group et al., 2007; Prince et al., 2007; Saxena, Thornicroft, Knapp, & Whitford, 2007). In Rwanda, policymakers and the international community are primarily focused on promoting economic development and stability for the country (Obura, 2003; Tikly et al., 2003). Frequently, issues such as HIV/AIDS or poverty are targeted in isolation from other domains, despite the correlation between poor physical health, economic instability, and high rates of mental disorders (Patel & Kleinman, 2003; Saraceno et al., 2007).

However, research underscores that addressing the mental health consequences of adversities such as genocide and HIV/AIDS is a critical component of other health care services, which may not be fully accessible to those impaired by problems like depression, substance use, or psychosis (Patel, 2007; Prince et al., 2007). In addition, it has been shown that *prevention* of mental health problems can help decrease the factors that aggravate poor outcomes in other life domains by helping patients improve their help seeking, problem solving, coping skills, and degree of community engagement (Saxena, Jane-Llopis, & Hosman, 2006). To initiate such preventive services for at-risk children and families, stakeholders and policymakers should consider the role of primary health care organizations, which can work to integrate basic medical care and ART with mental health care, including initiatives to prevent mental health problems in families directly and indirectly affected by illness and other forms of adversity (Murray & Jenkins, 1998; Rotheram-Borus, Gwadz, Fernandez, & Srinivasan, 1998; Warner et al., 2009). Incorporated into an existing package of services, prevention programs can be initiated for at-risk families identified by primary care providers and can work to provide a first line of defense against the mental health risks facing children (Mwape et al., 2010; Saxena et al., 2007).

Applicability of Western Interventions to Non-Western Cultures

To design such interventions for low-resource settings, research can capitalize on the existing evidence based on mental health interventions and assessments. Given that the vast majority of intervention studies come from industrialized countries, this work requires methods that integrate current clinical knowledge and knowledge of local psychopathology to create culturally suitable interventions in low and middle countries, particularly in sub-Saharan Africa (Bass, Bolton, & Murray, 2007). In particular, an understanding of how culture affects the expression of mental health problems and protective processes is critical. For any given setting, qualitative examination of local perceptions of mental health problems and resources contributing to resilient outcomes is the critical first step in designing both assessment measures and interventions. Once such information is available, assessment tools originally intended for other populations may be reviewed and selected or adapted using culturally relevant terminology (Bolton, 2001; Bolton & Tang, 2002;

Ungar, Liebenberg, & Brown, 2005). By contrast, qualitative work may also reveal that local problems differ greatly from expressions of psychopathology studied in more industrialized nations and that no existing mental health assessments apply to certain populations (Tempany, 2009). In this case, researchers may elect to design measures derived directly from qualitative data (Betancourt et al., 2009). Similarly, qualitative research may be used to adapt evidence-based interventions to other populations that express similar problems (Bolton et al., 2007).

Planning and Evaluating Mental Health Services in Culturally Diverse Settings: A Conceptual Mixed-Methods Model

In our approach to intervention development, we used qualitative research as the starting point for developing both contextually appropriate quantitative assessment measures and identifying treatment modalities that have the potential to be culturally acceptable. As demonstrated in Figure 6-1, this process begins with qualitative inquiry into relevant mental health problems, protective processes, and their local manifestation. In the second step of the model, the qualitative data are used to select, adapt, and create assessment measures as appropriate. Information on common mental health problems and modifiable protective processes that mitigate risks for disorders can then be used to identify intervention models that are potentially a good fit to the setting. Where possible, it is important to also conduct a validation study of the measures. In the third step of the model, the culturally informed intervention is then assessed using the culturally informed measures and the most rigorous scientific methodologies possible. Such evaluations may include, but are not limited to, randomized controlled designs. Once those initial stages have been carried out, this model can be refined and used in other settings to understand mental health services needs and preferences and as potential intervention models in many other situations of adversity.

Another important feature of intervention development under this approach involves mechanisms to ensure input and collaboration with local service providers, community leadership, and potential beneficiaries. To date, we have established CABs to provide another source of guidance and insight in the intervention development process. Through this iterative approach, the FSI-R benefited from the integration of traditional healing resources within more formal clinical intervention strategies.

This mixed-methods process is described in detail and illustrated with examples from our work in Rwanda in this chapter. This approach has the potential to make contributions to improving assessment of mental health services needs, as well as protective processes, and informing intervention

FIGURE 6-1: A Model for Designing and Evaluating Mental Health Services in Diverse Cultural Settings

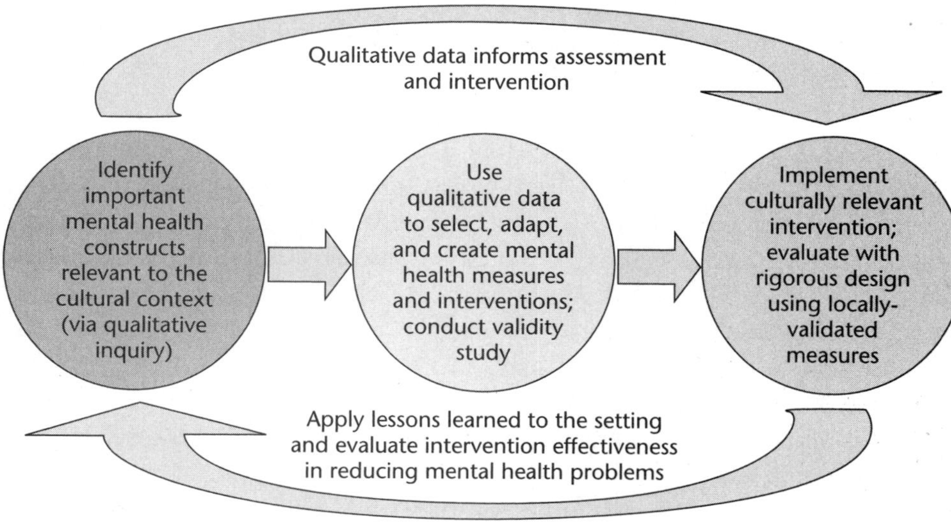

models that build on local strengths. By using local terminology and integrating locally relevant protective processes into the context of interventions, this approach also has the potential to improve treatment, engagement, and acceptability of services models to assist children and families facing adversity.

From Conceptual Methodology to Reality: Developing the FSI-R

Qualitative Studies

To better understand local conceptions of mental health syndromes and protective processes in Rwanda, cultural context was paramount. Following the mixed-methods model laid out in the preceding section, our work to develop an intervention for the Rwinkwavu setting began with two qualitative studies to investigate local perceptions of mental health among Rwandan youths and families. Given the effects of the genocide and alterations in family organization due to HIV/AIDS, mental health issues generally go unaddressed within Rwandan culture. Personal or family challenges are mostly kept secret and, in the absence of formal mental health services, many families turn to religious organizations for help. In many communities, discussions of mental health problems are highly stigmatized. The view of mental disorders as spirit "possession" or "madness" is common. Individuals who suffer from mental health disorders are often stigmatized and neglected. To begin planning how to address mental health in this community, we aimed to unpack the commonly recognized mental health problems that exist among this population and to explore the protective processes that help to combat them.

Mental Health Problems

Our first qualitative study was launched in January 2007 (Betancourt, Rubin-Smith, et al., 2011). Our goals were to explore local perceptions of mental health problems facing HIV/AIDS-affected youths in postgenocide Rwanda. Children (ages 10 to 17 years) ($N = 71$) and their caregivers ($N = 57$) were interviewed using free listing and key informant (KI) methods; this rapid qualitative assessment approach has been used in previous cross-cultural mental health research in sub-Saharan Africa (Betancourt, Speelman, Onyango, & Bolton, 2009; Bolton, 2001; Bolton & Tang, 2002; de Jong & Van Ommeren, 2002; Fernando, Miller, & Berger, 2010; Miller et al., 2006). All interviews and data analyses were conducted in Kinyarwanda (the local language) and were documented from the participants' points of view, using their own concepts and terminology. Rwandan research assistants (RAs) facilitated interviews, participated in data analysis, and assisted nonlocal staff in organizing and synthesizing the collected data to select and adapt measures and the design of intervention models. Throughout this process, our Rwandan RAs also offered insights and explanations of Rwandan culture.

The research identified several categories of locally defined syndromes indicative of the mental health needs of children in this setting. *Agahinda kenshi* (persistent sorrow) was explained as quite common among HIV/AIDS-affected children and adolescents and genocide survivors. When coupled with rejection and stigma, it could also lead to problems such as *umushiha* (constant irritability/anger), which feeds a cycle of social withdrawal and isolation. Agahinda kenshi was also linked by respondents to delinquent and high-risk behavior *(uburara)*, such as dropping out of school, fighting, early sexual debut, and the use of drugs and alcohol. Hopelessness and suicidal ideation (*kwiheba*) were described as serious manifestations of mental health problems in youths. Some participants also discussed *ihahamuka,* a term describing the effects of extreme trauma such as the genocide or the diagnosis of HIV (for example, feeling out of control or feeling entirely overwhelmed and numb).

Many of these problems emerged as severe and disabling; in particular, the symptoms of kwiheba showed strong relationships to those for major depressive disorder (as defined by standard criteria from the *DSM-IV* (American Psychiatric Association, 2000), including depressed mood, recurrent thoughts of suicide, and somatic complaints without medical cause. One KI commented that

> [In a child with kwiheba], what shows is that he is worried, he always thinks that his future is not good, so he cannot plan for it. A child who has lost hope is always sorrowful; he is always complaining and feels that he has no confidence in himself. He never has joy. (27-year-old man from Ruramira)

KIs also spoke to conduct problems and high-risk behavior, commenting that these symptoms are often linked to disrupted family structures and orphanhood. One 16-year-old girl from Kayonza spoke about "delinquent" children, saying,

> These children adopt bad behavior such as sexual [behavior], alcoholism, smoking, and drugs, which lead them to a loose life. Often this behavior depends on how adoptive families don't take care of them. They feel forsaken by everyone, like no one hears them.

An older man from the Ruramira district commented on the lack of support for children struggling with problems:

> The children become delinquent: This is due to hard life. Without anybody to take care of them, they get involved in criminality . . . The children portray melancholy, they easily get bad tempered, and they seem to be disgusted by life, as they are victims of discrimination. There is nobody to provide them with good education . . . Those children abandon school because their parents or tutors are poor. (45-year-old man)

Community stigma around HIV/AIDS also emerged as an important risk factor for and contributor to these mental health problems. Speaking about umushiha, the problem of constant irritability, one woman from Kayonza district commented:

> [Children] are easily irritated because of the many problems for which they do not find responses. They regret that they were born and abandoned in such a life. They are isolated, misunderstood by others who mock them because they are AIDS patients . . . They're stigmatized, so they feel hopeless and abandoned. But there is no other option except to keep silent . . . There is an example of a child who lost his parents because of AIDS; when he was playing with his colleagues, he fell down and was wounded. Then his adoptive family sent him away, saying that he intended voluntarily to contaminate their children. (35-year-old woman)

In general, KI interviews highlighted the importance of strong family and community support and the consequences that result from a lack of these networks. Several KIs underscored how widespread misunderstanding of HIV and its modes of transmission contribute to discrimination and, by extension, to children's isolation, loneliness, and hopelessness for the future. Findings showed that these poor outcomes are compounded when parents are absent, incapacitated, or unable to provide for their children.

Protective Processes

A second qualitative study was completed in January 2008 to identify the protective processes that children and families engage in during times of hardship (Betancourt, Meyers-Ohki, et al., 2011). This study replicated methods used in the prior investigation of mental health problems. In addition, focus group methodologies were used to identify and examine strengths and sources of resilience in individuals and families at risk for psychosocial difficulties due to hardships like HIV/AIDS and genocide. Maximum variation sampling was used to complete free-listing exercises ($N = 21$), KI interviews ($N = 68$), and focus groups ($N = 9$) among adults and children (ages 10 to 17 years) from HIV/AIDS-affected families in the southern Kayonza district. This study identified local Kinyarwanda terms for protective resources, their indicators, and local perceptions of how to foster these strengths in children, families, and communities. The five primary resources included individual factors such as perseverance/coping and self-esteem/self-confidence, family factors such as family connectedness and good parenting, and larger community factors such as social support.

High self-esteem was often tied to good parenting. For instance, one young female KI described children who experience a good upbringing as "always jolly, always respectful, not boastful to other children . . . They think of studying, they think of their parents and to help the country and friends." During other interviews with adult KIs, several participants stressed that positive spousal relationships and good parental functioning have a positive impact on children and the family unit:

> It's simple that a good caregiver will be a role model for their child, and they will not just let their children be involved in quarreling. This can be seen if the parents themselves do not have conflict between them. (adult female)

* * *

> A caregiver who is not well-mannered himself cannot bring up his children well . . . a good caregiver should understand the times that we are living in so that [he] can teach the child. (adult female)

Individual traits such as perseverance were also related to good community participation and lack of community stigma. When asked to describe the factors that help people make it through difficult times, one young KI said,

> I think it's important for people to get closer to people who have problems. I also think it is important to console them and let them know that there is someone out there who is thinking about them and to let them know that there is a solution to their problems. (17-year-old male)

An interview with a village elder illustrated how the community may intervene when families are in conflict:

> I had a trial of a daughter and her mother. The daughter goes to pray and, when she is back, her mother quarrels saying [the girl] does not cook for her . . . [The mother] does not want her to go to pray again . . . With people together, we told the mother that what she was doing for her child was not good, that she was hindering her rights—she did not deliver her child to work. She accused her child of not cultivating for her, and the child answered that she does her best according to her strength. When people meet, they discuss all of these things and make some decisions.

The same KI described how a troubled child may be helped through supports outside of the family:

> If the child was sad, now he is happy and his face tells you. If he used to come tell you his problems, now he comes and suggests how you can help him solve them. His thoughts are known through his actions. When you discuss, you notice that he is calm.

He offered another example:

> A child who lost his mother some days ago, he was so troubled that he failed in class, whereas he used to be the first. However, during the last term, he overcame his sorrow and became first again . . . I think what helped that child was [his] talking with people. They came to him and told him: 'take it easy, such things exist, do not worry, we are near you, we are siblings.' You try to console [orphans like him] slowly and, finally, he can open up his heart to you and tell you his worries.

Applying Qualitative Findings to Intervention Design

Our qualitative findings on protective mechanisms suggest strong interactions between children's mental health, family communication, good parenting, and community connectedness. This interrelatedness between protective processes in the family, further ability to navigate community resources, and children's mental health indicates that, to promote emotional and behavioral health among youths, interventions must work to improve functioning and communication skills within the entire family. Given the central importance of the local constructs of family unity, good parenting, and strong social support, we viewed these protective processes as platforms on which intervention activities might build. We therefore aimed to leverage and enhance naturally occurring resources through a family-strengthening intervention, rather than a group-based or individual one. In addition, KI discussion of community networks highlighted that good communication between community members, community leaders, and troubled individuals is essential to helping families navigate resources, and to normalizing hardships related to genocide and HIV/AIDS (Denison, McCauley, Dunnett-Dagg, Lungu, & Sweat, 2009). Because many KIs underscored how misunderstanding of HIV transmission leads to community stigmatization of affected children, we concluded that psychoeducation would be an important component of the intervention.

The potential for using local protective processes as key ingredients in the intervention solidified our focus on a strengths-based approach. Strengths-based models have been shown to successfully target modifiable protective processes to promote well-being and good mental health (Tedeschi & Kilmer, 2005). The theoretical model proposed by the stress-adjustment paradigm (Bell et al., 2008; Biddlecom, Awusabo-Asare, & Kankole, 2009; Lazarus & Folkman, 1984b) (see Figure 6-2), provides foundational support for these strengths-based interventions. The paradigm holds that changes in life events create stress, which, if mismanaged, can lead to emotional and behavioral problems. In the Rwandan cultural context, these stressors may be due to past genocide-related trauma, HIV/AIDS, or both in the family. Problematic reactions to these stressors may include high-risk behaviors, social isolation, or expression of anxiety and depression-like symptoms. In contrast, the paradigm also proposes that when stressors are managed well, the likelihood of mental health problems may be reduced (Lazarus & Folkman, 1984a). According to this theory, families and children turn to a variety of resources to manage stress, including aspects of the individual (such as coping, self–esteem), the family (such as connectedness, communication, good caregiving), and the community (such as social support). Our second round of qualitative data confirmed that local protective processes promote resilience in Rwandan families and better mental health adjustment in children. These resources are evidenced at the individual, family, and community levels and offer a natural starting point for translating the stress-adjustment paradigm to intervention development.

Selecting an Intervention Model

To support our inclination toward a family and strengths-based intervention, we examined the broad cross-cultural literature on family interactions and their impact on child development. Across a range of settings and cultures, findings underscored that positive family and larger community interactions

FIGURE 6-2: Stress-Adjustment Paradigm

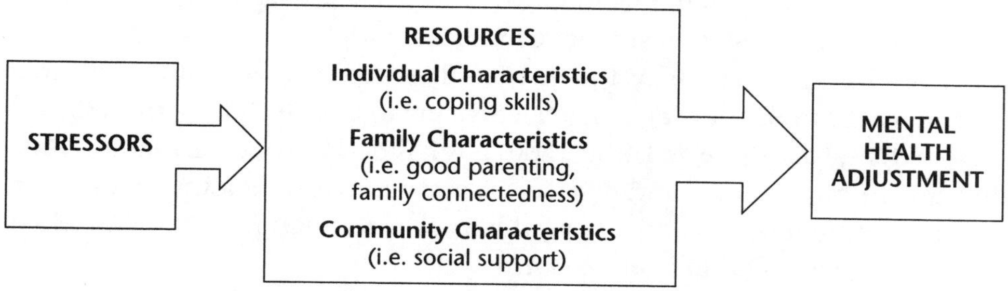

Note: Developed to illustrate Lazarus and Folkman' (1984) theory.

are critical enabling factors for good child and adolescent mental health (Aguilar & Retamal, 2009; Barrett, Rapee, Dadds, & Ryan, 1996; Peleg-Popko & Dar, 2001; Solantaus, Paavonen, Toikka, & Punamäki, 2010; Tamplin & Goodyer, 2001). In particular, early risks for childhood mental health problems are often associated with early family adversity such as parental mental health problems, poverty, exposure to violence, chronic illness, and social isolation (Aguilar, Sroufe, Egeland, & Carlson, 2000; Campbell, Shaw, & Gillion, 2000; Luthar & D'Avanzo, 1999; Luthar & Goldstein, 2004).

Strengths-based preventive interventions focus not only on addressing these types of risk factors, but also on strengthening resilience and cultural strengths to facilitate positive outcomes (see Figure 6-2) (Campbell-Sills, Cohan, & Stein, 2006; Luthar & Brown, 2007; Weine, 2008). A strengths-based perspective has informed a large base of interventions in low-, middle-, and high-income settings (Bayer et al., 2009; Riley et al., 2008; Shepard & Dickstein, 2009), including programs that focus on preventing mental health problems in children affected by HIV/AIDS (DeGennaro & Zeitz, 2009; Messam, McKay, Kalogerogiannis, Alicea, et al., 2010). In addition, many preventive programs look beyond the immediate family system and also aim to improve community relations and provide psychoeducation to larger populations to raise awareness and expand local networks of support (Institute of Medicine, 1994). However, such interventions for low-resource and non-Western populations are lacking. In particular, to our knowledge, no family-based prevention programs have been developed for use in sub-Saharan Africa.

Despite the absence of existing strengths-based, family-based prevention programs for sub-Saharan Africa, an examination of Western interventions revealed strong synergies between our primary protective processes of interest (family connectedness and communication, caregiving skills, and access to social support) and those leveraged by the family-based preventive intervention (FBPI) developed by Dr. William Beardslee of Children's Hospital Boston.

The FBPI focuses on identifying and enhancing resilience in families and was one of the earliest programs to adopt an ecological approach to chronic family illness (Beardslee, 1998; Beardslee, Gladstone, Wright, & Cooper, 2003). The intervention was also one of the first family-based mental health preventive interventions to demonstrate effectiveness in large-scale efficacy trials (Beardslee, Wright, Gladstone, & Forbes, 2007). It has demonstrated sustained effectiveness in low-resource and diverse cultural settings, including among low-income Latino mothers and among the Blackfeet Indian Nation (D'Angelo et al., 2009; Llenera-Quinn et al., 2006).

Trials of FBPI have found it to be acceptable, feasible, and related to long-term changes including greater child understanding of caregivers' symptoms, improved family functioning, increased recognition and treatment of subsequent symptoms, and decreased internalizing symptoms in youths (Llenera-Quinn et al., 2006; Podorefsky, McDonald-Dowdell, & Beardslee, 2001). This model has demonstrated sustainability through integration within existing public health service systems in Finland and Costa Rica (Larivaara et al., 2004; Solantaus et al., 2010), and it is recognized by the National Registry of Effective Programs and Practices (see http://nrepp.samhsa.gov/Search.aspx).

We elected to use the FBPI as a foundational model for our Family-Strengthening Intervention in Rwanda (FSI-R) and sought to adapt it using qualitative data and ongoing community feedback. Different national and international adaptations of the FBPI have produced standardized manuals and training materials, which we used as the basis for the FSI-R.

What Is the FBPI Framework?

The FBPI model focuses on identifying and strengthening family resilience, delivering psychoeducation, improving family communication and parenting skills, and helping families to better navigate formal and nonformal resources and services. Although the original FBPI was designed to address caregiver depression, we have found that the six guiding principles to intervention development identified by Beardslee and colleagues (Beardslee, 1998; Beardslee & Gladstone, 2001) are applicable to diverse situations. First, education must provide information about diagnosis and treatment of chronic family illness and should address ways of destigmatizing illness and its emotional consequences in families. Psychoeducation should reinforce strengths and resources and appeal to a positive outlook rather than emphasize negative potential outcomes. Second, good prevention programs for at-risk groups should comprise treatment and support approaches for both caregivers and children. Third, common concerns about death and, by extension, children's futures, must be addressed. Fourth, family support and education should bolster protective processes, thus increasing the resources a child can marshal to achieve resilient outcomes. Fifth, preventive intervention efforts for children should recognize the possibility of comorbid syndromes and should target a wider spectrum of issues. Sixth, effective interventions should take a public health approach.

To address these six main points, the FBPI uses the development of a shared family narrative to facilitate discussion about difficult events in the past and the family's ability to draw on individual and collective strengths to manage them. The exercise also allows families the opportunity to reflect on their unique sources of resilience, which are critical to helping them to make it through their current challenges. This activity merges different family members' perspectives on past events to create a common timeline. The goal is to illustrate how chronic illness affects entire families, and that families can reorient toward a shared future and being successful caregivers and healthy children despite illness (Beardslee et al., 2003). In addition, psychoeducation is flexibly integrated into the modules in response to families' concerns or discussions of chronic illness. This process is extremely important for integrating the experience of genocide with the current crisis from HIV/AIDS in the family. As different family participants participate in constructing the family narrative, they are encouraged to identify core issues and milestones. At each point along the narrative where a major crisis was survived, participants are encouraged to reflect on the individual, family, or societal resources that helped them through that difficult time. In this manner, a full portrayal of the presence of protective resources and strengths operating in the family is detailed and honored. Culturally specific elements such as spiritual beliefs, ancestral links to family characteristics, and cultural aspects of how the local community functions (such as seeking guidance from village leaders) are encouraged.

Adapting the FBPI to Create the FSI-R

Developing the FSI-R's Core Components

The FSI-R is a culturally adapted Rwandan family strengthening intervention that builds on the FBPI framework by using a family narrative to elucidate the family's experience of genocide and current experience of HIV/AIDS. The intervention is centrally focused on increasing family resilience by bolstering naturally occurring strengths; in particular, it focuses on traditional mechanisms that have been affected by HIV/AIDS and genocide, such as family unity and good parenting. Many of the themes endorsed by our qualitative studies will be used to spur discussion of problems such as stigma, shifting family roles, and other negative effects of impaired parenting due to mental illness, trauma, and HIV/AIDS. The FSI-R integrates local terminology, songs, proverbs, role play, and other means of transmitting Rwandan cultural views of self-esteem to strengthen families. As in the FBPI, our FSI-R uses a family focus to attend to the reality that HIV/AIDS is a family disease and to show that individual, familial, and community resources may help families to succeed despite chronic illness and the legacy of genocide in families and communities.

Core components of the FSI-R (see Figure 6-3) were chosen to address the key risk factors our qualitative data identified as threatening to families facing the dual adversities of the legacy of genocide and chronic illness due to HIV. The major risk factors included misinformation and fear of HIV/AIDS, foreshortened sense of the future, lack of communication among family members, and family social and economic stress.

To combat these risk factors, or stressors, intervention core components were built on local protective processes (family unity, good parenting, community resources), such that activities incorporate and underline positive coping strategies indicated during qualitative data collection.

Building Parenting Skills and Improved Family Communication. The FSI-R includes separate preliminary meetings with caregivers and children (divided by older and younger children, and possibly by gender) to prepare for a larger family meeting. In meeting separately with children and caregivers, the interventionist identifies key points of worry or concern that caregivers and children have for one another and for themselves. In these separate modules, the interventionist helps caregivers and children prioritize concerns or key messages that they most want to share with the other party. Role play and discussions are used to impart improved parenting and communication skills and to prepare children and caregivers for family meetings. In the family meetings, children and caregivers share their concerns with one another and develop a shared family narrative, which integrates past events into a singular story with shared goals and a future orientation. These family modules also discuss the services and supports (formal and nonformal resources) that the family will engage with to achieve their shared goals. Other examples of improved family communication may involve having caregivers validate the fear and confusion that children in the family felt upon learning of a family member's diagnosis, or their own if relevant. Caregivers also may recognize the great strength shown by children during this difficult time and offer reassurance that family members are receiving the medical care they need to live a long life. Songs and proverbs suggested by the CABs as a common means of Rwandan caregiver–child communication are used to help address hopes, share feelings, and impart knowledge (Betancourt et al., 2009; Dybdahl, 2001a, 2001b).

Development of a "Family Narrative," or a Time Line, to Build Family Connectedness and Highlight Sources of Resilience. The FSI-R uses the family narrative as a means of eliciting key concerns and identifying sources of strength that have helped

FIGURE 6-3: Core Components of the Family-Strengthening Intervention for Rwanda (FSI-R)

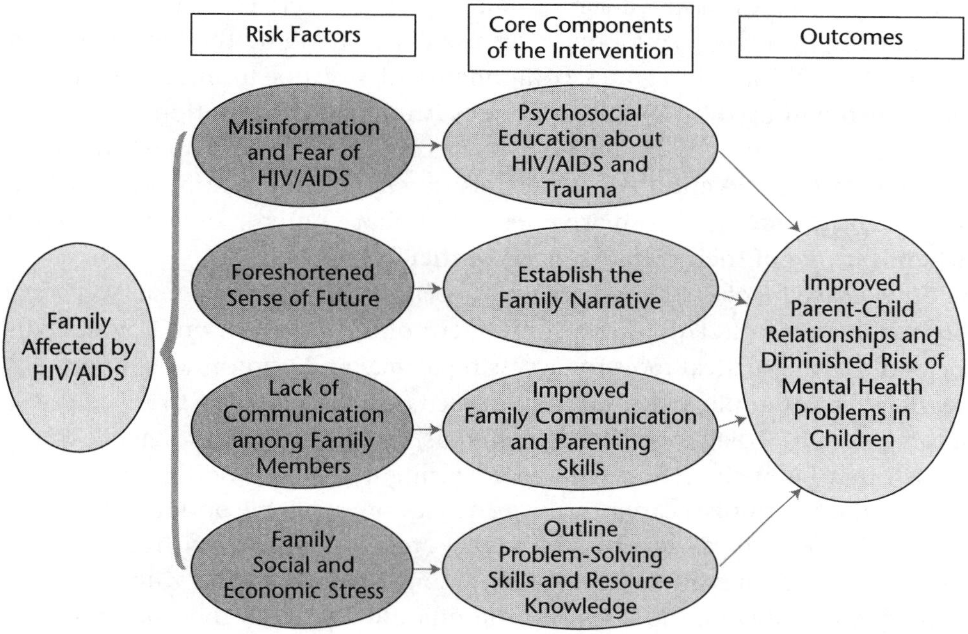

the family to make it through difficult times, including the genocide. Using a family narrative also allows family members to control the degree of information that they choose to share about sensitive or traumatic events, including experiences of loss and displacement that took place during the genocide (Beardslee et al., 1998; Rousseau, Singh, Lacroix, Bagilishya, & Measham, 2004). In telling the narrative, the interventionist encourages participants to identify and reflect on strengths and resources that helped them to make it through difficult events. This family narrative threads the themes of each module together and helps families to use past lessons, experiences, regrets, and triumphs to inform a future-oriented perspective and set of goals. The exercise is a good fit to the Rwandan tradition of telling tales and proverbs to transmit cultural content and teachings. It also allows for integration of other past family experiences, including loss due to the genocide and the experience of all family members, who are old enough to speak for themselves, about the effects of HIV/AIDS on the family. Individual caregivers and children are given the chance to establish their own versions of the family narrative; the family then comes together to discuss their strengths as a unit. These family modules may reveal discrepancies among different individuals' narratives and can thus serve to underscore the benefits of continued communication and shared family goals.

Provision of Psychoeducation on Trauma and HIV. Given the frequent miscommunication that can occur in families affected by trauma and chronic illness, the FSI-R provides basic education about genocide-related trauma and HIV by drawing from counseling materials used at PIH and by the Rwandan government. The FSI-R integrates components of psychoeducational materials developed and used by Rwandan nongovernmental organizations to address normative responses to traumatic events, coping skills, cognitive reframing, and self-care. Intervention materials also include information on how HIV is transmitted and the normative responses that family members may have when learning of their own diagnosis or that of loved ones.

Strengthened Problem-solving Skills and Ability to Access Formal and Nonformal Support and Services. This fourth component of the intervention provides participants with practical tools for accessing formal and nonformal support and services. For example, if a child has dropped out of school due to despair over a caregiver's HIV diagnosis, family members, including the child, may express a wish that he or she return to school. During individual modules with caregivers, interventionists can introduce and explore available options to address this challenge, such as government services to assist families with school fees. The family modules are then used to lay out a plan for achieving this goal. Subsequent follow-up modules allow families to report on their progress and troubleshoot as needed.

Using CABs

We invited the direct involvement of local community members to help us create a culturally acceptable intervention that can successfully address family dynamics within the Rwandan context. Community participatory research used in other settings has been shown to enhance feelings of partnership between researchers and communities and has had positive effects on community endorsement of intervention implementation (Ellis, Kia-Keating, Yusuf, Lincoln, & Nur, 2007; Israel, Schulz, Parker, & Becker, 2001; Israel et al., 2003). Given the strong community networks in Rwanda, as highlighted by our qualitative research, we viewed community support and input as critical to intervention design. In particular, we sought to obtain feedback from a variety of community members of different ages and backgrounds to address both the clinical and cultural components of the FSI-R.

In 2009, we established four 10-person CABs to assist in adapting the FBPI's core material and concepts to the Rwandan cultural context and to the situation of HIV/AIDS-affected families. The four distinct CABs comprise (1) Rwandan clinical staff (nurses, physicians, and social workers suggested by hospital leadership), (2) community leaders (community health workers, elected representatives of local organizations), (3) adult representatives from the surrounding communities, and (4) youth representatives (ages 10 to 17 years) from those same areas. To recruit youth representatives, children from community organizations were asked to elect and vote for peers. Two children from each village in the catchment area were elected, along with two children elected to represent the sector. These youths then attended an information session with a caregiver about their potential participation.

Recruitment of adult CAB members was facilitated by the local sector executive secretary and by the community health worker department at PIH. Using the registry of parent organizations at the village and sector levels, the secretary created a list of adults renowned for their involvement in community activities and knowledge of intervention subject matter (mental health/HIV/AIDS). Similarly, PIH/Inshuti Mu Buzima (IMB) recommended 10 community health workers who were considered active members of the community and generally supportive of child health care. Potential participants were invited to attend an information session; interested parties were subsequently invited to take part in the community and caregiver CABs. In addition, PIH/IMB clinicians who specialized in pediatrics, social work, mental health, or HIV/AIDS-infected or -affected children were asked to participate in a CAB of health care experts.

In the early stages of intervention development, CAB input was used to finalize the format of the intervention delivery: group or family based. Participants agreed that the intervention's use of a home-based format would exert a broader influence within the family and might be particularly helpful in imparting the comfort level necessary for improving family communication. They emphasized that, given Rwanda's large average family size, family- and home-based models have the potential to involve all children in the family by avoiding barriers inherent in long-range transportation. The clinician CAB also underscored that a family-based format will allow greater flexibility in scheduling, which is critical to ensuring the involvement of fathers. The community and caregiver CABs viewed father involvement as essential to success. In addition, because routine home visits are included as part of PIH's usual care, a home-based format fits well with existing delivery systems and has less risk of stigmatizing participants.

CABs also met to discuss the FSI-R content. At each of these meetings, the research coordinator and local project manager presented an overview of the core themes and content of an intervention module and asked for feedback on how to address certain topics (for example, psycho-education, family narrative/communication). Participants broke out into small working groups to review FSI-R materials for cultural appropriateness, acceptability, and significance. CAB participants were prompted to endorse intervention elements that they considered good or beneficial and to critique elements that needed further exploration or modification. On reconvening, the entire group discussed its responses and generated a list of suggested modifications, including culturally relevant concepts or themes. When there was lack of consensus between CAB participants or across CABs on a recommendation, the groups were invited to further explain and explore the diversity of opinions being expressed. For example, CAB group members could not come to a consensus related to parenting skills. Some caregivers believed that communicating with a child is better than the alternative, beating the child. The CABs were asked to take a vote on their final recommendation. This process was repeated until all CAB groups agreed that the adapted materials reflected the interests and culture of Rwandan children and families. In the end, the materials contained discussions regarding the importance of good communication with children and alternatives to beating children. Although a minority of CAB members initially identified beating as a part of the tools that a parent may use to raise their children well, extended CAB discussions determined that this was not a majority opinion and that safer and more supportive alternatives to beating could be readily identified in high-functioning Rwandan families and were integrated into the content of the intervention manual.

Piloting the FSI-R

The FSI-R will first be piloted among a small number of families, who will provide feedback on the intervention's cultural and contextual acceptability. Interventionists facilitating the sessions will be trained social workers with prior experience working in home-based services. The intervention will be revised to reflect participant input and will be repiloted among an expanded sample size in preparation for a larger randomized controlled trial (RCT) facilitated by community health workers. This RCT will be powered to allow for statistical analysis of intervention effectiveness, evaluated through validated assessments for measuring local mental health problems and protective processes.

Measuring Success

Evaluating the mental health status of participants will require the use of measures sensitized to the cultural-specific expression of local problems (Fisher & Ball, 2005). As discussed, qualitative data on mental health problems revealed several syndromes common to this population, and the results of this qualitative study were used to guide the development of measures (detailed later). These evaluations are designed to be used during pre-, post-, and follow-up assessments of the intervention. The follow-up assessments will monitor the prevention (or absence of onset) of mental health problems. In addition, protective processes will also be measured at pre-, post-, and follow-up time points to assess whether or not the FSI-R contributes to increased levels of processes that contribute to more resilient outcomes in individuals and families.

Developing Mental Health Measures for Use with Rwandan Children and Families

Qualitative data analysis resulted in lists of symptoms and indicators commonly understood to demonstrate a single overarching syndrome or protective process. For instance, symptoms of agahinda kenshi (persistent sorrow) included sadness, loneliness, unhappiness, crying, anger, antisocial behavior, gloominess, low energy, forgetfulness, and suicidal tendencies. We used the indicator lists of each local mental health syndrome or protective construct to make comparisons to standard measures of similar mental health symptomatology. For instance, a scale item such as "I feel sad" was matched to the agahinda kenshi symptom "sadness." Each item was discussed by the American–Rwandan team to ensure that both native-Kinyarwanda and native-English speakers understood the concepts being measured.

The number of local symptoms measured by the standardized scale was divided by the total number of symptoms to generate a percent-match. Scales were also evaluated for generalizability; for example, assessments that referenced activities such as "sharing CDs" or "flying on an airplane" were considered culturally inappropriate and would need cultural and contextual adaptation. In most cases, we were able to find at least a 50 percent match between items in our qualitative data and a standard measure. Some instances indicated that a much greater match was possible, but in some instances low matching (below 50 percent) indicated that it was necessary to use the qualitative data to create a more appropriate measure of the construct of interest. Once finalized, all standard measures were translated and backtranslated according to a rigorous protocol informed by the best practices cited in the literature (Alegria et al., 2004; Bolton, 2001; Canino & Alegria, 2008; Canino & Bravo, 1994; Matias-Carrelo et al., 2003). This process included forward translation by independent translators, backtranslation by a third translator, and review by bilingual translation committee. Where possible, survey items were modified to include conceptually equivalent, qualitatively derived Kinyarwanda indicator terms, such that the local language distilled from qualitative data was used in lieu of a direct translation from English. For example, the local symptom "gloominess" was considered to be conceptually linked to the item "I feel sad and blue"; subsequently, forward translation of the measure used the qualitatively derived Kinyarwanda term for "gloomy" and *not* the direct translation of "sad and blue."

Following translation, we implemented culture-specific additions to improve the sensitivity and relevance of the selected instruments. New items to measure context-specific symptoms conformed to the structure, tense, and response format of original versions. These additions were placed at the end of the measure and arranged to create a flow, building from less intense items to more intense items (such as those about suicidal ideation) and ending with less difficult questions. Thus, for our measurement of depression-like problems, we added the problem of "thinking too much," which was described as linked in our qualitative data to depression-like syndromes such as agahinda kenshi and kwiheba.

When no corresponding standard measure was found, we created new scales based on qualitative data. Each question on these new scales was designed to measure the constellation of relevant symptoms or indicators as derived from several in-depth KI interviews. All measures were then cognitively tested among small groups of six children ages 10 to 17 years and small groups of caregivers. Measures were revised according to participant feedback to maximize clarity and comprehensibility, and to eliminate problematic vocabulary. A validity study will examine the test–retest and interrater reliability of these measures prior to use with FSI-R pilot participants.

Potential for Integrating the FSI-R within Existing Systems of Care

Because the FSI-R has been developed in context with a strong emphasis on local culture and terminology, we hope it will be immediately more engaging and feasible than importing other family-based intervention models from other cultures. The foundational intervention, the FBPI, was originally designed to be implemented by a wide range of mental health workers, and a similar spirit is emulated in the FSI-R. Although initial feasibility trials of the FSI-R will be implemented by well-trained and experienced social workers (to optimize our learning and ensure participant safety), we intend for the intervention to eventually be refined and implemented by well-trained and supervised community health workers. Such an approach is also intended to build on the system of care that exists at the Rwandan government district hospitals and IMB, which places a strong emphasis on systems of community-based services. These systems rely heavily on community health workers and community outreach to ensure access to care despite limited human resources for health.

Conclusion

Described is a collaborative, participatory process for intervention development in a situation in which families have been affected by the dual adversities of the Rwandan genocide and chronic illness due to HIV and AIDS. Should our intervention prove effective, potential benefits include improved family functioning, social support, and caregiver–child relationships and reduced risk of mental health problems in children and caregivers.

Globally, over 1 billion children live in countries affected by armed conflict; of these, approximately 300 million are under the age of five (Office of the Special Representative of the Secretary General for Children and Armed Conflict, 2007). A large percentage of these children are orphans and displaced or separated from caregivers due to war; many are regularly overlooked or underserved by educational, justice, and health systems (UNICEF, 2008). These limitations, in addition to the stressors of widespread infectious diseases and illness-related community stigma, present huge challenges to young people struggling to adjust to the postconflict environment. However, despite these risk factors, many children successfully achieve healthy functioning in settings of compounded adversity. Promising results from recent research show that children are bolstered by caregiver support and guidance, by integration within community networks, and by engagement in school and educational programs, which serve to equip children with life skills and healthy coping strategies (UNICEF, 2009). Interventions like the FSI-R that work to rebuild informal systems of support and facilitate access to more formal services can begin to address the compounded effects of conflict and chronic illness on children.

Overall, the major goal of the research presented in this chapter was to develop a family-based intervention to prevent mental health problems in children affected by dual forms of adversity and to present this intervention as an opportunity for integrating mental health care within larger health systems in Rwanda (in this case, routine HIV testing and care). The complexity of this and similar resource-poor and war-affected settings demands that we pay particular attention to interventions' cultural validity, feasibility, and acceptability. Given the lack of formal evaluations of family-based prevention inventions for children in sub-Saharan Africa, our study endeavored to establish ethically and culturally sensitive systems for guiding intervention development; in particular, we used community perspectives, recommendations, and feedback to inform all stages of research design. CABs have helped to expand our understanding and appreciation of cultural disconnects that can increase interventions' risk of harm and have provided positive feedback about preventive interventions' potential benefits to individuals, families, and the larger community. These local experts have provided insightful commentary on the various needs of local children and families dealing with adversity, applying a broader perspective that complemented and enhanced our qualitative KI and focus group data. CABs will continue to be important during and after implementation of the FSI-R, as they can serve as channels for sharing study findings and results with the community and networks of service providers. Because interventions must be built on foundational knowledge of local problems, and can work most effectively by leveraging naturally occurring resources, iterative community participation is critical to achieving any study design that is grounded in cultural context.

Given the immense numbers of children in low-resource settings affected by armed conflict and chronic illness, family-based interventions like the FSI-R have great potential to strengthen healthy family functioning and improve outcomes for children and caregivers. Although the specific challenges may vary cross-culturally, adversity in many settings can be addressed through the framework adopted by the FSI-R: psychosocial education, multigenerational support for all family members, recognition of natural sources of strength and potential risk factors, and a public health approach should all be considered as integral to intervention design.

References

Aguilar, B., Sroufe, L. A., Egeland, B., & Carlson, E. (2000). Distinguishing the early-onset/persistent and adolescent-onset antisocial behavior types: From birth to 16 years. *Development and Psychopathology, 12,* 109–132.

Aguilar, P., & Retamal, G. (2009). Protective environments and quality education in humanitarian contexts. *International Journal of Educational Development, 29*(1), 3–16.

Alegria, M., Vila, D., Woo, M., Canino, G., Takeuchi, D., Vera, M., et al. (2004). Cultural relevance and equivalence in the NLAAS instrument: Integrating etic and emic in the development of cross-cultural measures for a psychiatric epidemiology and services study of Latinos. *International Journal of Methods in Psychiatric Research, 13,* 270–288.

Americal Psychiatric Association. (2000). *Diagnostic and statistical manual of mental disorders* (4th ed-text rev.). Washington, DC: Author.

Bachmann, M. O., & Booysen, F. L. (2003, April 1). Health and economic impact of HIV/AIDS on South African households: A cohort study. Retrieved from http://www.biomedcentral.com/1471-2458/3/14

Barenbaum, J., Ruchkin, V., & Schwab-Stone, M. (2004). The psychological aspects of children exposed to war: Practice and policy initiatives. *Journal of Child Psychology and Psychiatry, 45,* 41–62.

Barrett, P. M., Rapee, R. M., Dadds, M. M., & Ryan, S. M. (1996). Family enhancement of cognitive style in anxious and aggressive children. *Journal of Abnormal Child Psychology, 24,* 187–203.

Bass, J. K., Bolton, P. A., & Murray, L. K. (2007). Do not forget culture when studying mental health. *Lancet, 370,* 918–919.

Bauman, L. J., Foster, G., Silver, E. J., Berman, R., Gamble, I., & Muchaneta, L. (2006). Children caring for their ill parents with HIV/AIDS. *Vulnerable Children and Youth Studies, 1*(1), 56–70.

Bayer, J., Hiscock, H., Scalzo K, Mathers, M., McDonald, M., Morris, A., et al. (2009). Systematic review of preventive interventions for children's mental health: What would work in Australian contexts? *Australian and New Zealand Journal of Psychiatry, 43,* 695–710.

Beardslee, W. R. (1998). Prevention and the clinical encounter. *American Journal of Orthopsychiatry, 68,* 521–533.

Beardslee, W. R., & Gladstone, T. R. (2001). Prevention of childhood depression: Recent findings and future prospects. *Biological Psychiatry, 49,* 1101–1110.

Beardslee, W. R., Gladstone, T. R., Wright, E. J., & Cooper, A. B. (2003). A family-based approach to the prevention of depressive symptoms in children at risk: Evidence of parental and child change. *Pediatrics, 112,* e119–e131.

Beardslee, W. R., Swatling, S., Hoke, L., Rothberg, P. C., van de Velde, P., Focht, L., & Podorefsky, D. (1998). From cognitive information to shared meaning: Healing principles in prevention intervention. *Psychiatry, 61,* 112–129.

Beardslee, W. R., Wright, E. J., Gladstone, T. R., & Forbes, P. (2007). Long-term effects from a randomized trial of two public health preventive interventions for parental depression. *Journal of Family Psychology, 21,* 703–713.

Bell, C. C., Bhana, A., Petersen I, McKay, M. M., Gibbons, R., Bannon, W., & Amatya, A. (2008). Building protective factors to offset sexually risky behaviors among black youths: A randomized control trial. *Journal of National Medical Association, 100,* 936–944.

Betancourt, T. S., Bass, J., Borisova, I., Neugebauer, R., Speelman, L., Onyango, G., & Bolton, P. (2009). Measuring local instrument validity and reliability: A field-based example from northern Uganda. *Social Psychiatry and Psychiatric Epidemiology, 44,* 685–692.

Betancourt, T. S., Meyers-Ohki, S. E., Stulac, S. N., Barrera, A. E., Mushashi, C., & Beardslee, W. R. (2011). Nothing can defeat combined hands (Abashize hamwentakibananira): Protective processes and resilience in Rwandan children and families affected by HIV/AIDS. *Social Science & Medicine, 73,* 693–701.

Betancourt, T. S., Rubin-Smith, J. E., Manzi, A., Stulac, S. N., Fayida, I., & Safren, S. A. (2011). Understanding locally, culturally, and contextually relevant mental health problems among Rwandan children and adolescents affected by HIV/AIDS. *AIDS Care, 23,* 401–412.

Betancourt, T. S., Speelman, L., Onyango, G., & Bolton, P. A. (2009). Qualitative study of mental health problems among children displaced by war in northern Uganda. *Journal of Transcultural Psychiatry, 46,* 238–256.

Biddlecom, A., Awusabo-Asare, K., & Bankole, A. (2009). Role of parents in adolescent sexual activity and contraceptive use in four African countries. *International Perspectives on Sexual and Reproductive Health, 35*(2), 72–81.

Bolton, P. (2001). Cross-cultural validity and reliability testing of a standard psychiatric assessment instrument without a gold standard. *Journal of Nervous Mental Disease, 189,* 238–242.

Bolton, P., Bass, J., Betancourt, T. S., Speelman, L., Onyango, G., Clougherty, K. F., et al. (2007). Interventions for depression symptoms among adolescent survivors of war and displacement in northern Uganda: A randomized controlled trial. *JAMA, 298,* 519–527.

Bolton, P., & Tang, A. M. (2002). An alternative approach to cross-cultural function assessment. *Social Psychiatry and Psychiatric Epidemiology, 37,* 537–543.

Boris, N. W., Thurman, T. R., Snider, L., Spencer, E., & Brown, L. (2006). Infants and young children living in youth-headed households in Rwanda: Implications of emerging data. *Infant Mental Health Journal, 27,* 584–602.

Brouwer, C. N., Lok, C. L., Wolffers, I., & Sebagalls, S. (2000). Psychosocial and economic aspects of HIV/AIDS and counselling of caretakers of HIV-infected children in Uganda. *AIDS Care, 12,* 535–540.

Campbell, S. B., Shaw, D. S., & Gillion, M. (2000). Early externalizing behavior problems: Toddlers and preschoolers at risk for later maladjustment. *Development and Psychopathology, 12,* 467–488.

Campbell-Sills, L., Cohan, S. L., & Stein, M. B. (2006). Relationship of resilience to personality, coping, and psychiatric symptoms in young adults. *Behaviour Research and Therap, 44,* 585–599.

Canino, G., & Alegria, M. (2008). Psychiatric diagnosis—Is it universal or relative to culture? *Journal of Child Psychology and Psychiatry, and Allied Disciplines, 49,* 237–250.

Canino, G., & Bravo, M. (1994). The adaptation and testing of diagnostic and outcome measures for cross-cultural research. *International Review of Psychiatry, 6,* 281–286.

D'Angelo, E. J., Llerena-Quinn, R., Shapiro, R., Colon, F., Rodriguez, P., Gallagher, K., Beardslee, W. R. (2009). Adaptation of the preventive intervention program for depression for use with predominantly low-income Latino families. *Family Process, 48,* 269–291.

Danieli, Y. (2007). Assessing trauma across cultures from a multigenerational perspective. In J. Wilson & C. Tang (Eds.), *Cross-cultural assessment of psychological trauma and PTSD* (pp. 65–89). New York: Springer.

DeGennaro, V., & Zeitz, P. (2009). Embracing a family-centered response to the HIV/AIDS epidemic for the elimination of pediatric AIDS. *Global Public Health, 4,* 386–401.

de Jong, J. T., & Van Ommeren, M. (2002). Toward a culture-informed epidemiology: Combining qualitative and quantitative research in transcultural contexts. *Transcultural Psychiatry, 39,* 422–433.

Denison, J. A., McCauley, A. P., Dunnett-Dagg, W. A., Lungu, N., & Sweat, M. D. (2009). HIV testing among adolescents in Ndola, Zambia: How individual, relational, and environmental factors relate to demand. *AIDS Education and Prevention, 21,* 314–324.

Doku, P. (2009). Parental HIV/AIDS status and death, and children's psychological wellbeing. *International Journal of Mental Health Systems, 3*(1), 26. doi: 10.1186/1752-4458-3-26

Duffy, L. (2005). Suffering, shame, and silence: The stigma of HIV/AIDS. *Journal of the Association of Nurses in AIDS Care, 16,* 13–20.

Dybdahl, R. (2001a). Children and mothers in war: An outcome study of a psychosocial intervention program. *Child Development, 72,* 1214–1230.

Dybdahl, R. (2001b). A psychosocial support programme for children and mothers in war. *Clinical Child Psychology and Psychiatry, 6,* 425–436.

Dyregrov, A., Gupta, L., Gjestad, R., & Mukanoheli, E. (2000). Trauma exposure and psychological reactions to genocide among Rwandan children. *Journal of Traumatic Stress, 13,* 3–21.

Earls, F., Raviola, G. J., & Carlson, M. (2008). Promoting child and adolescent mental health in the context of the HIV/AIDS pandemic with a focus on sub-Saharan Africa. *Journal of Child Psychology and Psychiatry, 49,* 295–312.

Ellis, B. H., Kia-Keating, M., Yusuf, S. A., Lincoln, A., & Nur, A. (2007). Ethical research in refugee communities and the use of community participatory methods. *Transcultural Psychiatry, 44,* 459–481.

Feldman, D. A., Friedman, S. R., & Des Jarlais, D. C. (1987). Public awareness of AIDS in Rwanda. *Social Science & Medicine, 24,* 97–100.

Fernando, G. A., Miller, K. E., & Berger, D. E. (2010). Growing pains: The impact of disaster-related and daily stressors on the psychological and psychosocial functioning of youth in Sri Lanka. *Child Development, 81,* 1192–1210.

Fisher, P., & Ball, T. (2005). Balancing empiricism and local cultural knowledge in the design of prevention research. *Journal of Urban Health, 82,* iii44–iii55.

Institute of Medicine. (1994). *Reducing risks for mental disorders: Frontiers for preventive intervention research.* Washington, DC: National Academy Press.

Israel, B. A., Schulz, A. J., Parker, E. A., & Becker, A. B. (2001). Community-based participatory research: Policy recommendations for promoting a partnership approach in health research. *Education for Health, 14*(2), 182–197.

Israel, B. A., Schulz, A. J., Parker, E. A., Becker, A. B., Allen, A. Jr., & Guzman, R. (2003). Critical issues in developing and following community-based participatory research principles. In M. Minkler & N. Wallerstein (Eds.), *Community-based participatory research for health* (pp. 47–66). San Francisco: Jossey-Bass.

Jacob, K. S., Sharan, P., Mirza, I., Garrido-Cumbrera, M., Seedat, S., Mari, J. J., et al. (2007). Mental health systems in countries: Where are we now? *Lancet, 370,* 1061–1077.

Karen, A., & Joy, D. O. (2003). Parenting after trauma: Supporting parents and caregivers in the treatment of children impacted by violence. *Infant Mental Health Journal, 24,* 111–125.

Kayirangwa, E., Hanson, J., Munyakazi, L., & Kabeja, A. (2006). Current trends in Rwanda's HIV/AIDS epidemic. *Sexually Transmitted Infections, 82*(Suppl. 1), i27–i31.

Keogh, P., Allen, S., Almedal, C., & Temahagili, B. (1994). The social impact of HIV infection on women in Kigali, Rwanda: A prospective study. *Social Science & Medicine, 38,* 1047–1053.

Lancet Global Mental Health Group, Chisholm, D., Flisher, A. J., Lund, C., Patel, V., Saxena, S., Thornicroft, G., & Tomlinson, M. (2007). Scale up services for mental disorders: A call for action. *Lancet, 370,* 1241–1252.

Larivaara, P., Taanila, A., Aaltonen, J., Lindroos, S., Vaisanen, E., & Vaisanen, L. (2004). Family-oriented health care in Finland: Background and some innovative projects. *Families, Systems, & Health, 22,* 395–409.

Lazarus, R. S., & Folkman, S. (1984a). The coping process: An alternative to traditional formulations. In *Stress, appraisal, and coping* (pp. 141–180). New York: Springer.

Lazarus, R. S., & Folkman S. (1984b). *Stress, appraisal, and coping.* New York: Springer.

Lester, P., Rotheram-Borus, M. J., Lee, S. J., Comulada, S., Cantwell, S., Wu, N., & Lin, Y. Y. (2006). Rates and predictors of anxiety and depressive disorders in adolescents of parents with HIV. *Vulnerable Children and Youth Studies, 1*(1), 81–101.

Llenera-Quinn, R., Shapiro, R. L., Bravo, M., Lora, A., D'Angelo, E., & Beardslee, W. (2006). *Adapted manual for the Prevention of Depression in Families Program for use with Latino families.* Boston: Children's Hospital Boston.

Luthar, S. S., & Brown, P. J. (2007). Maximizing resilience through diverse levels of inquiry: Prevailing paradigms, possibilities, and priorities for the future. *Developmental Psychopathology, 19,* 931–955.

Luthar, S. S., & D'Avanzo, K. (1999). Contextual factors in substance use: A study of suburban and inner-city adolescents. *Development and Psychopathology, 11,* 845–867.

Luthar, S. S., & Goldstein, A. (2004). Children's exposure to community violence: Implications for understanding risk and resilience. *Journal of Clinical Child and Adolescent Psychology, 33,* 499–505.

Lyons-Ruth, K., Wolfe, R., & Lyubchik, A. (2000). Depression and the parenting of young children: Making the case for early preventive mental health services. *Harvard Review of Psychiatry, 8,* 148–153.

Matias-Carrelo, L. E., Chavez, L. M., Negron, G., Canino, G., Aguilar-Gaxiola, S., & Hoppe, S. (2003). The Spanish translation and cultural adaptation of five mental health outcome measures. *Culture, Medicine, and Psychiatry, 27,* 291–313.

Messam, T., McKay, M. M., Kalogerogiannis, K., Alicea, S., & Hope Committee Champ Collaborative Board MHHC. (2010). Adapting a family-based HIV prevention program for homeless youth and their families: The HOPE (HIV prevention Outreach for Parents and Early Adolescents) Family Program. *Journal of Human Behavior in the Social Environmemt, 20,* 303–318.

Miller, K. E., Omidian, P., Quraishy, A. S., Quraishy, N., Nasiry, M. N., Nasiry, S., et al. (2006). The Afghan symptom checklist: A culturally grounded approach to mental health assessment in a conflict zone. *American Journal of Orthopsychiatry, 76,* 423–433.

Murphy, D. A., Greenwell, L., Mouttapa, M., Brecht, M. L., & Schuster, M. A. (2006). Physical health of mothers with HIV/AIDS and the mental health of their children. *Journal of Developmental and Behavioral Pediatrics, 27,* 386–395.

Murray, J., & Jenkins, R. (1998). Prevention of mental illness in primary care. *International Review of Psychiatry, 10,* 154–157.

Mwape, L., Sikwese, A., Kapungwe, A., Mwanza, J., Flisher, A., Lund, C., & Cooper, S. (2010). Integrating mental health into primary health care in Zambia: A care provider's perspective. *International Journal of Mental Health Systems, 4*(1), 21. doi: 10.1186/1752-4458-4-21

Nampanya-Serpell, N. (2000). *Social and economic risk factors for HIV/AIDS-affected families in Zambia.* Paper presented at the AIDS and Economics Symposium, July 7–8, 2000, Durban, South Africa.

Obura, A. (2003). *Never again: Educational reconstruction in Rwanda.* Paris: International Institute for Educational Planning.

Odejide, A. O., Morakinyo, J. J., Oshiname, F. O., Omigbodun, O., Ajuwon, A. J., & Kola, L. (2002). Integrating mental health into primary health care in Nigeria: Management of depression in a local government (district) area as a paradigm. *Seishin Shinkeigaku Zasshi, 104,* 802–809.

Office of the Special Representative of the Secretary General for Children and Armed Conflict. (2007). *Ten years on, Machel review cites continued abuse against children in conflicts.* Retrieved from http://www.un.org/children/conflict/pr/2007-10-17167.html

Patel, V. (2007). Mental health in low- and middle-income countries. *British Medical Bulletin, 81,* 81–96.

Patel ,V., & Kleinman, A. (2003). Poverty and common mental disorders in developing countries. *Bulletin of the World Health Organization, 81,* 609–615.

Peleg-Popko, O., & Dar, R. (2001). Marital quality, family patterns, and children's fears and social anxiety. *Contemporary Family Therapy, 23,* 465–487.

Podorefsky, D. L., McDonald-Dowdell, M., & Beardslee, W. R. (2001). Adaptation of preventive interventions for a low-income, culturally diverse community. *Journal of the American Academy of Child and Adolescent Psychiatry, 40,* 879–886.

Prince, M., Patel, V., Saxena, S., Maj, M., Maselko, J., Phillips, M. R., & Rahman, A. (2007). No health without mental health. *Lancet, 370,* 859–877.

Riley, A. W., Valdez, C. R., Barrueco, S., Mills, C., Beardslee, W., Sandler, I., & Rawal, P. (2008). Development of a family-based program to reduce risk and promote resilience among families affected by maternal depression: Theoretical basis and program description. *Clinical Child and Family Psychology Review, 11*(1–2), 12–29.

Rotheram-Borus, M. J., Gwadz, M., Fernandez, M. I., & Srinivasan, S. (1998). Timing of HIV interventions on reductions in sexual risk among adolescents. *American Journal of Community Psychology, 26,* 73–96.

Rousseau, C., Singh, A., Lacroix, L., Bagilishya, D., & Measham, T. (2004). Creative expression workshops for immigrant and refugee children. *Journal of the American Academy of Child & Adolescent Psychiatry, 43,* 235–238.

Saraceno, B., van Ommeren, M., Batniji, R., Cohen, A., Gureje, O., Mahoney, J., et al. (2007). Barriers to improvement of mental health services in low-income and middle-income countries. *Lancet, 370,* 1164–1174.

Saxena, S., Jane-Llopis, E., & Hosman, C. (2006). Prevention of mental and behavioural disorders: Implications for policy and practice. *World Psychiatry, 5*(1), 5–14.

Saxena, S., Thornicroft, G., Knapp, M., & Whiteford, H. (2007). Resources for mental health: Scarcity, inequity, and inefficiency. *Lancet, 370,* 878–889.

Seeley, J., & Russell, S. (2010). Social rebirth and social transformation? Rebuilding social lives after ART in rural Uganda. *AIDS Care, 22*(Suppl. 1), 44–50.

Simbayi, L. C., Kalichman, S., Strebel, A., Cloete, A., Henda, N., & Mqeketo, A. (2007). Internalized stigma, discrimination, and depression among men and women living with HIV/AIDS in Cape Town, South Africa. *Social Science & Medicine, 64,* 1823–1831.

Solantaus, T., Paavonen, E., Toikka, S, & Punamäki, R. (2010). Preventive interventions in families with parental depression: Children's psychosocial symptoms and prosocial behaviour. *European Child & Adolescent Psychiatry, 19,* 883–892.

Stein, J. A., Riedel, M., & Rotheram-Borus, M. J. (1999). Parentification and its impact on adolescent children of parents with AIDS. *Family Process, 38,* 193–208.

Stulac, S. (2006, October 31–November 4). *The accompagnateur model for community-based interventions for pediatric TB-HIV coinfection in Rwanda.* Paper presented at 2006 IUATLD World Conference, Paris.

Stulac, S. N., Harrington, E. K., Niyigena, P. C., Kwizera, D., Uqamahoro, L., Epino, H. M., et al. (2006, August 13–18). *Implementing pediatric antiretroviral therapy as part of comprehensive HIV care in rural Rwanda.* Paper presented at the 16th International AIDS Conference, Toronto.

Tamplin, A., & Goodyer, I. M. (2001). Family functioning in adolescents at high and low risk for major depressive disorder. *European Child & Adolescent Psychiatry, 10*(3), 170–179.

Tedeschi, R. G., & Kilmer, R. P. (2005). Assessing strengths, resilience, and growth to guide clinical interventions. *Professional Psychology: Research and Practice, 36,* 230–237.

Tempany, M. (2009). What research tells us about the mental health and psychosocial wellbeing of Sudanese refugees: A literature review. *Transcultural Psychiatry, 46,* 300–315.

Tikly, L., Lowe, J., Crossley, M., Dachi, H., Garrett, R., & Mukabaranga, B. (2003). *Globalisation and skills for development in Rwanda and Tanzania.* London: Department for International Development.

Ungar, M., Liebenberg, L., & Brown, M. (2005). The International Resilience Project: A mixed methods approach to the study of resilience across cultures. In M. Ungar (Ed.), *Handbook for working with children and youth: Pathways to resilience across cultures and contexts* (pp. 211–226). Thousand Oaks, CA: Sage Publications.

UNICEF. (2008). *State of the world's children 2008*. New York: Author.

UNICEF. (2009). *Machel Study 10-year strategic review: Children and conflict in a changing world*. New York: Author.

Warner, K. E., Boat, T., Beardslee, W. R., Bell, C. C., Biglan, A., Brown, C. H., et al. (2009). *Preventing mental, emotional, and behavioral disorders among young people: Progress and possibilities*. Washington, DC: Institute of Medicine.

Weine, S. (2008). Family roles in refugee youth resettlement from a prevention perspective. *Child and Adolescent Psychiatric Clinics in North America, 17*, 515–532, vii–viii.

SECTION 3

Practice Implications for Social Workers

The chapters in this section discuss practice issues with individuals and families from Africa affected by armed conflict. The chapters describe the impact of trauma on individuals and communities and inform about treatments to address the effects of trauma. Attention is given to understanding the meaning and significance of the traumatic experience within the individual's and family's social and cultural perspective.

Chapter 7 describes the impact of traumatic experiences on individuals and the society, with attention to the role of culture in shaping meaning and serving a protective function against trauma. Specific trauma symptoms are explored and interventions are identified and described. Chapter 8 explores the role of African traditional practices in the healing of populations affected by armed conflict. Examining the purpose of these practices may help social workers consider how such practices support individual and communal functioning. Chapter 9 presents an ecological framework for identifying and exploring the complexity of issues that social workers will encounter when working with African populations affected by armed conflict. Using such a framework can help social workers see important strengths and stressors for the individual during the course of the migration process as well as identify areas of risk that need to be addressed in the current context.

7

Assessment and Treatment Issues for Children Affected by Armed Conflict:
Effects on Children, Family, and Culture

Joan Granucci Lesser

"To redeem one person is to redeem the world."

—Frieda Fromm Reichmann

This chapter addresses assessment and treatment issues related to armed conflict and the conscription of children into the rebel militia that has disrupted the lives and fabric of Ugandan children, families, and culture. It is the collective wisdom of our Ugandan colleagues with whom I had the privilege to engage in conversation with during their visits to Smith College School for Social Work in 2006 and the scholarly contributions of African-centered scholars, Western theoretical models of psychotherapy, and postmodern thinkers. I believe that the treatment of such massive trauma requires such a collaborative humanitarian effort. Definitions of key terms will be presented, followed by discussion of clinical assessment and treatment.

Trauma

A *trauma* is an event or events that are so extreme, severe, powerful, harmful, or threatening that they demand extraordinary coping efforts. Trauma can result in altered chemical functioning in the brain that produces disturbances in memory, learning, attention, concentration, cognition, and motor development (Allen, 2001). Although there are various types of traumas (for a more complete description of trauma, see McFarlane & van der Kolk, 2007). This chapter addresses trauma that has been deliberately caused by humans.

These traumatic experiences generally cause greater victimization; often cause feelings of shame, guilt, and worthlessness; and may lead to long-standing interpersonal and characterological problems (Meichenbaum, 1994).

The personal meaning of a traumatic experience for an individual is influenced by the social context in which it occurs (Salzman, 2001). Victims and the significant people in their surroundings may have different perceptions about the reality of what happened and of the extent of the victims' suffering. This difference in perceptions may result in conflicting desires to repair, forget, or take revenge, and a perpetuation of the trauma in a larger social setting in which the issues of blame and responsibility become the central issue (McFarlane & van der Kolk, 2007). Culture is one aspect of a social setting that is affected by trauma.

Cultural Trauma

Culture can be defined as "the symbolic and learned non-biological aspect of human society, including language, custom, and convention, by which human behavior can be distinguished. It guides how people live; what they generally believe and value, how they communicate; what their habits, customs, and tastes are. It also organizes our cognitions, emotions, and behaviors in both subtle and obvious ways that may be beyond awareness" (Ayonrinde, 2003, p. 234). Culture can serve as a psychological defense against existential terror. Salzman (2001) introduced the concept of a "cultural anxiety buffer" and described two aspects associated with it. "The first is a worldview in which one has absolute faith in and a set of standards for being and acting in the world that, if achieved, will lead to self-esteem" (pp. 189–190). The traumatic disruption of the individual and collective psychological defense that is culture increases anxiety and the motivation to engage in anxiety-reducing behaviors. Cultural trauma, therefore, "as opposed to psychological or physical trauma, refers to a dramatic loss of identity and meaning, a tear in the social fabric, affecting a group of people that has achieved some degree of cohesion" (Eyerman, 2001, p. 2). Cultural trauma creates profound discontinuity in the order and predictability that culture has brought to daily life and social situations. Such disruptions can wreak havoc on traditional ways of life and can leave people without a "meaningful framework in which to construct their suffering and their lives" (Bracken, Giller, & Summerfield, 1995, p. 1078). Cultural trauma may include cultural loss and bereavement, cultural clash or traumatic stress, cultural challenges, cultural reorganization, cultural stability, or cultural extinction (Dawes & Honwana, 1996; Nader, Dubrow, & Stamm, 1999). The role of a therapist is to support the collective and individual construction of meaning through individual, group, and community intervention services that reinstate their standards, values, and cultural worldview. Understanding the impact of trauma on the collective memory of a community is important in supporting the well-being of individuals and communities.

Cultural Trauma and Collective Memory

Collective memory is defined by Stamm, Stamm, Hundall, and Higson-Smith (2004) as "the collective understanding of a shared history, by people from a socio-historical context" (p. 8). This understanding creates a type of social solidarity in the present as there is a unique biographical memory to draw on (Weinstein, Fucetola, & Mollica, 2001). Collective memory is a social necessity. It specifies the temporal parameters of past and future: where we came from, where we are going, and why we are here now. Individual identities are shaped within the narrative provided by collective memory, embedded within narratives of the past, the present, and the future. "This socially constructed, historically rooted collective memory functions to create social solidarity in the present . . . thus while there is always a unique, biographical memory to draw upon, it is described as always rooted in collective memory" (Eyerman, 2001, p. 6). Grief may be unresolved when traditional cultural solutions are suppressed or lost, contributing to the multigenerational transmission of trauma (Salzman, 2001). Therefore, more work must be done to ensure that the social, political, and cultural contexts within which traumatic experiences occur are understood. This will help to ensure that the psychological dimensions of traumatic reactions are not isolated from the somatic and cultural or interpersonal. These contextual issues should be considered fundamental to assessment and treatment as they "structure the context in which violence occurs" (Bracken et al., 1995, p. 1077).

Acute Stress Disorder and Posttraumatic Stress Disorder

Both acute stress disorder and posttraumatic stress disorder (PTSD) are Western psychological constructs (see the *DSM-IV-TR* [American Psychiatric Association, 2000]) for the complete criteria for each of these conditions). Much of the theory, research, and measurement of PTSD have been generated by North American, European, Israeli, and Australian researchers and professionals (Marsella, Friedman, & Spain, 1994; Weine et al., 2002). When these concepts are applied to non-Western peoples, especially those who practiced and are identified with cultural traditions, there is a serious danger of "ethnocentric bias" (Marsella et al., 1994). Definitions of normality and health vary globally within and across national, geographical, cultural, and subcultural boundaries, influencing societal perception of the appropriateness of social behavior, health, illness, and disease (Ayonrinde, 2003). Bracken et al. (1995) also raised questions about the universality of the concept of individuality implied in the diagnostic category of PTSD. They also wondered to what extent this concept emphasizes both the similarities and differences in responses to trauma between different cultural groups. We must therefore be careful of ethnocentric diagnostic classification systems that may further alienate survivors from their culture's view about suffering and misfortune and impose a worldview that may violate the cultural survival of the people who have been traumatized. However, we must also recognize that, although not culture specific, the *DSM* has evolved since its initial inception. It now includes an overview of cultural assessment and impact on diagnosis and care. This includes attention to the cultural explanation of the individual's illness, including predominant idioms of distress, meaning of symptoms, perceived severity of symptoms in relation to cultural norms, perceived causes or explanatory models of illness, past experiences of care, and current preferences of care. There are also cultural factors related to the psychosocial environment and levels of functioning: for example, interpretation of social stressors, availability of social support, and level of functioning/disability. Ayonrinde added that the cultural elements of the relationship between an individual and clinician need to be considered, such as differences in cultural and social status, problems associated with these differences, communication, elicitation of symptoms, cultural significance, and negotiating relationship. Salzman (2001) introduced the term "cultural trauma syndrome"—a conceptual framework for understanding the common suffering experienced by peoples whose cultural foundations have been assaulted and disrupted (described in section under Cultural Trauma). This may more appropriately describe what the children and families have suffered in Uganda.

Cross-Cultural Partnership, Culture, and Community

There are dilemmas in making a culturally relevant diagnosis when the clinical picture is complex. There may be a difference between cultural bereavement and PTSD. There may also be comorbidity. Survivors can develop disabling symptoms that may mimic PTSD but will not be ameliorated by Western therapeutic methods alone. When trauma occurs on such a pervasive scale, children can develop new disorders, the meaning of which is not known in their culture of origin, thereby presenting a cultural challenge for those who have long relied on traditional healing practices (Monteiro, 1996; Nader et al., 1999). Importance must therefore be given to intercultural or cross-cultural communication. Stamm et al. (2004) suggested that consideration be given to how people understand and come to be understood, that when a message is produced in one culture and has to be produced in another culture, it may be misrepresented; attention must be given to issues of nonverbal communication, the importance of psychological privacy (with whom and under what conditions thoughts and feelings are shared), and social privacy (control of social contacts to manage interactions and maintain status divisions, appropriate conversational topics, and style of conversation).

The partnership that developed between the U.S. team of researchers/clinicians and our Ugandan colleagues is a useful cross-cultural model for treatment and intervention. Understandably, most indigenous trauma counseling programs use trained, supervised lay counselors to help people come to terms with their lives following individual, family, and cultural disruption. In many African and other developing countries, most therapy directly involves other family members and the wider community, and the individual's recovery is bound up with the recovery of the entire community (Bracken et al., 1995). However, an "over-socialized concept of man" (Harrell-Bond, 1986) can also lead to problems in recognizing and intervening with individual suffering. It is indeed a dilemma. Given the severity of the impact of the crisis in Uganda, we united in a human, collective concern—or cross-cultural partnership—building a "human infrastructure" (Stamm et al., 2004) with attention to cultural heritage, strengths, and a vision for the future. This was done through a process of skilled dialogue involving an "anchored understanding of diversity" and "the skill of third space." An anchored understanding of diversity included acknowledging the range and validity of our diverse perspectives, establishing interactions that allowed an equal voice for all our perspectives, and communicating an understanding that each other's perspectives had a positive intent. The skill of third space involved staying in relation and conversation with the tension of our differing perspectives, creating opportunities for equalizing power across our many interactions, and collaboratively crafting a response that integrated the collective strength of our diverse perspectives (Barrera & Corso, 2002).

Language differences often exist when clinicians are working with clients from other countries, and cultural interpreters are often relied on to translate communication when the language is not shared. Translation is the ability to exchange words from one language to another while retaining the meaning. It requires a reasonable fluency in both languages, literacy in both languages, awareness of nonverbal communications, the ability to work as a team member, and an understanding of the purpose of the interpretation. The triangular relationship between the client, the interpreter, and the clinician depends on the combined experience of the clinician and the competence of the interpreter. Both verbal and nonverbal communication must be considered. Medical and psychological terms can be difficult to translate, making it difficult for the same meanings to be retained. Good interpreter skills should include an understanding of the task, its purpose, and the means of achieving success (Stamm et al., 2004). Hays (2008) also cautioned against the clinician and the interpreter talking during the session with the client unless it relates to discussing a conceptual or linguistic difference, and then being sure to inform the client. She reminds us to "be aware of cultural, class, and political differences between the interpreter and the client that might affect the interpreter's work" (Hays, 2008, p. 121).

Assessment within a Cross-Cultural Framework

The cultural influences on children's social and cognitive functioning occur within a developmental context. Some common developmental tasks and requirements in socialization, such as learning to understand and respond appropriately to social and cultural standards and acquiring personal independence, may lead to cross-culturally similar patterns in human development. This view of interaction between cultural context and developmental factors may help practitioners understand the complex processes through which traumatized children with certain dispositional features can be helped in the context of their culturally constructed socioecological setting. Children's exposure to war and disaster, community violence, kidnapping, and hostage situations (among other traumatic events) may affect the course of development by shaping "children's expectations about the world, the safety and security of their interpersonal life, and their sense of personal integrity" (Pynoos, 1994, p. 65). The appraisal of external danger, the tolerance of internal danger, the expectations of outside intervention, and self-efficacy and the degree to which these are influenced by reliance on parents, adult caretakers, siblings, and peers all vary with the maturation of the child. Traumatic stressors interact with the child's emerging personality in a number of significant ways: achievement of psychological and physiological maturation; hierarchical integration of competencies; intrapsychic structure of internal and external dangers; inner representation of self and others; mechanisms of cognitive and emotional regulation; schematization of security, safety, risk, injury, loss, prevention, and intervention; behavioral attributes of fear, courage, and fearlessness; and evolving intervention fantasies and their relationship to internal scripts, actions, and creativity (Pynoos, 1994). Three projective questions that can be helpful in assessing the impact of traumatic events on children are as follows:

1. If you had three wishes, what would you wish for? (the assessor may be able to gain insight as to whether the child has any hope for the future).
2. If a baby bird fell out of the nest, what might happen? (this question may indicate what the child feels about ability to depend on others for safety).

3. If you were going on a rocket ship to the moon, and you could take only one person with you, who would that person be? (the child's response is expected to reveal the most important person in his/her life; but it may also reflect the child's judgment about who would be most helpful in this special situation)." (Pynoos, p. 66)

Webb (1999) offers the following tripartite assessment model designed to guide the clinician in assessing trauma in children and adolescents.

The Nature of the Crisis Situation

a. Psychosocial/environmental problems
b. Anticipated versus sudden crisis
c. Single event versus recurring
d. Natural disaster, accidental disaster, deliberately caused disaster
e. Solitary versus shared experience
f. Proximity to the crisis
g. Presence of loss factors
   1. Separation from family members
   2. Death of family members
   3. Loss of familiar environment
   4. Loss of familiar role/status
   5. Loss of body parts or function
h. Presence of violence
   1. Witnessed and/or experienced
   2. Element of stigma
I. Presence of life threat to self/family/others

Individual Factors

a. Age
   1. Developmental factors
   2. Cognitive level
   3. Moral level: The proximal impact of extended trauma on moral development can be profound. It can interfere with the development of moral concepts that can result in behaviors either overly regulated by concepts of good and bad or amoral.
   4. Temperamental characteristics
b. Pre-Crisis Adjustment
   1. Home
   2. School
   3. Interpersonal
   4. Medical

c. Coping style/ego development/resilience
d. Past experience with crisis
e. Global assessment of functioning (*DSM,* Axis 5)
f. Specific meaning of the crisis

Factors in the support system
a. Nuclear family
b. Extended family
c. School
d. Friends/community
e. Culture/religions (p. 5)

Symptoms of Traumatic Stress in Children

Traumatic stress refers to the constellation of biological, psychological, and behavioral manifestations of posttrauma events (Pynoos, 1994). Children in conditions of war and political violence display both externalizing behaviors and internalizing symptoms that may differ according to their developmental age and stage. Some of these are listed here (Lesser & Pope, 2011):

Middle Childhood (Ages 5 to 11)

- Sleep problems, headache, and nausea, visual, or hearing problems
- Distractibility, fighting, aggressive behaviors, and angry outbursts
- Concerns about safety
- Repetitious traumatic play and retelling
- Feelings of responsibility and guilt
- Loss of interest in activities
- Generalized fear, specific fears, anxiety about death
- Specific trauma-related fears
- Marked regressive behaviors
- Cognitive confusion
- Helplessness and passivity

Early Adolescence (Ages 11 to 14)

- Withdrawal, isolation, retreat from others in order to manage inner turmoil
- Memory gaps
- Depression, suicidal ideation
- Aggressive behaviors, substance abuse
- Appetite disturbance
- Self-consciousness

- Trauma-driven acting out behaviors, including life threatening reenactment
- Excessive activity and involvement with others
- Rebellion at home or at school
- Accident proneness

Adolescence (ages 14 to 18)
- Confusion, withdrawal, isolation, depression
- Antisocial behavior
- Substance abuse
- Hallucinations
- Distractibility
- Obsessional thinking
- Withdrawal into heavy sleep or night frights
- Eating disorders
- Trauma-driven acting out
- Retreat from others in order to manage inner turmoil
- Life-threatening reenactment
- Accident proneness (p. 420)

James (1989) developed a framework of nine "traumagenic states" that outline the dynamics, psychological impact, and behavioral manifestations of trauma that should be evaluated and addressed in treatment. The psychological components of these states are listed below:

Traumagenic States

1. Self-Blame
   Psychological impact: Guilt, shame, belief that self is bad
2. Powerlessness
   Psychological impact: Anxiety, fear, depression, lowered sense of efficacy, perception of self as victim, need to control, identification with aggressor, experiencing part of self as being split off (dissociation)
3. Loss and Betrayal
   Psychological impact: Numbing of emotions, denial, suppressed longing, guilt, rage, distrust of self and others
4. Fragmentation of Bodily Experience
   Psychological impact: Numbing of emotions, denial, suppressed longing, guilt, rage, distrust of self and others
5. Stigmatization
   Psychological impact: Guilt, shame, lowered self-esteem, feels different from peers, self-loathing

6. Eroticization
   Psychological impact: Preoccupation with sexual issues; confusion about sexual identity; confusion about sexual norms; confusion of sex with love or caregiving or care getting; negative association to sexual activities and arousal sensations; positive association to exploitative sexual activities
7. Destructiveness
   Psychological impact: Reinforces self-blame, guilt, shame; frightening loss of impulse control; confusion regarding self-concept; confusion regarding values, morals, addictive cycle; destructive or abusive acts relieve tensions caused by destructive or abusive acts
8. Dissociative Disorder
   Psychological impact: Fragmentation of personality; inconsistent and distorted development; depersonalization; feels alienated from others; encapsulates intense emotions
9. Attachment Disorder
   Psychological impact: Cannot trust needs will be met; cannot find comfort or security in relationships; isolated, lonely, depressed, low self-esteem, lacks secure base from which to explore the universe, unable to develop a sense of mastery

Dissociation

Dissociation is a broad descriptive term that often accompanies severe trauma. It includes a variety of mental mechanisms or defenses involved in disengaging from the world: distraction, avoidance and numbing, daydreaming, floating, assuming the persona of heroes or animals, fainting, or catatonia. When a child's physical and psychological integrity begins to be compromised, the child may turn to these self-protective defense mechanisms that allow him or her to physically and psychologically distance from what is happening, to feel it is not happening, to control autonomic arousal and anxiety, and to protect certain ego functions. The child attempts to ward off any sense of active participation in these violations through a process of dissociation that may require disclaiming affective needs and desires.

It is important to consider that dissociation, like other defenses, may not necessarily be positive for a child's mental health, especially over the developmental trajectory. Factors contributing to vulnerability may likewise not necessarily be negative. For example, lack of empathy may lead to less overt distress but may contribute to antisocial conduct and more difficulties reconnecting with family and community. Dissociative, delusional processes in response to being uprooted must be interrupted; everything should be done to prevent the problem from becoming chronic; otherwise, dissociation can result in a more serious dissociative or disordered identity disorder.

According to James (1989, p. 105), the more serious manifestations of dissociative identity include the following:

- Spontaneous trance states
- Use of another name
- A claim not to be himself/herself or a claim of dual identity
- Referring to self as "we"
- Change in ability to perform tasks
- Denial of behavior that has been observed by others
- Changes in vision, handwriting, style of dress
- Drastic changes in behavior, unexplained outbursts, disorientation
- Hearing voices
- Loss of time
- Drawing self as multiple persons
- Describing self as "unreal" or an "alien"
- Describing surroundings as becoming altered
- Getting lost coming home from school or friend's house

Trauma Bond

Another concept important to understanding the experiences of the children who have returned from captivity is that of the trauma bond (Dutton & Painter, 1981). This provides a sociopsychological explanation based on the notion that powerful reinforcement mechanisms interact with the emotional and cognitive consequences of an imbalanced power structure within the relationship to produce a traumatically based bond between captor and hostage. The children may return with what appears to be attachment relationships to their captors, but we need to be careful not to confuse attachment relationships and trauma bonds. The cognitive and affective consequences of the abuse operate to mutually reinforce each other and contribute to the victim's sense of psychological servitude. The attachments formed in such situations manifest themselves in positive feelings and attitudes by the subjugated party for the maltreating or abusing party. The help provided to the affected children will be more effective if helpers are aware of the psychological dynamics that characterize the relationship the children had with their captors.

Treatment within a Cultural Context

Cultural Trauma Model

Several authors (Stamm et al., 2004) have collaborated on the construction of a cultural trauma model that provides a useful template for considering how to intervene with children, families, and communities. The traumatic stressors in this model include exposure to warfare, extreme loss, sexual assault, violence, and other life threats. There are 15 constructs or domains in this model (see Stamm et al., p. 103, for the complete model). Those constructs that may be particularly relevant to working with the Ugandan children, their families, and their community are listed here:

- Depression (the discontinuity of experience and loss of cultural memory)
- How the problem started (warfare, beliefs)
- How the problem is sustained (discontinuity of experience, loss of cultural memory, diminished economic opportunities)
- Functional social support (adequacy of social network, economy, governmental systems, access to needed services and supports)
- Structural social supports (family and social network, traditional dress and clothing)
- Cultural identity (language, beliefs, family systems)
- The ability to envision a new world (preservation of original culture, ability to make choices)
- The ability to reconcile (cognitive flexibility, belief system, cultural identity)
- The willingness for reconciliation (the ability to make choices, increased family stability, renewed sense of health, spiritual resurgence)
- Spirituality (belief system, language, symbols)

These authors make the important point that although fragmentation is disrupting to the routines of a culture, these ruptures can be "entry points for intervention."

Goal of Therapy with the Children

The goal of any trauma therapy is to help the individual resolve traumatic material and restore self-esteem. Resolving traumatic material involves being able to remember the trauma and not reexperience it or, in other words, to mentalize or experience the trauma as a memory (Figley, 1999). This implies the ability to distinguish between past and present. We must focus on changing thoughts and feelings within the context of a relationship that enables thinking and reflective functioning. The therapeutic relationship provides the experience of mental involvement with another human being without the threat of overwhelming mental anguish.

Clinical interpretation serves a useful function when it is hard to establish engagement with survivors of extreme situations. One needs to recognize the power of internal aggression and its accompanying guilt, as well as the need to interpret it, contain it, and find ways to make reparation for it. This provides the psychological space necessary to engage in the process of resolving trauma. The dismissal of a survivor's sense of guilt undermines the treatment process. It dismisses the need for reparation. Opportunity for reparation must become an intrinsic part of any ongoing treatment if the survivor is to bear the sequelae of extreme experience (Sklarew, Twemlow, & Wilkinson, 2004). Psychological space must also be made for the community as a whole to mourn its losses and to cleanse those who feel dirty from exposure to violence, whether victim or perpetrator. The African literature on survivors reports that sometimes people feel so overwhelmed by guilt that they cannot accept or participate in traditional healing and may become engaged in negative and antisocial behavior; they may also commit suicide (Dawes & Honwana, 1996; Monteiro, 1996). Keilson (1992) referred to this as sequential traumatization, when the transition from war to peace poses its own problems. Children need to learn to understand their behaviors symbolically. Performing symbolic acts of sufficient reparative power enables them to feel worthy of good. These children must also learn concretely useful skills. This must all be done within the context of cultural familial and cultural supports that allow the children to think through and moderate the violent propensities of their own murderous superegos. The re-establishment of symbolic places and culturally prescribed behaviors is important to help re-establish previously learned cultural rules and reinstate members of the community in role functions appropriate to their places in the life cycle. A prerequisite for reconnection of the children with the community and the individuals within it is helping the children mourn the loss of attachment figures through abduction. This may also include anger at family members and community elders who may be held accountable for not protecting the children. The family and larger culture need help and guidance to ensure they do not collude with the children in avoiding the work of mourning and in suppressing their grief because of their own feelings of sadness, guilt, and helplessness that may be evoked in them by the child's pain (Figley, 1999). The multiculturally competent therapist must help the traumatized child and his or her community reconnect around their pain and then move beyond it by recontextualizing the trauma in a safe and controlled way. When trauma has been resolved, appropriate and realistic meaning has been given to the trauma. There is disengagement from the trauma that frees up energy for the present and the future; a sense of identity, competence, belonging, and stability are apparent, and hope is restored.

Trauma and Reenactments

Traumatized children generally have two conflicting drives: one to master difficult and emotionally painful material and the other to avoid and suppress it. Children with unresolved traumatic material usually demonstrate their preoccupation or engagement with that material through behavior or play. Reenactment behaviors are manifested by specific behavioral responses to subsequent situations or cues that are associated with trauma-related actions (Gil, 2006; James, 1989, 1994). They may represent a developmental tendency toward what Terr (1983) referred to as "action memories." These reenactments represent both an "anticipatory bias" in response to perceived threat and "unconscious efforts" to ward off the original moments of traumatic helplessness. Older children may actually seek out opportunities to engage in reenactments, including aggressive and violent actions. Difficulties in modulating aggression can also make these children more irritable and easy to anger.

Reenactment behaviors can serve the children in a number of ways:

- Survival
- Gaining an understanding of his or her own victimization
- Gaining mastery by reenactment, sometimes as the aggressor
- Addiction to the sensation (power, excitement, fear)
- Attempting to hold onto a positive image of his or her own abuser (trauma bond)
- Revenge
- Power
- Reinforcement of self-blame, guilt, shame
- Need to be punished, hurt, killed by another
- Reenacting learned behavior
- Need for affection and emotional closeness (James, 1989, p. 78)

When the behavioral reenactments of trauma are unrecognized, the culture and the helps can become destructive repetitions of the trauma in which the child is again disconfirmed and left alone with his or her pain (James, 1989, 1994). The goal of therapeutic work with children is to help the children identify the needs being met by these behaviors, meet their needs in a more appropriate way, identify the underlying conflicts or trauma experiences; and help them achieve some degree of resolution of those experiences.

Treatment Techniques

Survivors of disaster and trauma need psychosocial intervention that is culturally appropriate and promotes psychological stability and the reempowerment of individuals, families, and communities. The following treatment techniques have been selected for their utility in doing this.

Eye Movement and Desensitization and Reprocessing (EMDR)

This technique, developed by Francine Shapiro, PhD, integrates a number of theoretical frameworks—including cognitive–behavioral, body-based, interpersonal, and psychodynamic—into standard clinical protocols that make it accessible to training and implementation on a large scale. Its attention to affect, attachment behavior, biological information processing, and somatic variables makes it especially relevant to work with trauma, especially trauma that has occurred on a large scale. Several authors have written on the use of EMDR after natural or human-provoked disasters (Jarero & Artigas, 2002; Kristal-Andersson, 2000; Samec, 2001; Shapiro, 2001; Wilson, Tinker, Hofmann, Becker, & Marshall, 2000). van der Kolk (2002) highlighted the significance of any therapeutic technique designed to help people deal with traumatic experiences that does not rely on a trusting relationship, as this may circumvent the threat of traumatic reenactment. He also shared other observations such as how EMDR seems to loosen up free associative processes, giving rapid access to memories and images of the past, possibly allowing a person to associate current painful life experiences with prior life events that have been successfully mastered. EMDR also seems to be able to accomplish its therapeutic action without the traumatized individual having to articulate in words the source of his or her distress. Finally, EMDR seems capable of softening the pain of past experience and enhancing feelings of pleasure and serenity associated with others.

Spirituality

Traumatic events often lead to dramatic change in the survivors' world so that fundamental assumptions about meaningfulness, goodness, and safety shift negatively. For those whose core values are theologically founded, traumatic events often give rise to questions about the fundamental nature of the relationship between the Creator and humankind. How can belief in a loving, all-powerful God be sustained when the innocent are subjected to traumatic victimization? (Drescher & Foy, 2006). Children who have experienced profound or frightening changes in their lives need to understand that they are more than their families, their possessions, or their bodies. They need to feel that there is a core to their being that cannot be taken away and that they have an inner wisdom on which they can rely (Jacobs, 2011). The knowledge of a spiritual self can be nourished using examples from the natural world; for example, "If a tree loses its leaves, is it still a tree?" (Drescher & Foy, 2006). From an African perspective, "spirit" "is as important as the physical manifestations of the self. Spirit refers to that incorporeal, animating principle and energy that reflects the essence and sustenance of all matter" (Parham, 2002, p. 14). Parham goes on to explain that in the African cultural worldview, "it is the condition of *being* spirit, not merely practicing spirituality—the human being not only *has* spirit, he or she *is* spirit" (p. 17).

Spiritual manifestations of traumatic experiences can include the following (Drescher & Foy, 2006; Hodge, 2006):

- Feelings of abandonment and emptiness
- Magical thinking such as seeking magical solutions
- Doubt in religious beliefs
- Feeling unforgiven
- Survivor guilt
- Cynicism about specific activities or life in general
- Need to prove one's self-worth

Some treatment techniques incorporating spirituality include the following:

- Spiritual autobiography (oral or written; individually or in groups)
- Spiritual exercises (meditation, guided imagery, silent prayers)
- Religious and cultural rituals described by Parham in which the therapist and client join together "to develop a collective consciousness around the issue at hand" (Parham, 2002, p. 107)
- Selecting readings, poetry, prose, and storytelling which act as "symbolic representations of the subject" (Parham, 2002) providing a language to express affective and intellectual sentiments
- Religious services
- Using music to help a person "to stay on the move spiritually" (Parham, 2002, p. 109)

Narrative Therapy

Survivors of disaster and trauma need psychosocial intervention that is culturally appropriate and promotes psychological stability and the reempowerment of communities and individuals. Narrative therapy is compatible with the Afrocentric treatment concept of "metaphor" (Parham, 2002). Use of the story metaphor involves the therapist in a reformulation of the child or adolescent's memories. This includes the deconstruction of social power (in the narrative) and the hold these powers have had on the person's life and how these practices have caused clients to feel about themselves and their relationships with others (Cooper & Lesser, 2008). In this deconstruction state, the client is also encouraged to take responsibility for his or her own behaviors, which may be helpful for those children who cannot forgive themselves or who others may either not forgive or continue to fear. The therapist engages the client in a retelling of the original story, called new meaning making (Cooper & Lesser, 2008), that promotes psychological stability and reempowerment by supporting construction of a coherent narrative understanding of what has happened. Sliep, Weingarten, and Gilbert (2004) used an interactive community narrative approach called "narrative theater" to address the issue of domestic violence in a refugee camp in northern Uganda. The forum theater, the facilitator, and the audience mutually engaged in a "scene" that was recognizable to all present. They were then invited to comment on what they had witnessed and replay any of the actors at any point to share their own perspectives about the scene (Cooper & Lesser, 2011). Denborough (as cited in Cooper & Lesser, 2011) also suggested using "collective narrative practice" to respond to communities that have experienced trauma. Two techniques include convening definitional ceremonies (such as community storytelling, and public rituals) and group murals and collective narrative documents (such as proverbs, sayings, songs, and images from family and culture) that privilege values or knowledge from the culture.

Psychodynamic Techniques

Other metaphor or storytelling techniques (O'Connor & Braverman, 2009) come out of the psychodynamic tradition. Included among these are the following:

Storytelling. The child is encouraged to tell a story individually or in a group setting. The children are told that the story should have a beginning, a middle, and an end and a lesson or moral. The therapist then follows the child's story with one of his or her own that offers a more adaptive coping response or a more productive resolution.

Mutual Storytelling. The therapist starts the story, pauses, and then prompts the child to continue it. When the child falters, the therapist can pick up the story thread, pause, prompt again, and so on. Consider including helpful elements in the story that pinpoint mastery and hope. Creating a storybook and including artwork to accompany storytelling is also productive.

Positive Reminiscing. It is helpful to ask parents and other community members to incorporate into routine conversation mention of places and occurrences that took place when the children were with them, before the abduction and traumatic events occurred. It could be helpful to recover lost positive memories when there are less intense angry feelings or when the children felt more attached to their family and community.

Negative Reminiscing. This helps the child to remember the repressed events and associated feelings that are limiting the child's repertoire of behaviors. It may help the child to work through internalized negative memories that are otherwise resulting in reenactment behaviors.

Expressive Art and Physical Activity

The following expressive arts therapeutic techniques can be especially helpful for children and adolescents who do not have words to express their experiences; they are often speechless. This technique may also be of benefit when the child and the therapist do not speak the same language.

Music and Dancing. Parham (2002) talked about how music contributes to a spiritual awakening and how its "rhythms help to illustrate the need for sustaining movement and momentum in the face of personal struggle and how it helps a person to stay on the move spiritually in the face of intellectual, emotional, behavioral, or spiritual pain" (p. 109). It is also helpful with letting out feelings of anger as the physicality of dancing to music burns off energy. James (1989) wrote about how movement allows children to express and explore feelings and conflicts in an indirect and safe way and lessen their sense of lonely isolation. Joining in communal dances that allow the children to give expression to their emotions and to relieve body trauma and tension through movement are also beneficial when the children and the community are ready for this conjoint activity.

Thought Feeling Hoop. This is another physical activity that involves pairing identifying thoughts and feelings with shooting a basketball. Crumpled up balls of paper or stones and a wastebasket or bucket can suffice. The child is instructed to share his or her thoughts and feelings before and after he or she takes a shot. This practice enables the children and the helper to connect to situations, thoughts, and feelings.

Murals. Creating a mural that tells the children's story can be helpful for those children who are not able to talk about their experiences. Encouraging children to draw their experiences before, during, and after the abduction can be helpful to give a sense of mastery over the events. Telling the story through the mural in a community setting could be particularly healing if the community recognizes and validates what occurred.

Making Masks. Making masks is a way to help children tell their story from a different voice, especially if their own has been silenced and they are unable to find it. This is also a way for children who carry self-blame and shame to tell their story behind a mask. The person the child creates for himself or herself with the mask should be someone powerful who can help the child solve a problem or express a feeling.

Thought Feeling Bookmarkers or Posters. This art activity involves decorating the object with a coping statement that serves a self-instructional function. For example, "Things change," "I can handle challenges," and "Feelings change."

Color Your Life. The child is provided with a long strip of paper that represents his or her life. The child expresses his or her feelings and experiences with colors, beginning at the left side, representing when he or she was born, and continuing to the right side, identified as the present time. The paper becomes a legend associating a color with a feeling.

Cognitive–Behavioral Therapy

This type of therapy assumes a reciprocal interaction between what we think, how we feel, and how we behave. Thoughts determine feelings, which then determine behaviors. A typical cognitive–behavioral approach to treating trauma in children would target specific behaviors that are a focus for change, considering when and how often the behaviors occur, setting goals to change the behaviors, intervening, giving exercises that reinforce the change, and instituting a plan for relapse prevention (Friedberg & McClure, 2002; March & Mulle, 1998).

Self-Instructional Approaches

- Sample Treasure Chest: Ask the child to make a small box or "treasure chest" and put positive coping statements inside.
- Star of Courage: Helping children face their fears
  Draw a star and, on each one of the five points, ask a question:
  What was a fear I faced?
  How long did I face my fear?
  How many times did I face my fear?
  How did I feel after I faced my fear?
  What did I do to help myself face it?
- Taking Command or Blaming Yourself
  Draw a "thought bubble" and ask the child his or her thoughts (about certain events that occurred). Then ask the child if this is a thought that "takes command" or "blames" self. For example, if the child says "I'm bad," this would be a thought that is self-blaming and would be addressed by the therapist. If the child said, "Just because I did bad things doesn't mean I am bad," this would be a thought that is "taking command." Draw a line to show whether the thought is a way to take command or a way to blame yourself.

Community-oriented Techniques

Through community-oriented activities, the children can help each other through identification and by providing some of the advantages of group work when a group is not available. They can share their experiences by giving another child a piece of artwork, a written or shared story, and so forth. They can also be helped to write articles or make videotapes to be shown to other children (James, 1989).

Vicarious Traumatization: Impact of Trauma on Helpers

Repeated exposure to trauma material of this magnitude may expose helpers to what Pearlman and Saakvitne (1995) described as vicarious traumatization: "the repeated exposure to trauma material in the context of empathic connection with the survivor client" (p. 299). In essence, it challenges the therapist's worldview in much the same way as trauma affects the worldview of the clients. The therapist may feel confused, angry, sorrowful, overwhelmed, and hopeless. The trauma therapist, community healer, or lay person working with the profound trauma in Uganda may question the point of working with individual children and adolescents who need help so desperately. If this occurs, the therapist loses his or her greatest therapeutic tool—hope, as well as his or her greatest therapeutic joy—engaging hope in the traumatized children. The trauma therapist and all those working or engaging in this work can help guard against vicarious traumatization through peer consultation with colleagues; limiting the number of traumatized clients they see; emotional, physical, and spiritual forms of self-care; creating some boundaries between work and home; and recognizing the positive feelings associated with being able to help children who have been so cruelly maltreated. All of these things can result in what Medeiros and Prochaska (1988) called "optimistic perseverance."

Summary

The challenges faced by those working with children, families, and communities in Uganda continues on many levels. More work is needed to ensure that the social, political, and cultural context within which traumatic experience occur are understood. This understanding will help to ensure that the psychological dimensions of traumatic reactions are not isolated from the somatic, the interpersonal, and the cultural. These contextual issues should be considered fundamental to assessment and treatment as they "structure the context in which violence occurs" (Bracken et al., 1995, p. 1077). However, Keilson (1992) reminded us that often what is considered to be political can be very personal. Therefore, we must be mindful of the suffering of individuals while attending to the needs of the group as a whole.

References

Allen, J. G. (2001). *Traumatic relationships and serious mental disorders.* New York: John Wiley & Sons.

American Psychiatric Association. (2000). *Diagnostic and statistical manual of mental disorders* (4th ed., text rev.). Washington, DC: Author.

Ayonrinde, O. (2003). Importance of cultural sensitivity in therapeutic transactions: Considerations for healthcare providers. *Disease Management & Health Outcomes, 11*(4), 233–248.

Barrera, I., & Corso, R. M. (2002). Cultural competence as skilled dialogue. *Topics in Early Childhood Special Education, 22*(2), 103–113.

Bracken, P. J., Giller, J. E., & Summerfield, D. (1995). Psychological responses to war and atrocity: The limitations of current concepts. *Social Science & Medicine, 40,* 1073–1082.

Cooper, M. G., & Lesser, J. G. (2008). *Clinical social work practice: An integrated approach* (2nd ed.). Boston: Allyn & Bacon.

Cooper, M. G., & Lesser, J. G. (2011). *Clinical social work practice: An integrated approach* (4th ed.). Boston: Allyn & Bacon.

Dawes, A., & Honwana, A. (1996). *Children, culture, and mental health: Intervention in conditions of way.* Keynote address at Rebuilding Hope Congress on Children, War and Persecution, Maputo, Mozambique.

Drescher, K. D., & Foy, D. W. (2006). Spirituality and trauma treatment: Suggestions for including spirituality as a coping resource. *NCP Clinical Quarterly, 5*(1), 1–5. Retrieved from www.ncptsd.va.gov/publications/cq/v5/n1/drescher.html

Dutton, D., & Painter, S. L. (1981). Traumatic bonding: The development of emotional attachments in battered women and other relationships of intermittent abuse. *Victimology: An International Journal, 6*(1–4), 139–155.

Eyerman, R. (2001). *Cultural trauma: Slavery and the formation of African American identity.* Boston: Cambridge University Press.

Figley, C. R. (1999). *Traumatology of grieving.* Philadelphia: Brunner/Mazel.

Friedberg, R. D., & McClure, M. (2002). *Clinical practice of cognitive therapy with children and adolescents.* New York: Guilford Press.

Gil, E. (2006). *Helping abused and traumatized children: Integrating directive and nondirective approaches.* New York: Guilford Press.

Harrell-Bond, B. (1986). *Imposing aid: Emergency assistance to refugees.* New York: Oxford University Press.

Hays, P. A. (2008). *Addressing cultural complexities in practice: Assessment diagnosis and treatment* (2nd ed.). Washington, DC: American Psychological Association.

Hodge, D. R. (2006). A template for spiritual assessment: A review of the JCAHO requirements and guidelines for implementation. *Social Work, 51,* 317–326.

Jacobs, C. (2011). Spiritual development through the life cycle. In J. G. Lesser & D. S. Pope, *Human behavior and the social environment: Theory and practice* (2nd ed., pp. 226–242). Boston: Allyn & Bacon.

James, B. (1989). *Treating traumatized children: New insights and creative interventions.* New York: Free Press.

James, B. (1994). *Handbook for the treatment of attachment trauma problems in children.* New York: Free Press.

Jarero, I., & Artigas, L. (2002). *The seven phases model: An approach for mental health interventions in disaster situations.* Retrieved from http://www.amamecrisis.com.mx/articulo/index.htm

Keilson, H. (1992). *Sequential traumatization in children.* Jerusalem: Magnes Press, Hebrew University.

Kristal-Andersson, B. (2000). *Psychology of the refugee, the immigrant and their children: Development of a conceptual framework and applications to psychotherapeutic and related support work.* Lund, Sweden: University of Lund Press.

Lesser, J. G., & Pope, D. S. (2011). *Human behavior and the social environment: Theory and practice* (2nd ed.). Boston: Allyn & Bacon.

March, J. S., & Mulle, K. (1998). *OCD in children and adolescents: A cognitive–behavioral treatment manual.* New York: Guilford Press.

Marsella, A. J., Friedman, M. J., & Spain, E. H. (1994). Ethnocultural aspects of posttraumatic stress disorder. In R. S. Pynoos (Ed.), *Posttraumatic stress disorder: A clinical review* (pp. 17–36). Lutherville, MD: Sidran Press.

McFarlane, A. C., & van der Kolk, B. A. (2007). Trauma and its challenge to society. In B. van der Kolk, A. McFarlane, & L. Weisaeth (Eds.), *Traumatic stress: The effects of overwhelming experience on mind, body, and society* (pp. 24–47). New York: Guilford Press.

Medeiros, M. E., & Prochaska, J. O. (1988). Coping strategies that psychotherapists use in working with stressful clients. *Professional Psychology: Research and Practice, 19*(1), 112–114.

Meichenbaum, D. (1994). *A clinical handbook/practical therapist manual for assessing and treating adults with posttraumatic stress disorder (PTSD).* Waterloo, Canada: Institute Press.

Monteiro, C. (1996, July 31). *Cultural issues in the treatment of trauma and loss: Honoring differences.* Paper prepared for the Christian Children's Fund, Richmond, VA.

Nader, K., Dubrow, N., & Stamm, B. H. (Eds.). (1999). *Cultural issues and the treatment of trauma and loss: Honoring differences.* New York: Brunner-Routledge.

O'Connor, K. J., & Braverman, L. D. (Eds.). (2009). *Play therapy theory and practice: Comparing theories and techniques* (2nd ed.). New York: John Wiley & Sons.

Parham, T. A. (2002). *Counseling persons of African descent: Raising the bar of practitioner competence.* Irvine, CA: Sage Publications.

Pearlman, L. A., & Saakvitne, K. W. (1995). *Trauma and the therapist: Counter transference and vicarious traumatization in psychotherapy with incest survivors.* New York: W.W. Norton.

Pynoos, R. S. (1994). Traumatic stress and developmental psychology in children and adolescents. In R. S. Pynoos, *Posttraumatic stress disorder: A clinical review* (pp. 65–98). Lutherville, MD: Sidran.

Salzman, M. B. (2001). Cultural trauma and recovery: Perspectives from terror management theory. *Trauma, Violence, & Abuse, 2,* 172–191.

Samec J. (2001, December). The use of EMDR safe place exercise in group therapy with traumatized adolescent refugees [Special edition]. *EMDRIA Newsletter, 6,* 32–34.

Shapiro, F. (2001). *Eye movements desensitization and reprocessing: Basic principles, protocols, and procedures.* New York: Guilford Press.

Sklarew, B., Twemlow, S. W., & Wilkinson, S. M. (Eds.). (2004). *Analysts in the trenches: Streets, schools, war zones.* Hillsdale, NJ: Analytic Press.

Sliep, Y., Weingarten, K., & Gilbert, A. (2004). Narrative theatre as an interactive community approach to mobilizing collective action in northern Uganda. *Families Systems & Health, 22,* 306–320.

Stamm, B. H., Stamm, H. E. IV, Hundall, A. C., & Higson-Smith, C. (2004). Considering the theory of cultural trauma and loss. *Journal of Loss & Trauma, 9,* 89–111.

Terr, L. (1983). *Too scared to cry.* New York: Harper & Row.

van der Kolk, B. A. (2002). Beyond the talking cure: Somatic experience and subcortical imprints in the treatment of trauma. In F. Shapiro (Ed.), *EMDR: Promises for a paradigm shift* (pp. 66–70). Washington, DC: American Psychological Association.

van der Kolk, B. A. (2005). Developmental trauma disorder: Toward a rational diagnosis for children with complex trauma histories. *Psychiatric Annals, 35,* 401–408.

Webb, N. B. (1999). Assessment of the child in crisis. In N. B. Webb (Ed.), *Play therapy with children in crisis: Individual, group and family treatment* (pp. 3–29). New York: Guilford Press.

Weine, S., Danieli, Y., Silove, D., Van Ommeren, M., Fairbank, J. A., & Saul, J. (2002). Guidelines for international training in mental health and psychosocial interventions for trauma exposed populations in clinical and community settings. *Psychiatry, 65,* 156–164.

Weinstein, C., Fucetola, R., & Mollica, R. (2001). Neuropsychological issues in the assessment of refugees and victims of mass violence. *Neuropsychology Review, 11,* 131–141.

Wilson, S., Tinker, R., Hofmann, A., Becker, L., & Marshall, S. (2000, November). *A field study of EMDR with Kosovar-Albanian refugee children using a group treatment protocol.* Paper presented at the annual meeting of the International Society for the Study of Traumatic Stress, San Antonio, TX.

8

African Approaches to Healing Children and Families Affected by Armed Conflict: *Implications for Western Practice*

Joanne Corbin

The use of Western psychological and social approaches with individuals affected by armed conflict in non-Western societies has received much attention in recent literature. Interest in culturally appropriate and effective interventions with such individuals is likely to continue because civilians are increasingly involved in such violence (United Nations Security Council, 2005). There are approximately 30 to 32 armed conflicts worldwide (Ploughshares, 2006; United Nations Security Council, 2005), with children making up 75 percent of these armed forces (Human Security Center, 2005). In addition to the psychological and social effects on individuals, families, and communities, these conflicts result in massive dislocations of populations. The effects of armed conflict are concerns for social service professionals in international settings as well as those in U.S. settings due to the relocation of refugees and immigrants from war-affected regions. Mental health practitioners in countries affected by armed conflict face impoverished conditions and under-resourced services (Annan, Blattman, & Horton, 2006). They are eager to build their capacity to handle the psychological and social consequences of armed conflict on a population. Western-trained mental health practitioners willing to meet this need often bring the psychotherapeutic approaches that they are familiar with to their work as trainers and consultants in such countries. When practitioners in the United States encounter children and families from international contexts of armed conflict, they may be unaware of the complex cultural contexts of these families. Both situations may result in interventions that are culturally dissonant if Western psychotherapeutic models are applied to individuals with non-Western cultural orientations.

The purpose of this chapter is to use two key concepts from psychotherapeutic approaches to trauma that are familiar to Western practitioners—empowerment and reconnection (Herman, 1997)—to analyze whether and how two traditional cleansing ceremonies from northern Uganda address these same concepts. By using concepts familiar to Western practitioners, I aim to enhance their understanding of non-Western practices so they can better integrate culturally syntonic practices into their work with non-Western populations.

In an earlier study (Corbin, 2008) on resettlement experiences of children involved in armed conflict in northern Uganda, I found that, as a coping strategy, respondents did not speak about their experiences as child soldiers or have any significant contact with counselors. However, most respondents had participated in traditional cleansing ceremonies as a part of returning to their communities and reported that these practices settled their minds and re-connected them with their family and social networks. As a result, I became interested in understanding more about the role of these ceremonies in supporting recovery from trauma experiences. In this chapter I will identify commonalities between this specific ethnic group and African cultural beliefs more generally to broaden the application of this chapter to African societies that have holistic and collectivist cultural orientations. A description of the armed conflict in northern Uganda to provide context will be followed by a summary of the goals of psychotherapeutic approaches to trauma. An analysis and discussion of how traditional practices address the psychotherapeutic goals in trauma work is conducted, concluding with implications for practice.

Background

Children become actively involved as combatants in armed conflict due to desperate economic and political conditions, coercion and threats of violence, and abduction by armed forces (Human Security Center, 2005). In northern Uganda, children have been abducted by armed forces. Beginning in 1988, the Lord's Resistance Army (LRA), a political opposition group, used violence against the population in the north by abducting adults and children and forcing them into the LRA as combatants (Behrend, 1999). The LRA attacked villages for food, equipment, and people. During these attacks, the LRA often killed, wounded, and maimed those in the villages. Child abductions by the LRA escalated in frequency and severity in the early 1990s (Behrend, 1999), culminating with approximately 25,000 to 30,000 children, under 18 years of age, forced into armed conflict (Human Security Center, 2005). The LRA conflict ended in 2007 with attempts to reach a peace agreement.

This violence affected everyone who lived in this area of northern Uganda. In 1996, the Ugandan government created Internally Displaced Persons (IDP) camps, designed to provide protection from the LRA. At the height of the conflict, 80 percent of the population in this area lived in an IDP camp. Conditions were deplorable with overcrowding, limited water, and inadequate food. LRA attacks and abductions continued. Over 95 percent of formerly abducted children and adolescents reported that their village had been attacked by the LRA prior to their own abduction, and 88 percent indicated that a close friend or sibling had been abducted (MacMullin & Loughry, 2002). Among children who were not abducted, 75 percent had been robbed, two-thirds had a family member disappear, two-thirds witnessed a beating or torture, and one-third had a parent die violently (Annan et al., 2006).

More than one-third of male and one-sixth of female individuals among one sample in northern Uganda had been abducted by the LRA (Annan et al., 2006). Children witnessed others being killed and endured abusive actions (Annan et al., 2006; Derluyn, Broekaert, Schuyen, & De Temmerman, 2004). Approximately 20 percent to 25 percent of abducted children may have been forced to commit violent attacks or killings (Annan et al., 2006). Among children who had experienced abduction in northern Uganda, there has been a range in clinical outcomes, including high rates of posttraumatic stress syndromes and clinically significant Impact of Event Scale scores (Derluyn et al., 2004). Thirty-three percent of abducted children experienced high levels of emotional distress, and 10 percent had poorer psychosocial functioning and increased aggression (Annan et al., 2006).

Although not everyone forced into armed conflict develops clinically significant levels of posttraumatic stress disorder, the trauma experiences can affect all aspects of an individual's life (Elliot, Bjelajac, Fallot, Markoff, & Reed, 2005). Both children involved as combatants and those who were not involved endure the traumatic experiences of living through the violence and social, cultural, and economic disruption of armed conflict. This chapter will first discuss two common goals of Western psychotherapeutic approaches to trauma, setting the foundation for examining the African approaches. Practitioners are more likely to understand the meaning, function, and importance of traditional healing practices if they can be linked to familiar Western psychotherapeutic concepts commonly used when addressing trauma.

Goals of Psychotherapeutic Approaches to Trauma Recovery

Individuals living through such experiences of violence have been exposed to acts of inhumanity that cause them to question their values and beliefs and to reexamine basic assumptions about themselves and their relationship to the world (Gerrity & Solomon, 1996). The effects of traumatic experiences on individuals can result in disempowerment and disconnection (Herman,

1997). Regaining a sense of empowerment and reconnection to others is the focus of intrapersonal and interpersonal recovery from such experiences (Herman, 1997). Developing autonomous and conscious control over one's actions restores one's sense of empowerment (Saakvitne, Tennan, & Affleck, 1998). Forming safe, consistent, and nurturing relationships establishes genuine and intimate reconnection to others (Elliot et al., 2005). Psychotherapeutic approaches address the goals of empowerment and reconnection by establishing safety, redefining identity, and creating a narrative of the trauma experience.

Safety is conceptualized along the physical, emotional, social, and moral dimensions (Bills, 2003; Herman, 1997). Establishing physical safety and eliminating risk of further trauma is essential before beginning psychological work. Initial steps in regaining physical safety include removing oneself from an unsafe physical environment or abusive relationships. Access to appropriate health services is another physical safety issue. Emotional safety involves protecting oneself from situations or experiences that overwhelm one's coping ability. Emotional safety is strengthened when an individual gains the skills to control his or her behavioral and emotional difficulties resulting from the trauma and trusts that he or she can effectively use these skills (Bills, 2003; Herman, 1997; Saakvitne et al., 1998). Bills (2003) identified two additional aspects of safety: social and moral. Social safety refers to the individual having a supportive and available social network. Moral safety refers to the individual's faith in a moral order of the community and a system of protection. This may be an official system of justice, a traditional system, or a religious system.

Redefining one's identity, a second task of psychotherapeutic approaches for recovery, involves developing a sense of self that is independent and a sense of self that is interdependent (LaFrombiose, Coleman, & Gerton, 1993). Identity develops through an interaction of developmental, social, and cultural influences (Miller & Garran, 2008). Developing a sense of self that is independent includes knowing one's strengths, weaknesses, likes, and dislikes. One's identity is largely shaped by the roles one has in society and the value attached to those roles. Identity is also influenced by one's sense of competence gained through purposeful activity in the society. A sense of self that is interdependent refers to a person's identity as a result of relationships with others. Cultural identity is an example of a type of sense of self that is interdependent (LaFrombiose et al., 1993) and is experienced when one incorporates the norms, values, attitudes, and behaviors of the group (Yeh & Hwang, 2000).

A third psychotherapeutic task of recovery is the creation of a narrative incorporating the trauma experience. Remembering and verbally expressing the trauma experience to the therapist is considered a necessary step in the healing process. The narrative helps the individual make connections between his or her life before the trauma experience, during the trauma experience, and the hopeful story of life after the trauma in a cohesive and psychologically integrated way (Herman, 1997; van der Kolk, McFarlane, & van der Hart, 1996). The narrative allows the therapist and others within the support network to provide validation to the individual. Through the cognitive and affective work of creating the narrative, a person identifies, acknowledges, and mourns the many losses associated with the experience, including one's former sense of self. Developing the narrative helps the individual reexperience a sense of personal power in relation to himself or herself and connection to others (Saakvitne et al., 1998), providing a foundation for empowerment and reconnection.

Two traditional African cleansing ceremonies will now be examined to explore whether and how the goals of empowerment and reconnection are addressed within these non-Western approaches to healing. A brief description of the Acholi culture will set the context for understanding these two traditional practices. Commonalities with African culture will be identified to allow generalization of this discussion beyond the culture-specific examples.

Description of Traditional Ceremonies

The traditional ceremonies described in this chapter are specific to the Acholi ethnic group of northern Uganda. The Acholi are one of approximately 65 ethnic groups in Uganda (personal communication with A.J.B. Odama, Gulu Archdiocese, Gulu, Uganda, May 22, 2006), with a population of 1.2 million. The Acholi practice a communal lifestyle organized by clans. Before the LRA armed conflict, livelihood centered on producing food and cash crops and raising livestock. As a result of the war, self-sufficiency was replaced with dependency on humanitarian aid. The gradual return of peace is encouraging many families to move out of the IDP camps and reengage in farming.

Religion is deeply embedded in everyday life of the Acholi culture, from the personal to the political. An Acholi religious leader stated that, "The whole of the Acholi life is a spiritual life" (personal communication with F. R. Obol, parish priest, Awach Parish, Gulu, Uganda, May 22, 2006). "Every moment of her/his life is spent faithfully in the presence of his/her jok [spirit]. There is no moment that one is free from it" (Obol, 2006). Each chiefdom and clan had shrines for their jogi [plural of jok] that watched over the moral order of the community and were responsible for the collective well-being of the community (Behrend, 1999). According to the Acholi, to be human is to belong to the whole community, to be responsible to and in relationship with the whole community. This responsibility includes participation in religious practices and ceremonies. Not participating in such practices implies separation from the community, resulting in cultural death (Obol, 2006).

The spiritual nature of life for the Acholi includes respect and observance of the ancestors. Relatives who have died continue to be part of the living community and central to the day-to-day lives of families. Relatives who have died by violent means or in a distant location and have not received a decent burial are believed to seek vengeance on their living relatives through illness or misfortune (Behrend, 1999).

The integration of religion with all aspects of life is common to African belief systems. Religion is the strongest element in traditional African cultural and has the greatest influence on African people (Mbiti, 1990). The whole of the life is connected to religion, and there are prayers for every aspect of life including becoming pregnant, restoring life, and protection from danger (Kamya, 1997). These beliefs remain strongly embedded in African belief systems even with the widespread practice of Christianity and Islam (Kamya, 1997; Olupọna, 1991). African religions serve important psychological and social functions. Psychologically, they help people integrate various experiences into their lives and regain their equilibrium after experiencing distress (Mulago, 1991). Socially, these practices articulate a social order between the individual and the community. These practices are primarily for the well-being of the community, not the individual (Mbiti, 1990). Religion is central to the identity of the African, and separating oneself from the religion of the group means "to be severed from his roots, his foundation, his context of security, his kinships and the entire group of those who make him aware of his own existence" (Mbiti, 1990, p. 2).

Interconnection is also an important concept in African beliefs and values. Everyone and everything is interconnected (Kamya, 1997). People are recognized not as individuals but by their relationships to family and community (Honwana, 2006; Mbiti, 1990; Oosthuizen, 1991). One's existence is conceptualized by one's connection to others and relationship to the community. One's identity is a community identity. This interconnection extends to the crucial role and influence of ancestors in the lives of family, similar to that of the Acholi.

The interconnectedness of life is important for understanding health and illness for the Acholi. The Acholi believe in the power of spiritual forces, including the ancestors, to affect their lives positively and negatively. Community members may interpret events such as sickness, misfortunes, failure of crops, or poor hunting in terms of the ancestors being dissatisfied. Prayers, traditional practices, and ceremonies may be used to mediate effects of misfortunes (Harlacher, Okot, Obonyo, Balthazard, & Atkinson, 2006).

Similarly, across various African cultures, health is defined by the harmonious relationships between individuals and the spiritual world, among individuals, and within the community (Honwana, 2006). If these relationships are disrupted, then the health and well-being of the community is jeopardized. This conceptualization of health includes psychological and social well-being. Therefore, psychological distress is not conceptualized as an individual responsibility but, rather, as a responsibility of the whole community and inclusive of the spiritual world. "For Africans, therefore, coping, be it cognitive or social, emotional or physical, is derived from the personal and collective understanding of the spiritual in people's lives" (Kamya, 1997, p. 4).

Traditional practices are the means through which healing occurs in rural African communities (Honwana, 2006). Every African society has regulations and procedures about purification ceremonies and rituals that are used when an offense is committed. These beliefs are strongly held by Africans in traditional communities in Africa as well as by Africans who have immigrated to Western countries (Mbiti, 1990). Germane to this chapter's focus on individuals exposed to armed conflict, Honwana (2006) noted that people who are connected to types of death that violate community norms threaten the well-being of the community. Specific cleansing and protective ceremonies purify and restore the identity of the individuals within the community. For example, in Mozambique and Angola, traditional practices provide support in the aftermath of war, support "to heal decimated families, repair social bonds, and restore ecological balance in their environment" (Honwana, 2006, p. 156).

Two traditional Acholi ceremonies used with individuals returning to their communities after an absence are "Stepping on the Egg" and "Washing Away the Tears." These ceremonies are being used with individuals who were abducted by the LRA and have returned from abduction.

Stepping on the Egg

Stepping on the Egg is typically performed when a person returns to the community after being away from the community for a period of time or enters the parents' clan for the first time. The ritual can also be used to express welcome from the community and commitment on the part of the returnee if the person left on bad terms. The family or clan will organize this ceremony to "cleanse" the returning person of any impurities or spirits that he or she has encountered outside the community. These spirits have the potential of bringing misfortune to the community. The ritual is performed at the entrance to the clan settlement or before the person enters the home.

The ceremony involves a fresh raw egg, a Y-shaped branch from a tree (opobo) that is used to make soap, and a longer stick used to hold the top of the clan's granary open so that food can be taken out or put in. The Y-shaped stick is placed on the ground in front of the returning person, with the long end of the Y pointing away. The egg is placed at the base of the opening in the Y-shaped stick. The long end of the Y-shaped stick rests on the granary stick

(Harlacher et al., 2006). The returning person steps on to the raw egg with a bare foot and continues to walk over the opobo branch and the granary stick. The returning person's stepping on the egg represents innocence; he or she is made pure. Walking over the opobo stick symbolizes that all the spiritual impurities to which the person was exposed have been washed away, thereby cleansing the person (Harlacher et al., 2006). When the returning person walks over the granary stick, representing the food of the clan, it symbolizes the clan's taking responsibility for the returning person (Harlacher et al., 2006).

The ceremony is conducted by the family or clan and is recognized and accepted by the entire community and signals to community members that the individual has been welcomed back into the community (Harlacher et al., 2006). A slight variation of this practice has the returning person enter the home after walking through the egg as described earlier. As the person steps into the house, the mother or an elderly woman of the clan pours water down the thatch roof, again symbolizing cleansing. The returning person stays in the home and can now "feel at ease" because he or she has been cleansed and accepted by the family and community (personal communication with F. R. Obol, May 22, 2006). Family and clan members pray to the ancestors and tell them of the person's long absence and their pleasure at his or her return. The remaining water is poured on the western front of the home with the statement, "Let the sun set on all the misfortune of this family" (personal communication with F. R. Obol, May 22, 2006).

Washing Away the Tears

This ceremony is performed for a retuning person who was believed to have died. The family and community mourned the individual's death and later found out the person was still alive. This ceremony is often done in conjunction with the Stepping on the Egg ceremony for returning children thought to have died in the armed conflict. The community believes that harm would fall on the returning individual if the mourned tears are not returned to the individual, or *washed away*.

> The returning person would stay as if mad and not healthy. He would stay like a dead person . . . The ritual helps in washing away the bitterness of the people who mourned the person so that this bitterness does not bring problems such as sickness that doesn't cure. (Caritas, as cited in Harlacher et al., 2006, p. 71)

The ceremony entails washing the returnee's face with blessed water. The family slaughters a goat to be eaten during this ceremony. Some of the water used for washing the hands before and after the meal would be sprinkled on the returnee's body by each person, with the following blessing for health:

"We had already wept for you; we thought that you were dead. May our sorrow that made us weep for you not bring any problem to you. Today we have washed our tears so that you may stay healthy" (Caritas, as cited in Harlacher et al., 2006, p. 72). Some of the water is also poured on the thatch roof of the home as the returning person performs the ritual of entering and exiting of the home, another form of cleansing. The remaining water is used by the family members to wash away the tears that were shed for the child and any accompanying bad spirits (Harlacher et al., 2006).

Analysis and Discussion

Linking the aforementioned purification methods conceptually to Western psychotherapeutic trauma theory will expand Western practitioners' understanding about how African approaches facilitate recovery. Such understanding may help practitioners integrate aspects of such approaches into their work. However, before addressing these goals, the central role of the family and community in these traditional practices must be discussed. Western models have an individualistic orientation (Honwana, 2006) and extend to include the broader social systems. Traditional African societies have a collectivist orientation (Honwana, 2006) and recognize the individual primarily in relation to a family or clan (Mbiti, 1990). This collectivist orientation is the organizing framework for traditional approaches. The practices underscore the holistic conceptualization of healing in the Acholi culture. The community as a whole, rather than the individual, is the locus of repair. The role of the community will continue to be discussed as I explore how these traditional practices address the issues of safety, identity, and a healing narrative—tasks toward achieving empowerment and reconnection.

Establishing safety is a priority in both Western and traditional practices. Herman (1997) explained that people cannot recover from trauma experiences until they take charge of the material circumstances of their lives. This includes establishing a safe environment. However, in situations of armed conflict, achieving desirable levels of safety in the camps and villages is not possible. Adults have limited ability to protect their children and families. People living in such an environment may not be able to fully attain safety until there is a cessation of all violence and restoration of basic functions such as food production, provision of shelter, and health services.

Despite these contextual limitations, the returning person may experience a sense of safety simply by knowing that his or her family and community are arranging these ceremonies and preparing to receive him or her back into the community. Performance of the ceremonies and the presence of family provide the social support and supportive relationships that buffer the effects of trauma and provide a sense of cohesion (Silove & Zwi, 2005). Social safety is experienced through the social inclusion provided by the community's participation in these practices. The returning person also knows that he or she will receive the shelter of a family member or relative, even if temporarily, thus providing a sense of physical safety. In the Stepping on the Egg ceremony, the symbolism of walking over the granary stick implies that the basic needs of the returning person will be taken care of by the community.

These ceremonies can be viewed as addressing emotional safety because they provide external mechanisms of self-control (Littlewood, 1998). Participants in my earlier study said these practices psychologically *balance* the returning person. Stepping on the egg cleanses the person of the influence of the spirits, and returning the tears returns the individual's spirit. The returning person may feel that he or she, rather than the spirits, is in control of his or her actions. When these traditional practices are not performed, the community members may attribute the person's inappropriate behavior to the ceremony that was not performed. These practices also psychologically balance the community. Performing these ceremonies assures community members that everything within their control has been done to resolve disruptions in the natural and spiritual relationships.

Emotional and moral safety are supported through prayers and giving advice, ways of transmitting the social mores and values of the community. The advice can help a returnee to manage his or her behavior and emotions and stay within the bounds of appropriate behavior. Annan et al. (2006) suggested that Acholi family connectedness and social conformity contribute to low levels of aggression among war-affected youths. However, adhering to traditional norms may be difficult for many returning individuals as they had to make many difficult individual decisions during abduction. Returning to traditional norms may be restricting to these individuals, and they may experience a sense of disempowerment from the pressure to conform to the group norms (Annan et al., 2006).

Identity is reclaimed through the restoration of social and ethnic identity in both traditional practices. For example, washing the tears reconnects the person with the living; the person is no longer *dead* to the world. These ceremonies signal acceptance into a social network, thereby reducing anxiety and restoring hope (personal communication with F. R. Obol, May 22, 2006). Reentering the social network is often the first step in reengaging in social roles such as returning to school or involvement in farming or other income-generating activities. Such normative experiences provide individuals with a sense of security and stability, and hope for the future (Lorey, 2001).

Identity is viewed as a process of interdependence rather than separation and individuation in collectivist cultures (Dien, 2000; Markus & Kitayama,

1991). Western developmental identity theories tend to deemphasize the social context in shaping identity (Yeh & Hwang, 2000). Therefore, it is critical for Western practitioners to grasp the importance of social acceptance and social inclusion in a culture that values social identity over individual identity. Complicating this understanding of collective identity is the impact of urbanization and mass displacement on this population. Individuals may have grown away from the traditional practices and still have strong cultural beliefs. These demographic changes signal a need to consider recovery approaches that support a combination of individual identity and collective identity development.

The third task defined by psychotherapeutic approaches in the work toward empowerment and reconnection is the creation and communication of a narrative of the trauma experience. Western approaches encourage the development of an individual narrative to achieve cognitive and affective integration of the trauma experience. The Acholi traditional approaches are structured around a collective narrative. The violence that individuals committed during abduction was "not their will." The elders and community leaders educate other community members that these individuals were forced to do the violent actions. The cultural discourse provides a spiritual understanding of the social disruption of the abduction and associated violence and looks for a spiritual resolution to the distress. This worldview and the associated practices, the cleansings and the prayers, guide the community members on how to interact with the returned person (Saakvitne et al., 1998).

Mourning is built into these cultural narratives and begins with the public acknowledgment that the person is returning and needs to experience cleansing. In the ceremonies, there is also an aspect of forgiveness that appears necessary before the returning person is accepted back into the community (Zack-Williams, 2006). The returning individual's breaking the egg and walking over the opobo branch symbolizes the washing away of spiritual impurities and the restoration of innocence. One female religious leader stated that "with the sound of the breaking of the egg, all that the person has done in the past is silenced as well." Pouring water on the western side of the home also symbolizes that whatever the person was involved with will be a settled matter as the sun sets.

In the Washing Away the Tears ceremony, the family and community reflect on their premature mourning of the returning person. The community must make apologies for the premature grieving for the returning person. Although the initial and premature mourning of the person was painful, it provided a sense of closure for the family and community. With "washing the tears," this closure is reopened and the community must grieve this as well. The connection of mourning and forgiveness indicates a transactional process between the individual and the community that is structured into the cultural healing approaches. Completion of the actions within the ceremonies implies that the individual and the community can begin a renewed relationship.

It may not be easy for a new beginning to occur as the community can be a source of pain for returning individuals who experience the harassment of community members. A person who has been exposed to armed conflict may have been involved in actions that violate the social contract, for example, killing, maiming, abusing, torturing, and being sexually violated. Community members may know of the returning person's behavior or may have experienced violence caused by the returnee. Therefore, the impact of the trauma experience is felt by the entire community. The traditional practices begin to heal the relationship between the individual and the community. However, the recognition and mourning of traumatic experiences affecting the community will require massive community strategies of remembrance, grieving, and reconciliation.

In summary, the psychotherapeutic goals of empowerment and reconnection are achieved through these ceremonies. However, the Western conceptualization of empowerment as the conscious control over one's actions is not as clearly pictured in the traditional practices as is described in Western approaches. It is clear that the traditional approaches re-establish safety, redefine identity, and provide a collective narrative: the steps through which a sense of empowerment is regained. What is less clear is whether empowerment is conceptualized differently in more traditional cultures than in Western cultures. These traditional ceremonies provide the community with a sense of agency. Families and communities may experience a sense of powerlessness from the inability to protect those who were abducted. In the traditional approaches, the families and communities are taking action and reclaiming a sense of power by accepting the person back into the social structure. Hence, these ceremonies become opportunities for community empowerment. Further consideration must be given to exploring how empowerment is conceptualized and expressed in cultures that value collective identity over individual identity.

In psychotherapeutic approaches, this healing work occurs in the therapeutic relationship involving a trained professional who displays a neutral and nonjudgmental stance. In contrast, the community provides the healing relationship in traditional cultures, providing warmth, empathy, acceptance, and guidance for most of those returning from armed conflict. The traditional ceremonies are formalized systems for reorienting the returning person to his or her family, community, and culture. The community involvement and cultural orientation regarding illness and disease decreases stigmatization for the individual because the community has conceptualized the distress in a culturally compatible way (Elliot et al., 2005) and is engaged in the healing process (Silove, Steel, & Psychol, 2006).

Implications

The concept of collective identity as the primary identity is radically different from the concept of individual identity and is an important starting place for those working with clients from collectivist cultures. This was an important distinction in these African exemplars. Practitioners must explore how children and their families from African cultures conceptualize individual and collective identity before recommending interventions. The centrality of the family and the community in these examples highlights the transactional nature of healing and the need for Western practitioners to address the individual perspective and the community perspective, including the spiritual dimension in the healing process.

In addition, the locus of healing in the African practices was the relationship between the individual and the community. The collective narrative in these examples provided the community with an understanding of the trauma experience and a resolution to the disruption in the relationship. When working with families with collectivist cultural orientations, Western practitioners should consult with those who understand the client's worldview so that the culturally defined locus of healing is addressed (Silove et al., 2006).

Although this chapter recommends increased integration of non-Western cultural understanding and practices by Western practitioners, traditional practices should not be adopted uncritically. Many individuals coming out of armed conflict situations in Africa are not returning to traditional communities. They are relocating to more urbanized areas; in fact, some families sent their children to live in these areas during intense phases of armed conflict for protection. These children have grown up away from the traditional practices and may have ambivalence toward traditional beliefs.

Finally, contexts of armed conflict provide a unique challenge in which to address the psychosocial needs of children and families. There must be a combination of interventions planned for all levels of the ecological social systems. This chapter focused on individual, family, and community recovery issues; however, the work of healing and recovery must include attention to economic, cultural (Silove et al., 2006), and political recovery as well. Social service providers are especially challenged by the overwhelming poverty; the lack of food, water, and shelter; and the insufficiency of human, material, and educational resources. Addressing these needs is often a priority in such communities, well ahead of psychotherapeutic intervention.

Conclusion

The cultural concepts of the spiritual nature of life, collective identity, and interconnection of the natural and spiritual worlds are important touchstones in addressing trauma experiences with children and families from African cultures affected by armed conflict. Culturally competent social workers must increase their familiarity with the worldviews of children and families from such areas. It is hoped that the examination here of the Acholi cleansing rituals in the context of Western psychotherapeutic concepts will facilitate Western practitioners' understanding of how traditional African approaches can support healing from trauma experiences, particularly the re-establishment of safety, the redefinition of collective identity, and the use of a cultural narrative. The major distinction between African and Western approaches was that the African approaches placed the family and the community as the focus of healing, whereas Western approaches placed the focus on the individual. Collective identity was a key aspect in the African practices and will be important in developing culturally appropriate interventions. In summary, social workers and helping professionals in the United States can better aid clients from African cultures by understanding more about their worldviews, in particular, the spiritual nature of life, the interconnection of the natural and spiritual worlds, and collectivism.

References

Annan, J., Blattman, C., & Horton, R. (2006). *The state of youth and youth protection in Northern Uganda: Findings from the survey for war affected youth.* Kampala, Uganda: UNICEF.

Behrend, H. (1999). *Alice Lakwena & the holy spirits: War in Northern Uganda 1985–1997.* Oxford, United Kingdom: James Currey, Ltd.

Bills, L. J. (2003). Using trauma theory and S.A.G.E. in outpatient psychiatric practice. *Psychiatric Quarterly, 74,* 191–203.

Corbin, J. N. (2008). Returning home: Resettlement of formerly abducted children in northern Uganda. *Disasters, 32,* 316–335. doi:10.1111/j.0361-3666.2008.01042.x

Derluyn, I., Broekaert, E., Schuyen, G., & de Temmerman, E. (2004). Post-traumatic stress in former Ugandan child soldiers. *Lancet, 363,* 861–863.

Dien, D. S. (2000). The evolving nature of self-identity across four levels of history [Electronic version]. *Human Development, 43,* 1–18.

Elliot, D. E., Bjelajac, P., Fallot, R. D., Markoff, L. S., & Reed, B. G. (2005). Trauma-informed or trauma denied: Principles and implementation of trauma-informed services for women. *Journal of Community Psychology, 33,* 461–477.

Gerrity, E. T., & Solomon, S. D. (1996). The treatment of PTSD and related stress disorders: Current research and clinical knowledge. In A. J. Marsella, M. J. Friedman, E. T. Gerrity & R. M. Scurfield (Eds.), *Ethnocultural aspects of postraumatic stress disorder: Issues, research, and clinical applications* (4th ed., pp. 87–102). Washington, DC: American Psychological Association.

Harlacher, T., Okot, F. Z., Obonyo, C. A., Balthazard, M., & Atkinson, R. (2006). *Traditional ways of coping in Acholi: Cultural provisions for reconciliation and healing from war*. Kampala, Uganda: Intersoft Business Services, Ltd.

Herman, J. L. (1997). *Trauma and recovery*. New York: Basic Books.

Honwana, A. (2006). *Child soldiers in Africa*. Philadelphia: University of Pennsylvania Press.

Human Security Center. (2005). *Human security report: War and peace in the 21st century*. Retrieved from http://www.humansecurityreportinfo/HSR2005_PDF/Part1.pdf

Kamya, H. (1997). African immigrants in the United States: The challenge for research and practice [Electronic version]. *Social Work, 42,* 154–166.

LaFrombiose, T., Coleman, H.L.K., & Gerton, J. (1993). Psychological impact of biculturalism: Evidence and theory [Electronic version]. *Psychological Bulletin, 114,* 395–412.

Littlewood, R. (1998). Cultural variation in the stigmatization of mental illness [Electronic version]. *Lancet, 352,* 1056–1057.

Lorey, M. (2001). *Child soldiers: Care and protection of children in emergencies: A field guide*. Westport, CT: Save the Children Federation.

MacMullin, C., & Loughry, M. (2002). *An investigation into the psychosocial adjustment of formerly abducted child soldiers in Northern Uganda*. Washington, DC: International Rescue Committee.

Markus, H. R., & Kitayama, S. (1991). Culture and the self: Implications for cognition, emotion, and motivation [Electronic version]. *Psychological Review, 98,* 224–253.

Mbiti, J. S. (1990). *African religions and philosophy*. Portsmouth, NH: Heinemann Educational Books.

Miller, J. L., & Garran, A. M. (2008). *Racism in the United States: Implications for the helping professions*: Belmont, CA: Wadsworth.

Mulago, V. (1991). Traditional African religion and Christianity. In J. K. Olupọna (Ed.), *African traditional religions: In contemporary society* (pp. 119–134). New York: Paragon House.

Obol, R. C. (2006). *Peacebuilding*. Unpublished manuscript.

Olupọna, J. K. (1991). Major issues in the study of African traditional religion. In J. K. Olupọna (Ed.), *African traditional religions: In contemporary society* (pp. 25–34). New York: Paragon House.

Oosthuizen, G. C. (1991). The place of traditional religion in contemporary South Africa. In J. K. Olupọna (Ed.), *African traditional religions: In contemporary society* (pp. 35–50). New York: Paragon House.

Ploughshares. (2006). *Armed conflicts 2006 report summary*. Retrieved from http://www.ploughshares.ca/libraries/ACRText/Summary2005.pdf

Saakvitne, K. W., Tennan, H., & Affleck, G. (1998). Exploring thriving in the context of clinical trauma theory: Constructive self development theory. *Journal of Social Issues, 54,* 279–299.

Silove, D., Steel, Z., & Psychol, M. (2006). Understanding community psychosocial needs after disasters: Implications for mental health services [Electronic version]. *Journal of Postgraduate Medicine, 52,* 121–125.

Silvove, D., & Zwi, A. B. (2005). Translating compassion into psychosocial aid after the tsunami. *Lancet, 365,* 269–271.

United Nations Security Council. (2005). *Report of the secretary-general on the protection of civilians in armed conflict*. Retrieved from http://daccessdds.un.org/doc/ UNDOC/GEN/N05/610/43/PDF/N0561043.pdf?OpenElement van der Kolk, B. A., McFarlane, A. C., & van der Hart, O. (1996). A general approach to treatment of posttraumatic stress disorder. In B. A. van der Kolk, A. C. McFarlane, & L. Weisbeth (Eds), *Traumatic stress: The effects of overwhelming experience on mind, body, and society* (pp. 417–440). New York: Guilford Press.

Yeh, C. J., & Hwang, M. Y. (2000). Interdependence in ethnic identity and self: Implications for theory and practice [Electronic version]. *Journal of Counseling and Development, 78,* 420–429.

Zack-Williams, T. B. (2006). Child soldiers in Sierra Leone and the problems of demobilisation, rehabilitation and reintegration into society: Some lessons for social workers in war-torn societies. *Social Work Education, 25*(2), 119–128.

9

Ecological Framework for Social Work Practice with African Populations Affected by Armed Conflict

Joanne Corbin

African individuals and families affected by armed conflict may address a range of issues with social workers, such as exposure to conflict; loss of family and social networks; displacement; loss of means of livelihood; unaddressed health issues; language challenges; and differing cultural beliefs, values, and norms. Social workers can be overwhelmed by the complexity of the issues, clients' narratives of violence and oppression, the need to collaborate with many resources, and skills needed to address these areas (Gorman, 2001; Marotta, 2003; Woodcock, 2001). Providing social workers with a framework for assessing the many issues faced by African clients affected by armed conflict can help social workers develop a treatment plan based on clients' lived experiences (Gorman, 2001).

This chapter explores the biopsychosocial needs of African clients affected by armed conflict. An enhanced framework for identifying the multiple challenges to psychosocial functioning using the ecological perspective is presented; attention is given to the specific phases of the migration experience. Practice considerations for social workers will be explored.

Ecological Perspective

The ecological perspective will be used to consider the multiple levels of the social system (individual, microsystem, mesosystem, exosystem, and macrosystem) that social workers may encounter in their work with African individuals and families affected by armed conflict. The ecological model identifies the reciprocal interactions that occur between an individual and her or his social environment and provides a conceptual framework for understanding the impact of these transactions on the individual. Transactions can occur between one individual and another individual or social group (microsystem), between two or more social groups involving the individual (mesosystem), between two or more social groups not directly involving the individual (exosystem), and the overall societal context (macrosystem) (Bronfenbrenner, 1979). Using the ecological approach as a framework helps social workers identify the multiple systems that may be contributing to the individual's and family's current situation and determine at which levels they can most effectively intervene to support client needs.

Although the ecological model provides a useful framework to identify the multiple areas of consideration, this model must be adapted to reflect the critical phases of migration experiences of immigrants, refugees, and asylum seekers affected by armed conflict. The three phases presented in the literature are premigration, flight, and postmigration. (The terms "premigration," "transit," "postmigration," or "predisplacement," "displacement," and "postdisplacement" have also been used to describe the phases of migration.) Each of these phases has its own challenges and exposures to traumatic experiences affecting overall health, mental health and well-being (Brough, Gorman, Ramirez, & Westoby, 2003; Pine & Drachman 2005; Porter & Haslam, 2005; Schweitzer, Melville, Steel, & Lacherez, 2006; Silove & Ekblad, 2002). In addition, this chapter takes the preconflict experience of individuals and families into consideration as many individuals affected by armed conflict experienced a period of time before the violence of war affected their lives. The adapted model reflects the four phases of the migration experience and levels of the social systems to be considered. Using such a framework can help social workers identify the severity and sequence of issues to address rather than becoming overwhelmed by the totality of the issues presented.

Ecological Assessment

Prior to Conflict

Many individuals affected by armed conflict experienced life before war in their countries of origin. Several of the authors in this book describe their lives, relationships, and plans prior to the armed conflict. Exploring this period of time provides the social worker with information about community and family relationships, social systems, education, economics, employment, and religious and cultural influences that may allow social workers to understand the strengths and vulnerabilities that individuals and families had during periods of relative peace. Some individuals affected by armed conflict have only known life with war. Others have experienced cycles of war and peace: Many people affected by the recent Lord's Resistance Army armed conflict in Uganda also experienced the violence under Idi Amin's presidency in the 1970s.

Prior to Conflict: Macrosystem. History of the individual's country of origin, the economic and political tensions, and the social and cultural context in which the individual functioned is necessary information for practitioners. Such information can broaden a social worker's current perception of a client as being in distress. Clients may have been competent, productive, and respected members of their families and communities prior to the disruption of conflict. It can be useful for social workers to recognize the client embedded in these functioning systems. Another important consideration of history is information about the political and ethnic tensions among various groups in a client's country of origin that may help social workers understand that everyone from the same country will not have the same experience of armed conflict (Marotta, 2003). Some groups within countries experience political vulnerability and attack, and other groups within those countries are identified as the aggressors of the attack (Duyvesteyn, 2000). Such knowledge can be useful when enlisting cultural experts who may have different political backgrounds from those of clients.

Cultural orientation is a second macrosystem issue that shapes individuals' and families' beliefs, values, norms, roles, and attitudes (Lum, 2007; Triandis, 1995). Culture also influences individuals' conceptualization of health, mental health, wellness, and disease; hence, the interventions that would be used to address illness or poor functioning in the individual, family, or community (Honwana, 2006). Some of these interventions may include traditional practices that U.S. practitioners may be unfamiliar with. The predominant cultural orientation for individuals from Africa is collectivism (Honwana, 2006; Kamya, 1997; Mbiti, 1990). Attributes of collectivism include an interdependent conceptualization of the self; close alignment of personal and communal goals; social behavior guided by norms, obligations, and duties; and an emphasis on the maintenance of relationships (Triandis, 1995). Social workers can explore clients' culturally based values, beliefs, and expectations along these attributes. U.S. social workers will likely need to reconsider concepts that are central to social work, for example, self, self-determination, empowerment, and identity, when working with individuals from a collectivist cultural orientation.

A third macrosystem issue to consider is the context of social work in the client's country of origin. Social work is a developing profession in Africa, and clients may not have had prior exposure to social work or counseling as it is practiced in the United States. Clients may have beliefs of counseling being associated with stigma about mental illness (Wong et al., 2006) or be unfamiliar with practices such as follow-up for services (Gong-Guy, Cravens, & Patterson, 1991). Many individuals in Africa may associate counseling with *counseling* specific to HIV/AIDS programs; there are over 30,000 Voluntary Counseling and Testing centers in Africa (World Health Organization, 2011). Familiarizing clients with the nature of the counseling relationship and process can be a necessary and important first step in developing a working relationship.

Prior to Conflict: Exosystem. Social systems that affect individuals and families indirectly may include regional or area-level politics, and traditional political and authority structures such as tribal leaders who interface with the elected leaders. Individuals from Africa will be familiar with a different orientation around formal and informal power and authority. Exploring a client's expectations around legal, political, or employment decisions will help a social worker guide clients on policies and actions to take in the United States. Brown (2011) found that Liberian refugees viewed the U.S. government as a replacement of the transactional network of social, material, and instrumental support that they experienced in their communities in Liberia. Resource and supportive functions that they relied on their community for in Liberia were transferred to government systems in the United States.

Prior to Conflict: Mesosystem. The systems that individuals interface with routinely and that interact with one another include family and clan networks, work and livelihood networks, and religious or spiritual communities. These social systems looked out for people and took care of one another (Brown, 2011). For individuals coming from rural areas in which many activities of daily living are conducted in the social space of a community—farming, getting water from community sources—the mesosystem is a vital and necessary aspect of individuals' lives. *Community-as-a-whole* transactions are a way to describe these social and economic activities, which are different than individual acts of social or material support. It is the community-as-a-whole type of experience that is disrupted by armed conflict (Corbin, 2008).

Prior to Conflict: Microsystem. Interconnectedness among everyone in the community, including those who have died (ancestors), and the physical environment is a defining characteristic of traditional African culture (Kamya, 1997; Mbiti, 1990). (See chapter 4 for an expanded description of interconnection in northern Uganda.) It is necessary for social workers to identify the relationships that an African individual had prior to the conflict; understanding the significance and strength of these relationships can provide an understanding of the effects of armed conflict on these relationships for African clients holding a traditional cultural orientation. It is also important to pay attention to problems in these relationships that may be overshadowed by the experiences of armed conflict; these problems may recur in postconflict resettlement.

Prior to Conflict: Individuals. For many individuals from traditional African cultures, the individual is defined by a communal identity (Honwana, 2006; Kamya, 1997; Mbiti, 1990; Oosthuizen, 1991). Exploring an individual's connectedness to family, peers, community, and engagement in work or school and religious activities provides information about social and emotional well-being prior to the armed conflict. It is important to recognize that most individuals coming from Africa have significant strengths; they were deeply connected to family and community, involved in productive work and livelihoods, and supported their communities (Brown, 2011). An indication of such strengths was provided by one study that found that most African asylum seekers had some college education and spoke at least two languages (Piwowarczyk, Keane, & Lincoln, 2008).

Premigration

During premigration there is the increasing insecurity leading to violence and war. There is often the presence of opposition groups, government forces, fighting, violence, curfews, and closure of schools and places of employment or business. This phase in a country can be confusing for citizens; for example, in both Sierra Leone and Uganda the armed groups, the RUF and LRA, began with stated goals for reforming the countries' governments and then devolved into brutal violence and attacks on their populations (Denov, 2010; Finnström, 2008). Social workers can gain background information from media reports, a specific country's or neighboring countries' online newspapers, or the United Nations' Web site. Although this may appear to be a lot of information to gather, it is from this contextual information that social workers will have a basis to understand the nature of a client's or family's experiences during this time. Such information can expand or challenge a practitioner's preconceptions about a conflict situation (Marotta, 2003).

Premigration: Macrosystem. The macrosystem in which an individual is embedded changes with war; in fact, war becomes *the* overriding macrosystem issue affecting all aspects of life. The conflict disrupts communication and transportation systems as communication towers are destroyed, roads are ambushed, and land mines are planted. Food, gas, and supplies may not be able to get to markets due to the destruction and danger. Banks, schools, and places of employment are closed or too dangerous to attend. Livelihood activities are affected as farms are burned and livestock is stolen. It can take time for humanitarian efforts to be organized and reach the populations affected by the war. During these times, individuals and families living in these areas are on their own.

Premigration: Exosystem. During the premigration phase, regional or area-level politicians, traditional political and authority structures such as tribal leaders, and regional and district-level services may not be able to access needed resources at system levels above them due to safety issues. An example is that district and regional departments (exosystem) might identify social and medical needs of the conflict-affected areas, but national and international policy (macrosystem) will dictate that the regional programs cannot go into those dangerous areas. Such breakdowns may exacerbate feelings of isolation for conflict-affected populations from those who can help them.

Premigration: Mesosystem. The political instability and violence of armed conflict disrupts the functioning of family, clan, social, cultural, and economic social systems. The usual activities that ground people in their daily lives cease to function because of the insecurity or danger of meeting. Social and cultural activities become too dangerous to continue. Livelihood activities such as farming and getting water from boreholes stop because of the danger of attack or the possibility of stepping on land mines.

Premigration: Microsystem. As with the mesosystem issues, the violence and danger during armed conflict disrupt all social networks and connections. Families and individuals focus on survival and protection from political and civil instability, the unpredictability of daily life, and violence associated with armed conflict. Families may be separated from one another, and individuals may need to live apart from the family due to fears of safety. Families and social networks experience the abductions, disappearances, and killings of loved ones and friends.

Premigration: Individual. Many of the aspects of everyday life that provide safety, identity, and meaning for individuals—family, community, and social networks—are forever changed during premigration. Individuals are exposed to unspeakable violence and suffering. They experience murders of family members and friends; rape; torture; and lack of food, water, and shelter (Schweitzer et al., 2006). Experiences of trauma and violence in premigration are associated with poor mental health outcomes and somatization symptoms in individuals in postmigration (Hondius, van Willigen, Kleijn, & van der Ploeg, 2000; Sack, Clarke, & Seeley, 1996; Schweitzer et al., 2006). Depression in postmigration was associated with individuals who had a family member who experienced trauma in premigration (Schweitzer et al., 2006).

Individual-level factors have been associated with resilience and positive coping during premigration; these factors included religion and personal attitudes and beliefs. Religion helped individuals deal with events beyond their control and regain a sense of meaning (Schweitzer, Greenslade, & Kagee, 2007). Personal attitudes and beliefs helped people deal with adverse events; some refugees perceived themselves as becoming stronger with each challenge (Schweitzer et al., 2007).

Flight

Moving to another location or country to escape violence and war is unsettling and disruptive and can be traumatic. For some individuals and families, decisions to leave their home and country can occur over a period of time during which the armed conflict becomes increasingly violent. For others, there is no choice; the need to leave may happen quickly as violence erupts and citizens have to flee. Many people are unable to move, for example, elderly or ill individuals, and remain in the midst of the violence. Citizens may go to other areas of the country (internally displaced people [IDP]) or cross borders to other countries (refugees). The magnitude of flight from armed conflict is large in Africa; 10 million people are currently identified as refugees, asylum seekers, internally displaced, stateless, and repatriated (United Nations High Commissioner for Refugees [UNHCR], 2011). Many individuals experience multiple displacements.

The flight experience for those who are not refugees or asylum seekers may be different. Some may have the ability to live with friends or in communities outside of the conflict area until they are able to resettle in another country (see experience in chapter 3). However, the need to move from one's country of origin due to violence and fear of violence is a major psychosocial, cultural, and economic stressor for individuals and families.

Flight: Macrosystem. Macrosystem issues to be aware of during the flight phase include the emergency nature of people's experiences and the inability of the larger social systems in the countries to which people are displaced to address the enormity of human and social need. Refugees often travel long distances, bring few personal possessions, and do not know if they will return to their homes (Brough et al., 2003). The admission to refugee and IDP camps is confusing (Brough et al., 2003). These camps do not provide order and safety. Individuals and families continue to experience violence from the armed groups they sought to escape, opposition groups, or the army that is supposed to protect them (Achvarina & Reich, 2006).

When individuals and families are displaced, they are often moving to countries and areas that have different cultural norms, language, and political systems. These differences can be difficult to negotiate for individuals and families under extreme stress. Displaced populations can also experience hostility and prejudice from residents of the region or country that they have been displaced to (Schweitzer et al., 2007).

Flight: Exosystem. The exosystem-level resources are in disarray and may be inaccessible to those in refugee or IDP camps. Individuals might be unfamiliar with the political and economic systems in a different country. In flight they may be also interacting with international agencies such as UNHCR and humanitarian relief agencies that have different administrative systems from the country's system. The resources and services at this level of the system may be nonexistent, minimally functioning, or corrupted (World Vision, 2006). Sexual harassment and abuse of girls and women in refugee camps by those expected to protect them is common (World Vision, 2006). The breakdown in structures of authority and order can lead to further violence and insecurity (Brough et al., 2003).

Flight: Mesosystem. The social systems in which individuals were embedded prior to the armed conflict have fractured. Families and village members become separated from one another during the confusion of fleeing to any area of safety. Refugee camps or IDP camps can be disorganizing as individuals and families settle wherever they can find space, which may not be near anyone they know. Social and community groups that pulled together for collective livelihood and economic activities, cultural practices, and clan- and village-based activities cease to function due to members being dispersed, limited space, or risk of danger (Corbin, 2008). The community-as-a-whole networks that individuals relied on are no longer functioning.

Flight: Microsystem. During this period of flight, husbands become separated from wives, children from siblings and parents. Due to the crisis nature of this phase, individuals and families may not have had the opportunities to mourn the deaths of family members or friends or bury these loved ones in the culturally appropriate manner (Woodcock, 2001). Adding to the challenges of maintaining relationships during this time, Woodcock (2001) reminded us that individuals may also be escaping oppressive relationships or situations in the place of origin.

Families who had more choice, ability, or time to move from the area of conflict or country and who may not live in a refugee or an IDP camp are also affected by the loss of home and important social, economic, and familial networks. These individuals are also concerned for family and community members whom they became separated from or who remained in the conflict area.

Flight: Individual. The conditions under which people are forced to flee are traumatic; many people experience the violence associated with war, and others fear these experiences happening to them or family members (Brough et al., 2003). Individuals may be separated from family members and friends and surviving alone or with help from strangers. Over time, family members will try to find one another through word of mouth with others who might be familiar with the family. The period of flight and living in temporary sites can last years; individuals who were displaced longer experienced poorer mental health outcomes (Schweitzer et al., 2006). During this phase of migration, coping and resilience were supported by religious beliefs and personal attitudes and values (Schweitzer et al., 2007).

Postmigration

The postmigration phase is a time when individuals and families hope to re-establish their lives in a more permanent way. Those entering the United

States as refugees have received permission to enter for resettlement prior to arrival in the United States; the individual applies for this status during the period of flight or displacement, beginning with the UNHCR. If approved for refugee status, the individual arrives in the United States and can apply for permanent residency after one year and U.S. citizenship after five years (Bridging Refugee Youth and Children's Services, 2010). Individuals arriving in the country without refugee (or immigrant) status can apply for asylum on arrival at a border point (airport, seaport, border crossing). There is a lengthy process to determine whether someone meets criteria for receiving asylum; an average length of time for asylum decisions was 35 months (Marshall, Schell, Elliot, Berthold, & Chun, 2005). Uncertainty about immigration status can increase the stress of the postmigration phase. Unaccompanied children arriving in the United States are under the responsibility of the U.S. Citizenship and Immigration Services. Some children may be placed in the limited number of foster care services, but most are placed in a "soft detention" facility or children's detention center (Morton & Young, 2002). The facilities are institutional in nature, and children have access to educational programs (Morton & Young, 2002). Immigrants arriving with support of family members already in the United States or U.S. sponsors may receive guidance and have a different experience navigating their initial entry into a new country.

Postmigration: Macrosystem. Macrosystem factors that affect new arrivals to the United States are the policies regarding the economic and educational resources available to refugees and asylum seekers. Individuals who enter under immigrant status are eligible for social security, supplemental security income, and Medicare benefits. The Office of Refugee Resettlement (ORR) provides support around employability of refugees, such as skills training, language instruction, day care, transportation, and other resources—on a short-term basis—to help people make this transition (ORR, 2010). Asylum seekers do not receive these services. Medical assistance and cash assistance are available to refugees for up to eight months after their date of arrival in the United States or the date that asylum was granted for those seeking asylum (ORR, 2008, 2011). New arrivals with uncertain immigration status, such as asylum seekers and unaccompanied minors, may not be able to be employed or be eligible for needed health, mental health resources, educational, and legal services (Morton & Young, 2002). Asylum seekers cannot apply for work authorization until they have been in the United States for 150 days. Such policy affects asylum seekers' ability to take care of basic needs; those without work authorization were four times more likely to experience hunger than those with work authorization (Piwowarczyk et al., 2008).

Cultural orientation is another macrosystem-level issue that affects African new arrivals to the United States. The cultural orientation of the United States is predominantly individualistic; norms and values based on an individualistic orientation will be different for new arrivals from collectivistic cultures. Cultural differences are significant in regard to social and communal networks that provide a sense of belonging and identity in collectivistic cultures (Schweitzer et al., 2006). Some of the differences in cultural norms and practices may be experienced as enjoyable, especially for youths; however, the process of holding on to original cultural norms and accepting new cultural norms can be a source of tension between parents and children (Brough et al., 2003).

Receptivity of new arrivals by residents of the host country can affect the overall social climate for new arrivals. Immigrants, refugees, and asylum seekers can face hostility as residents of host countries have become *refugee fatigued* and less accommodating to new arrivals (Mupedziswa, 1997). Residents' prejudicial attitudes are fueled by fears that refugees and asylum seekers will gain economic and political power and they will lose that economic and political power; the new arrivals were viewed as a resource threat (Schweitzer, Perkoulidis, Krome, Ludlow, & Ryan, 2005). New arrivals also experience racial violence, which compounds any prior trauma experiences during premigration and flight (Brough et al., 2003).

Although individuals and families have moved to a new country, they are still connected to the countries of origin and affected by changes in political events in those countries. Refugees and asylum seekers had poorer mental health outcomes if the conflict in their countries of origin was ongoing or worsened (Porter & Haslam, 2005).

Postmigration: Exosystem. The relationships that refugees and asylum seekers establish with the refugee resettlement agency staff or government staff are significant. Staff members or volunteers with refugee resettlement organizations are the first people refugees and asylums seekers meet and interact with around all the basic needs of resettling. Refugee clients continued to be in regular contact with refugee resettlement agency staff after being transferred to county caseworkers (Brown, 2011). The relationships with the refugee resettlement agency staff were important and may replace the relationships that refugees lost during the migration process (Brown, 2011). Brown (2011) analyzed the discourse of Liberian refugees around citizenship and found that, for these refugees, the relationship with the U.S. government replaced the significant material and instrumental social networks that they had in their own country. From a collectivistic orientation these refugees conceptualized themselves in a transactional relationship with the U.S. government. One of Brown's participants perceived that the individualistic nature of the United States contributed to the need for the government to look after people because people do not help one another (Brown, 2011). Although this was the perception of this sample of African refugees, it is important to consider how other new arrivals who are not eligible for these resources understand their lack of connection to a system of resources.

Although refugees entering the United States are eligible to receive health, mental health, educational, and employment resources, they can experience barriers to access. There may be few services addressing the range of mental health needs of refugees and asylees, delays in services due to insufficient services to meet demand, lack of bilingual–bicultural staff (Gong-Guy et al., 1991), costs of services, lack of information about where to access services, and discrimination (Wong et al., 2006). In addition, clients' lack of language skills can prevent them from using public transportation systems to access treatment centers (Gong-Guy et al., 1991).

Postmigration: Mesosystem. As described earlier, the premigration and flight phases disrupt critical family, community, cultural, and social systems; this can be disorienting for those from African traditional cultures in which one's sense of identity and belonging are deeply connected to family and community networks (Schweitzer et al., 2006). This social and cultural disruption can be a continuing trauma for refugees (Marshall et al., 2005; Schweitzer et al., 2006). To mitigate these losses, African immigrants, refugees, and asylum seekers connect with others from their same ethnic group (Brough et al., 2003; Schweitzer et al., 2006). They create mutual aid societies and organizations to represent their political, economic, and social interests (Mupedziswa, 1997). It is important that social workers recognize the sense of agency that is demonstrated when African immigrants, refugees, and asylum seekers actively recreate these important systems that were disrupted. It is useful to note that although many African new arrivals prefer to connect with same-ethnic community groups, some individuals may prefer the broader community group because it reduces the expectation that they will follow traditionally accepted ways (Schweitzer et al., 2007).

Postmigration: Microsystem. Relationship with family and development of connections in the community are important during this phase. Important relationships may have been disrupted during resettlement in the United States. Africans who were married through traditional ceremonies and not legally married may be separated during this phase if only one spouse applied for or received refugee status (Brown, 2011). The presence of family and social support from others within the Sudanese community were significant factors for refugee psychological well-being (Schweitzer et al., 2006). Immigrants, refugees, and asylum seekers are still concerned about family members not living with them (Schweitzer et al., 2006). They will remain in contact with these members through phone calls and provision of financial support.

Postmigration: Individual. African immigrants, refugees, and asylum seekers experience individual-level strengths as well as challenges during postmigration.

Connections to family, community, and support networks are important for African new arrivals. The role of these connections can be seen in refugee youths who focused on their connectedness with their families, ethnic communities, and larger societies rather than focusing on the illness or problem areas (Brough et al., 2003). In addition, positive coping and resilience factors for some African refugees included their connection to religion, and personal beliefs and attitudes (Schweitzer et al., 2007).

Refugees and asylum seekers experienced challenges addressing basic needs of resettlement and mental health issues. Refugees' identified unmet needs included English language classes, dental care, and eyeglasses; for asylum seekers, the needs were food, jobs, dental care, and English language classes (Piwowarczyk et al., 2008). The fulfillment of basic needs can also have important social and emotional effects. A collaborative intervention to restore dental extractions in two African groups (voluntarily) provided individuals with the confidence to engage in job seeking and social interactions (Fox & Willis, 2010). The lower teeth extractions occurred during childhood in their country of origin and were a form of beauty. In the United States, this feature became a source of acculturation stress.

Social workers will need to pay attention to biopsychosocial aspects of working with clients and families as health issues are connected to the postmigration phase. In the process of adjusting to a new environment and culture, new arrivals can experience challenges affecting their physical health. High rates of hypertension and diabetes unrelated to obesity, trauma, or ethnicity have been identified among the refugees in one U.S. sample (Kinzie, 2009). Hunger can be an issue for those who are not able to work (such as asylum seekers) because of immigration status regulations (Piwowarczyk et al., 2008). For example, the lack of food affected asylum seekers' ability to take prescribed medications (Piwowarczyk et al., 2008).

The mental health of refugees is affected by the totality of the migration experience—premigration trauma, postmigration adjustment, and the biopsychosocial context in which the person is situated (Marshall et al., 2005; Schweitzer et al., 2006). Mental health outcomes for refugees from Africa were poorer than the outcomes for those from other regions, although more research is needed on this population (Porter & Haslam, 2005).

Predisplacement variables such as cultural capital, lower education, younger age, rural residence predisplacement, and greater distance from the original conflict were associated with positive mental health outcomes in postdisplacement (Porter & Haslam, 2005). Postmigration stressors such as temporary accommodation or lack of housing, uncertainty of financial security, and lack of employment were associated with poorer mental health outcomes (Porter & Haslam, 2005).

Poor English-speaking skills, unemployment, older age, being in retirement or having a disability, and living in poverty were associated with PTSD and major depression (Marshall et al., 2005). Living in the resettled country for less than one year was also associated with PTSD (Hondius et al., 2000). Trauma related to current context of refugees and asylum seekers is important as new exposures to violence compound the past effects of trauma. The neighborhoods in which refugees and asylum seekers are being placed are exposing many to significant levels of violence, such as seeing a dead body, experiencing a home invasion robbery, being threatened with a weapon, and other safety issues in their neighborhood (Marshall et al., 2005; Piwowarczyk et al., 2008).

Depression, anxiety, and somatization symptoms were predicted by postmigration difficulties—length of residency, employment status, social support from one's own ethnic group (Marshall et al., 2005; Schweitzer et al., 2006). Alcohol use disorder was significantly associated with exposure to trauma after immigration to the United States (Marshall et al., 2005).

The psychosocial effects of the migration experience can endure for years after resettlement in the new country. Refugees continued to be affected by premigration and postmigration trauma 14 to 20 years after migration to the United States (Chung & Bemak, 2002; Marshall et al., 2005; Steel, Silove, Phan, & Bauman, 2002). Rates of PTSD and depression remained high: both above 50 percent (Marshall et al., 2005).

Specific Groups

Comparison of immigrant children and youths with native-born children found no difference in terms of psychiatric disorders (Kirmayer et al., 2011). Immigrant children often achieved higher academically than native-born children (Kirmayer et al., 2011). Forty percent of child and adolescent refugees were estimated to have psychiatric disorders, and those experiencing war and violence in their countries of origin evidenced higher rates of PTSD, depression, and anxiety (Ehntholt & Yule, 2006). For youths, the symptoms of depression usually associated with postmigration stressors diminished significantly after six years (Sack et al., 1993). Refugee children with higher levels of emotional distress and depression, and unaccompanied children, were at high risk for mental health problems (Kirmayer et al., 2011).

Generally, refugee women had poorer mental health outcomes than did men (Porter & Haslam, 2005). One specific issue for helping professionals to be aware of is the identification and treatment of postpartum depression among immigrant, refugee, and asylum-seeking women. Immigrant women in a Canadian study were two to three times more like than native-born women to experience postpartum depression (Kirmayer et al., 2011). They are unlikely to seek treatment due to lack of familiarity with the illness, stigma, and fear of losing their children to authorities (Kirmayer et al., 2011).

Working with Clients

The ecological framework applied here allows social workers to recognize and understand individuals' and families' experiences at various phases of migration; all levels affect current functioning (see Figure 9-1). It is important to explore the interconnections among these different levels and across phases. The experiences of immigrants, refugees, and asylum seekers from Africa are not discrete events, and it would be a mistake to view them as such; they are a continuum of experiences (Brough et al., 2003). The social worker can develop an understanding of the individual's and family's areas of strength and resiliency as well as vulnerability over time that can be used in the development of interventions (Pine & Drachman, 2005).

While working with African individuals and families with experiences of violence and armed conflict, social workers must be aware of the following issues during the assessment process: the effect of violence and trauma on the clinical encounter, the effect of armed conflict on diagnosis, the effect of culture on diagnosis and treatment, the multiple roles of the social worker, and the effect of working with individuals exposed to conflict on the social worker.

Effect of Violence and Trauma on the Clinical Encounter. Social workers must gain a general awareness of the nature of clients' experiences of violence and armed conflict before working with them. Social workers may not know the specifics of an individual's or a family's experience of violence or conflict, but they can access reports or experts on a particular conflict. With such information, social workers can consider that the clinical interview or the arrangement of the interviewer's office might remind an individual of an interrogation, or the gender of the social worker may remind the individual of a rape or other traumatic experience (Kinzie & Fleck, 1987). Awareness of the contexts that clients may have been exposed to may help social workers minimize potentially stressful or retraumatizing experiences.

African clients who have experienced armed conflicts or other types of violence may be reluctant to provide information about themselves or their experiences due to mistrust of authority, fear of stigmatization, or consequences to relatives in the country of origin (Okitikpi & Aymer, 2003). Gorman (2001) found that practitioners often probe for detailed information too early in the counseling relationship. Clients may reveal specific information about past experiences of oppression, war, and violence only after the individual develops safety and trust in the relationship with the practitioner (Woodcock, 2001).

Effect of Armed Conflict on Diagnosis. The historical or political context of the client's experiences is very useful for helping practitioners determine

FIGURE 9-1: Ecological Framework for Populations Displaced Due to Armed Conflict

	Preconflict	Premigration	Flight	Post-Migration
Macrosystem	• Culture • History • Economic conditions	• Breakdown of country's infrastructure • Inability to support affected population	• Humanitarian crisis • Systems are overwhelmed • Political and language differences	• Resettlement policies • Status uncertainty • Cultural differences • Hostility and discrimination
Exosystem	• District political structures • Cultural leaders • International agencies	• Breakdown in regional district-level systems • Inability to access macro-level resources	• Temporary living conditions • Confusing and insecure structures • Hostile reception	• Barriers to services • Recreating system relationships to replace social systems lost
Mesosystem	• Community-as-a-whole activities • Cultural practices • Family and clan networks	• Disruption of family, clan, social, economic systems • Cultural and communal livelihood activities stop	• Social systems are fragmented • Villages/communities displaced to different areas	• Continuing effects of disruption of social networks • Connection to own ethnic group is important
Microsystem	• Family, clan, ancestors • School (teachers) • Religious leaders • Cultural leaders	• Disruption of family and peer supports • Focus on survival • Family members and friends abducted, killed	• Family members separated • Inability to mourn those who died • Prior relationship problems unresolved	• Family connection is important • Concern about family in country of origin
Individual	• Social and emotional well-being • Health issues • Educational experience	• Breakdown in all aspects of living • Exposure to or experience of violence • Religion and attitudes associated with resilience	• Exposure to/experience of violence • Individual factors associated with poorer functioning • Resilience factors	• Living conditions • Employment • Hunger • English language skills • Acculturation stress • Health concerns

appropriate diagnosis and treatment recommendations. A diagnosis such as paranoid personality may be reconsidered after evaluating an individual's experiences of violence and armed conflict (American Psychiatric Association, 2000; Woodcock, 2001). Although there is a focus on individual psychosocial functioning in the United States, Gorman (2001) reminded us that the experiences of abuse and violence of refugees and asylum seekers are abuses of the larger social and political contexts in which they occurred. To understand a client's experiences, the practitioner needs to understand the larger context and consider that larger context in the development of treatment (Gorman, 2001).

Effect of Culture on Diagnosis and Treatment. Clients from Africa may have a collectivist cultural orientation, which is significantly different from the individualist orientation of most U.S. practitioners. A significant aspect of collectivism is the embeddedness of individuals within the larger family; communal, natural, and spiritual systems; and the connectedness of these systems. Cultural orientation influences the nature, expression, and understanding of health, mental health, and well-being. Misdiagnosis can occur when social workers have expectations around expression of emotion that differ from the client's culture or if psychoemotional issues are expressed somatically rather than emotionally (Gong-Guy et al., 1991). In addition to the expressions of emotions, there can be conceptual differences in cultural understandings of concepts such as guilt and shame that can make a significant difference in diagnosis and treatment (Gorman, 2001).

A client with a collectivist conceptualization of self may prefer interventions that include others, such as family members, religious leader, or a group, providing a more culturally congruent experience (Gorman, 2001; Kelley, 1994; Weine, 2002). Practitioners who are predominantly individualistic in their cultural orientation must be willing to learn about and understand the individual's and family's beliefs and values as well as the significance of these beliefs and values.

Multiple Roles of the Social Worker. Social workers working with immigrant, refugee, and asylum-seeker populations may fill multiple roles such as counselor, caseworker, liaison with community resources, advocate in legal proceedings, support system as the client and family navigate activities of everyday life in a new country, and friend (Gorman, 2011). The need to fulfill multiple roles may be due to two reasons: (1) the practical nature of the activities that social workers may need to engage in with clients and (2) the traditional African cultural orientation about the nature of relationships. The practical nature of the work that is done with clients requires that someone in the social service system is attending to the issues—shelter, heat, clothes, food, money, employment, language issues—that affect mental health postmigration in addition to other psychoemotional needs. From a cultural perspective, it is through involvement in the activities mentioned earlier that relationships are formed with African clients. Sharing meals with families and interacting with the ethnic community around rituals or cultural stories are the ways of learning about clients' experiences (Woodcock, 2001). Social workers' involvement in these activities demonstrates commitment and interest in the client and the family and helps to create trust and rapport (Khamphakdy-Brown, Jones, Nilsson, Russell, & Klevens, 2006).

Effect of Working with Individuals Exposed to Conflict on the Social Worker. Clients' descriptions of frightening, oppressive, violent, and traumatic experiences during premigration, flight, and postmigration can be emotionally difficult for social workers and can contribute to burnout and vicarious traumatization. van der Veer (1998) specified that practitioners can be aware of their emotional reactions during three phases of the therapeutic work: during the therapeutic contact, shortly after the therapeutic contact, and long term. During the therapeutic encounter, therapists may have normal empathetic reactions that are unusual within the therapeutic context, for example, tearing up after listening to a client's experience of torture (van der Veer, 1998). Therapists might develop coping strategies to gain control over their reactions in the sessions that enable them to stay connected to the client and not burden the client with their emotional reaction. During and after sessions, therapists may recognize that they did not address or notice certain client comments (van der Veer, 1998). Such reactions may be ways that therapists unconsciously protect themselves from the horrific experiences they are hearing about (Marotta, 2003). Long-term effects on practitioners can include changes in beliefs, expectations, and assumptions about the world (van der Veer, 1998). Social workers engaged in work with war-affected populations will need to be aware of their reactions and develop a range of coping strategies to serve their clients and allow themselves to be effective in their work.

Another caution of listening to clients' descriptions of their difficult experiences is that social workers must be aware not to place more attention on the trauma narrative than the other narratives that the client may express (Papadopoulos, 2001). Immigrant or refugee families may seek treatment to help with negotiating the differences between parents and adolescents adapting to the host country (Brough et al., 2003) or addressing issues around employment or cultural adjustment.

Implications

The challenges that arise for social workers working with African clients affected by armed conflict require the use and support of a supervisory and collaborative network. The issues that are addressed in such work are many; these issues may be challenging in terms of the range of client needs, the number of systems to work with, culture, and language issues. Practitioner reflection on clinical encounters, use of process recordings, use of supervision, and participation on treatment teams are important ways to receive feedback, support, and perspective in one's work (Woodcock, 2001).

Social workers may need to work with an individual knowledgeable about the culture and language of the groups they are working with, to reduce misdiagnoses due to context issues, conceptual differences with words, culture-based expressions of emotion, and language differences (Kinzie, 2009). If working collaboratively is not possible, social workers may need to develop a network of cultural consultants to supplement their provision of mental health services (Khamphakdy-Brown et al., 2006).

The collaborative work of the social worker extends to the community. Social workers must know and establish relationships with as many community services and resources as possible. These community networks and resources are a vital aspect of the social relationships that African clients will need, and it is important for social workers to be familiar with them.

Conclusion

Social workers and other helping professionals working with African individuals and families from contexts of armed conflict are often challenged by the number and complexity of issues to address. The ecological perspective was used to develop a framework for identifying critical factors, experiences throughout the migration process, and cultural influences related to working with this population. Using such a framework enables social workers to take a long view of clients' experiences rather than focusing on a particular time period or phase of migration. Such a framework also allows social workers to identify areas of client strength, resilience, and vulnerability. Although it may be difficult to identify the specific macrosystem, exosystem, mesosystem, microsystem, and individual issues, not attempting to do so risks missing important aspects of people's lives. The integration of aspects of the collectivistic orientation in the framework highlighted the differences in conceptualization of relationships across all levels of the ecological system. This conceptualization of relationship provides a source of strength and empowerment for African immigrants, refugees, and asylum seekers and is salient for helping professionals' work with this population.

References

Achvarina, V., & Reich, S. (2006). No place to hide: Refugees, displaced persons and the recruitment of child soldiers [Electronic version]. *International Security, 31*(1), 127–164.

American Psychiatric Association. (2000). *Diagnostic and statistical manual of mental disorders* (4th ed., text rev.). Washington, DC: Author.

Bridging Refugee Youth and Children's Services. (2010). *Refugee 101*. Retrieved from http://www.brycs.org/aboutRefugees/refugee101.cfm

Bronfenbrenner, U. (1979). *The ecology of human development: Experiments by nature and design*. Cambridge, MA: Harvard University Press.

Brough, M., Gorman, D., Ramirez, E., & Westoby, P. (2003). Young refugees talk about well-being: A qualitative analysis of refugee youth mental health from three states. *Australian Journal of Social Issues, 38*(2), 193–208.

Brown, H. E. (2011). Refugees, rights, and race: How legal status shapes Liberian immigrants' relationship with the state. *Social Problems, 58,* 144–163. doi:10.1525/sp.2011.58.1.144

Chung, R. C.-Y., & Bemak, F. (2002). Revisiting the California southeast Asian mental health needs assessment data: An examination of refugee ethnic and gender differences. *Journal of Counseling & Development, 80,* 111–119.

Corbin, J. N. (2008). Returning home: Resettlement experiences of formerly abducted children in northern Uganda. *Disasters, 32,* 316–335.

Denov, M. (2010). *Child soldiers: Sierra Leone's Revolutionary United Front*. New York: Cambridge University Press.

Duyvesteyn, I. (2000). Contemporary war: Ethnic conflict, resource conflict or something else? *Civil Wars, 3*(1), 92–116.

Ehntholt, K., & Yule, W. (2006). Practitioner review: Assessment and treatment of refugee children and adolescents who have experienced war-related trauma. *Journal of Child Psychology and Psychiatry, 47,* 1197–1210.

Finnström, S. (2008). *Living with bad surroundings: War, history, and everyday moments in northern Uganda*. Durham, NC: Duke University Press.

Fox, S. H., & Willis, M. S. (2010). Dental restorations for Dinka and Nuer refugees: A confluence of culture and healing. *Transcultural Psychiatry, 47,* 452–472. doi: 10.1177/1363461510374559

Gong-Guy, E., Cravens, R., & Patterson, T. (1991). Clinical issues in mental health service delivery to refugees. *American Psychologist, 46,* 642–648.

Gorman, W. (2001). Refugee survivors of torture: Trauma and assessment. *Professional Psychology, Research & Practice, 32,* 443–451. doi:10.1037//0735-7028.32.5.443

Hondius, A.J.K, van Willigen, L.H.M., Kleijn, W.C., & van der Ploeg, H. M. (2000). Health problems among Latin-American and Middle Eastern refugees in the Netherlands: Relations with violence exposure and ongoing sociopsychological strain. *Journal of Traumatic Stress, 13,* 619–634.

Honwana, A. (2006). *Child soldiers in Africa*. Philadelphia: University of Pennsylvania Press.

Kamya, H. (1997). African immigrants in the United States: The challenge for research and practice [Electronic version]. *Social Work, 42,* 154–166.

Kelley, P. (1994). Integrating systemic and post-systemic approaches to social work practice with refugee families. *Families in Society, 75,* 541–549.

Khamphakdy-Brown, S., Jones, L. N., Nilsson, J. E., Russell, E. B., & Klevens, C. L. (2006). The empowerment program: An application of an outreach program for refugee and immigrant women. *Journal of Mental Health Counseling, 28,* 38–47.

Kinzie, J. D. (2009). A model for treating refugees traumatized by violence: A personal point of reference. *Psychiatric Times, 26*(7), 43–45.

Kinzie, J. D., & Fleck, J. (1987). Psychotherapy with severely traumatized refugees. *American Journal of Psychotherapy, 41,* 82–94.

Kirmayer, L. J., Narasiah, L., Munoz, M., Rashid, M., Ryder, A. G., Guzder, J., et al. (2011). Common mental health problems in immigrants and refugees: General approach in primary care. *Canadian Medical Association Journal, 183*(12), E959–E967. doi:10.1503/cmaj.090292

Lum, D. (2007). Culturally competent practice. In D. Lum (Ed.), *Culturally competent practice: A framework for understanding diverse groups and justice issues* (pp. 3–42). Belmont, CA: Thomson Brooks/Cole.

Marotta, S. A. (2003). Unflinching empathy: Counselors and tortured refugees. *Journal of Counseling & Development, 81,* 111–114.

Marshall, G. N., Schell, T. L., Elliot, M. N., Berthold, M., & Chun, C.-A. (2005). Mental health of Cambodian refugees 2 decades after resettlement in the U.S. *JAMA, 294,* 571–579.

Mbiti, J. S. (1990). *African religions and philosophy.* Portsmouth, NH: Heinemann Educational Books.

Morton, A., & Young, W. A. (2002). Children asylum seekers face challenges in the United States. *Refuge, 20*(2), 13–20.

Mupedziswa, R. (1997). Social work with refugees: The growing international crisis. In M. C. Hokenstad & J. Midgley (Eds.), *Issues in international social work: Global challenges for a new century* (pp. 110–124). Washington, DC: NASW Press.

Office of Refugee Resettlement. (2008). *Cash and medical assistance.* Washington, DC: U.S. Department of Health and Human Services, Administration for Children and Families. Retrieved from http://www.acf.hhs.gov/programs/orr/benefits/health.htm

Office of Refugee Resettlement. (2010). *Social services.* Washington, DC: U.S. Department of Health and Human Services, Administration for Children and Families. Retrieved from http://www.acf.hhs.gov/programs/orr/benefits/rss.htm

Office of Refugee Resettlement. (2011). *Health.* Washington, DC: U.S. Department of Health and Human Services, Administration for Children and Families. Retrieved from http://www.acf.hhs.gov/programs/orr/benefits/health.htm

Okitikpi, T., & Aymer, C. (2003). Social work with African refugee children and their families. *Child & Family Social Work, 8,* 213–222.

Oosthuizen, G. C. (1991). The place of traditional religion in contemporary South Africa. In J. K. Olupọna (Ed.), *African traditional religions: In contemporary society* (pp. 35–50). New York: Paragon House.

Papadopoulos, R. K. (2001). Refugee families: Issues of systemic supervision. *Journal of Family Therapy, 23,* 405–422.

Pine, B. A., & Drachman, D. (2005). Effective child welfare practice with immigrant and refugee children and their families. *Child Welfare, 84,* 537–562.

Piwowarczyk, L., Keane, T. M., & Lincoln, A. (2008). Hunger: The silent epidemic among asylum seekers and resettled refugees. *International Migration, 46*(1), 59–77. doi:10.1111/j.1468-2435.2008.00436.x

Porter, M., & Haslam, N. (2005). Predisplacement and postdisplacement factors associated with mental health of refugees and internally displaced persons: A meta-analysis. *JAMA, 294,* 602–612.

Sack, W. H., Clarke, G., Him, C., Dickason, D., Goff, B., Lanham, K., & Kinzie, J. D. (1993). A 6-year follow-up study of Cambodian refugee adolescents traumatized as children. *Journal of the American Academy of Child and Adolescent Psychiatry, 32,* 431–437.

Sack, W. H., Clarke, G. N., & Seeley, J. (1996). Multiple forms of stress in Cambodian adolescent refugees. *Child Development, 67,* 106–116.

Schweitzer, R., Greenslade, J., & Kagee, A. (2007). Coping and resilience in refugees from the Sudan: A narrative account. *Australian and New Zealand Journal of Psychiatry, 41,* 282–288. doi:10.1080/00048670601172780

Schweitzer, R., Melville, F., Steel, Z., & Lacherez, P. (2006). Trauma, post-migration living difficulties, and social support as predictors of psychological adjustment in resettled Sudanese refugees. *Australian and New Zealand Journal of Psychiatry, 40,* 179–187.

Schweitzer, R., Perkoulidis, S., Krome, S., Ludlow, C., & Ryan, M. (2005). Attitudes towards refugees: The dark side of prejudice in Australia. *Australian Journal of Psychology, 57,* 170–179. doi:10.1080/00049530500125199

Silove, D., & Ekblad, S. (2002). How well do refugees adapt after resettlement in Western countries. *Acta Psychiatrica Scandinavica, 106,* 401–402.

Steel, Z., Silove, D., Phan, T., & Bauman, A. (2002). Long-term effect of psychological trauma on the mental health of Vietnamese refugees resettled in Australia: A population based study. *Lancet, 360,* 1056–1061.

Triandis, H. C. (1995). *Individualism & collectivism: New directions in social psychology.* Boulder, CO: Westview Press.

United Nations High Commissioner for Refugees. (2011). *2011 regional operations profile—Africa.* Retrieved from http://www.unhcr.org/pages/4a02d7fd6.html

van der Veer, G. (1998). *Counseling and therapy with refugees and victims of trauma: Psychological problems of victims of war, torture and repression* (2nd ed.). New York: John Wiley & Sons.

Weine, S. (2002, January). Mental health and refugee families. *USA Today Magazine, 130*(2680), 26. Retrieved from Academic Search Premier database.

Wong, E. C., Marshall, G. N., Schell, T. L., Elliot, M. N., Hambarsoomians, K., Chun, C.-A., & Berthold, S. M. (2006). Barriers to mental health care utilization for U.S. Cambodian refugees. *Journal of Consulting and Clinical Psychology, 74,* 1116–1120.

Woodcock, J. (2001). Threads from the labyrinth: Therapy with survivors of war and political oppression. *Journal of Family Therapy, 23,* 136–154.

World Health Organization. (2011). *HIV/AIDS: Testing and counseling data and statistics.* Retrieved from http://www.who.int/hiv/topics/vct/data/en/index.html

World Vision. (2006). *Their future in our hands: Children displaced by conflicts in Africa's Great Lakes region.* Retrieved from http://www.worldvision.org/resources.nsf/main/greatlakes_conflicts_200702.pdf/$file/greatlakes_conflicts_200702.pdf?open&lid=greatlakes&lpos=main

Conclusion

Joanne Corbin

This book aimed to increase the awareness and knowledge of social workers and other helping professionals in the United States about the context and realities of children and families affected by armed conflict in Africa and the strategies used to address the needs of this population. The authors brought attention to the direct and indirect effects of armed conflict on populations; the effects on individuals, families, communities, and culture; and the micro- and macrosystems issues that must be included in intervention planning.

The focus on African populations is necessary due to the impact of conflict on the continent of Africa and the traditional cultural orientation that influences norms, values, and expectations. All individuals from Africa are not exposed to violence, nor will they all have had the experiences that are presented in this book. However, it is important that social workers in the United States develop awareness of the number of armed conflicts that occur in Africa and the impact these conflicts have on a country and its people and neighboring countries. The loss of life; the number of people wounded, disabled, maimed, and tortured; the breakdown of families; and the disruption of social, cultural, and economic systems are staggering. Social workers must be aware of such important contextual issues when working with families.

A second reason to focus on African populations is the predominant collectivistic cultural orientation that many individuals from Africa hold, which is different from the individualistic orientation that is predominant within the United States. What is important to be aware of is how a collectivistic orientation might shape an individual's views of self, relationships, well-being, health, and mental health. When social workers understand the perceptions, beliefs, and values that clients and families hold, they are better able to develop treatment plans and interventions that are cognitively and affectively congruent with the client.

Key Themes

The key themes that arose throughout this book include the following:

- Multiple factors to attend to when working with African individuals from contexts of armed conflict
- Complexity of factors
- Cultural understandings and influences
- Grounding interventions and programs in the local cultural understandings of health, mental health, and well-being
- Working collaboratively

Multiple Factors to Attend to When Working with African Individuals from Contexts of Armed Conflict

The authors identified many areas to consider when working with African clients affected by armed conflict. Clients' experiences before, during, and after the armed conflict influence mental health outcomes; they also provide information about client strengths and vulnerabilities. The description of relationships with family, peers, community, and the larger physical and spiritual worlds before the conflict allows social workers to understand the magnitude of loss and disruption of social networks clients may have experienced. Understanding the nature of the conflict and the exposure that clients had provides information about the impact of armed conflict on individuals' and families' psychological, social, physical, and economic worlds. Client experiences during the flight phase of migration and the length of time in the flight phase help the social worker to understand the continuing emotional, social, and physical assaults that clients were exposed to. Lastly, client experiences on arrival in the host country can provide continued stress and uncertainty. The living conditions, employment difficulties, language barriers, and unaddressed health and mental health issues will affect children and families and all will need to be attended to.

Complexity of the Many of Factors

In addition to the number of factors to consider when working with clients who have been affected by armed conflicts in Africa, social workers are faced with the complexity of many of these factors. For example, one individual's experience of armed conflict may be different from that of another individual from the same country. An individual's social and political associations may provide protection or vulnerability; family resources may provide protection or vulnerability around having shelter and food or being able to leave the violent areas. The complexity can also arise during assessment of mental health. Determining the impact of trauma experiences on the individual, the contribution of cultural aspects to this assessment, and the understanding of stressors related to current context can be difficult to discern.

Cultural Understandings and Influences

The explanations and descriptions of the traditional African cultural orientation on various aspects of individual, family, and community life were extremely useful. Descriptions of the traditional African cultures and practices by Ugandan and Rwandan authors provided a deep, rich, and nuanced explanation of these practices that is rarely understood. The African orientation of the individual embedded in the larger social, physical, and spiritual worlds is an important cultural concept for social workers to understand. This cultural concept expands social workers' concept of person-in-environment when working with individuals and families having a more traditional African cultural orientation.

Grounding Interventions and Programs in the Local Cultural Understandings of Health, Mental Health, and Well-Being

Related to the specific cultural understandings of self, relationships, well-being, and mental health is the importance of work with African individuals and families being informed by, if not grounded in, local cultural understandings. All of the interventions discussed in this book were developed within the local cultural understandings of well-functioning individuals and families and supportive and productive communities. For some, interventions that involved the family were more culturally congruent than those that focused on the community or an individual. In other examples, group interventions providing peer support were more accepted than family-based interventions. In all cases, understanding the cultural norms and practices from individuals within that culture is important.

Working Collaboratively

Authors identified the need for social workers to work collaboratively on several levels. First, it is important that social workers identify people knowledgeable about the client's language, culture, and context of the country of origin. Cultural experts or cultural consultants helped minimize misunderstandings that could occur from language differences or cultural conceptualizations around mental health and expectations of treatment. Second, social workers must consider working with African ethnic community groups, mutual aid societies, churches, and local resources such as food pantries. Connecting African new arrivals to these resources helps to recreate the significant social and cultural systems of support that were lost in the migration process. Working with African families to develop community connections also strengthens social workers' relationships with these families. Third, the chapters that described interventions and research developed in Africa focused on the involvement of the community in all aspects. Programs were not developed for communities but by communities and within communities. Collaboration occurred horizontally across administrative levels (national teams, district teams, community advisory boards) and vertically within communities. It is important to note that given the descriptions of the breakdown of social structures in conflict-affected areas, such community involvement and participation is a strength of these communities and for individuals coming from similar communities.

Implications

The key themes identified in this book speak to the need for social workers and helping professionals, more broadly, to develop frameworks to identify the important factors to attend to in their work with individuals who have been affected by armed conflicts in Africa. There can be a lot of information to pay attention to, and some of it may be very complicated. Developing a framework supports the social worker to pay attention to the broad range of issues that are being presented and reduces the tendency to prematurely identify an issue that is important to the social worker but not salient for the individual or the family. Frameworks need to be flexible enough to incorporate cultural influences and individual variables. The ecological perspective was offered as one possible framework.

Much more understanding of the African cultural orientation is needed. There are commonalities across African ethnic groups and there are differences. The authors detailed the understandings from the perspective with which they were most familiar. The perspectives that were presented provided information about the nature of interconnectedness among all levels of the social system and the transactional expectations of individuals. Social workers need more knowledge of specific ethnic groups' cultural perspectives to develop culturally congruent interventions.

Continued exploration and focus on the experiences of children and families coming from contexts of armed conflict in Africa is also needed. The number of individuals with this experience in the United States is not known;

however, demographic data provides some indication that this is a sizeable and growing number. Data are kept for refugees and asylum seekers but not for immigrants. Gaining more description of the experiences of Africans coming to the United States will help social workers develop a contextual understanding of the families with whom they are working.

Broader Implications

The content of this book grew out of a conference focusing on the needs of children and families affected by conflict in a few countries in Africa. Although the examples presented in this book are based on specific cultures, the identified themes have application to African children and families with similar experiences and navigating the challenging process of resettling in a new country with differences in culture, language, and practices. The hope is that the specific examples in this book enable helping professionals to understand the complexity of factors that they may need to address, the flexibility they may need to acquire to address these issues, and the importance of understanding the significance and nuance of culture in the totality of children's and families' lives.

Glossary

Acholi people One of the tribes within the Lwo ethnic group. The Lwo ethnic group also includes the Alur and Lwo (from Uganda, Sudan, and Kenya).

amnesty An official pardon for people who have been convicted of political offenses. (http://oxforddictionaries.com/definition/amnesty)

armed conflict A political conflict in which armed combat involves the armed forces of at least one state (or one or more armed factions seeking to gain control of all or part of the state), and in which at least 1,000 people have been killed by the fighting during the course of the conflict. (Project Ploughshares. http://www.ploughshares.ca/content/defining-armed-conflict)

asylum seeker A person who moves across borders in search of protection, has applied for protection in the host country, and is awaiting the determination of his or her status. An asylum seeker asks for protection after arriving in a host country, whereas a refugee is granted protective status outside of the host country. (http://www.unesco.org/new/en/social-and-human-sciences/themes/social-transformations/international-migration/glossary/asylum-seeker/)

Christian Children's Fund (now known as ChildFund) An international child sponsorship group that works in 31 countries with a mission centered on the belief that empowering children empowers the world around them. (http://www.childfund.org/about_us/)

collectivistic The characterization of social patterns of individuals who view themselves as closely linked, interdependent, and motivated by group norms and who give priority to group goals. (Triandis, H. C. [1995]. *Individualism & collectivism: New directions in social psychology.* Boulder, CO: Westview Press.)

demobilization The formal and controlled discharge of active combatants from armed forces or other armed groups. (http://www.unddr.org/iddrs/04/20.php)

IDP camp Internally Displaced Persons camp: A temporary or makeshift camp for people displaced within their country of origin.

immigrant A person who is lawfully admitted into a country (other than their country of origin) for permanent residence. (http://www.cbo.gov/ftpdocs/70xx/doc7051/02-28-Immigration.pdf)

individualistic The characterization of social patterns of individuals who view themselves as independent and motivated by personal needs and rights and who give priority to individual goals. (Triandis, 1995)

interstate Involving or existing between two states or countries.

intrastate Relating or existing within the boundaries of a state or country.

international war Any military confrontation between the military forces or two or more states, or the bombardment of one state by another state, or the invasion of one state by another state, including occupation. (http://www.adh-geneve.ch/RULAC/index.php) (http://www.slideshare.net/swissnexSF/international-law-in-times-of-armed-conflict)

orphan A child who has lost one or both parents. UNICEF and partner organizations began defining an orphan in this manner due to the increasing number of children that were losing parents due to AIDS. Single orphan refers to the loss of one parent; double orphan refers to the loss of both parents. (http://www.unicef.org/media/media_45279.html)

psychosocial The interrelation of social factors and individual thought and behavior. (http://oxforddictionaries.com/definition/psychosocial?region=us)

rehabilitation center A collection point in the first instance, where the psychosocial needs of children can be assessed in a nonmilitary environment before they are returned to their families. (http://www.unicef.org/media/media_14891.html)

reception centers The first place a formerly abducted youth is taken once he or she escapes or is freed from captivity. Reception centers provide basic human needs such as shelter, food, and clothing to formerly abducted youths.

refugee Any person who is outside his or her country of nationality who is unable or unwilling to return to that country because of persecution or a well-founded fear of persecution. (http://www.dhs.gov/files/statistics/stdfdef.shtm#0)

refugee camp A temporary, makeshift shelter established for refugees who are displaced from their country of origin.

reintegration The process of restoring to a position of as a part fitting into a larger whole. (http://english.oxforddictionaries.com/definition/reintegrate?region=us#m_en_us1284027.004)

reintegration programs Programs established to assist formerly abducted youths in returning to their communities and establishing a life as a noncombatant.

resident district commissioner A representative of the president whose constitutional mandate is to monitor the implementation of central and local government services in a given district, and the chairperson of the district security committee. (http://allafrica.com/stories/201104080101.html)

war-affected children Children whose lives have been physically, emotionally, psychologically, culturally, or spiritually disrupted by armed conflict.

Index

In this index, *f* denotes figure, *n* denotes footnote, and *t* denotes table.

S

About the Editor

Joanne Corbin, PhD, MSS, BA, is associate professor and chair of the research sequence at Smith College School for Social Work (SSW), in Northampton, Massachusetts. Dr. Corbin's current research focuses on children and families involved in armed conflict in northern Uganda. She has conducted research on the reintegration experiences of former child soldiers in northern Uganda and on the resettlement of internally displaced populations in northern Uganda. An outgrowth of this research was the development of a training-of-trainers program with service providers in northern Uganda addressing the psychosocial needs of individuals and families affected by armed conflict. Dr. Corbin developed a social work internship program in northern Uganda for students from Smith College School for Social Work, and she has written about the values conflicts that U.S.-based social workers experience in international settings. She has also explored global social work issues in South Africa, Tanzania, and Canada. In 2010, Dr. Corbin was appointed to the Council on Social Work Education's Council for Global Learning, Research and Practice, which seeks to develop social workers who are competent in international practice. Dr. Corbin is a clinical social worker and is trained in family therapy.

About the Contributors

William R. Beardslee, MD, is director of the Baer Prevention Initiatives at Children's Hospital Boston. He is a Gardner/Monks Professor of Child Psychiatry at Harvard Medical School and is the developer of the Family Talk intervention for families. Dr. Beardslee's research focuses on depression in children.

Jo Becker, MA, is advocacy director of the Children's Rights Division at Human Rights Watch. She is the founding chairperson of the international Coalition to Stop the Use of Child Soldiers, which campaigned successfully for an international treaty banning the forced recruitment of children under age 18 years and their use in armed conflict and helped secure U.S. ratification of the treaty in 2002. Becker is also an adjunct associate professor of international and public affairs at Columbia University.

Theresa S. Betancourt, ScD, MA, is assistant professor of Child Health and Human Rights in the Department of Global Health and Population at the Harvard School of Public Health. Dr. Betancourt is a member of the François-Xavier Bagnoud Center for Health and Human Rights, where she directs the Research Program on Children and Global Adversity. Her central research interests focus on the developmental and psychosocial consequences of concentrated adversity on children and families, resilience and protective processes in child mental health, health and human rights, and cross-cultural mental health research.

Felix Rwabukwisi Cyamatare, MD, is a physician and current interim clinical director at Partners In Health/Inshuti Mu Buzima in Rwanda. Dr. Cyamatare has worked at Partners In Health for four years, leading the Pediatric HIV and Prevention of HIV Mother-to-Child Transmission programs in combination with the Pediatric Chronic Diseases program.

Joan Granucci Lesser, PhD, MSW, LICSW, is founder and practicing clinician with the Pioneer Valley Professionals, a multidisciplinary mental health practice in Holyoke, Massachusetts. She is also adjunct associate professor at Smith College School for Social Work. Dr. Lesser is the coauthor of *Clinical Social Work: An Integrated Approach* and *Human Behavior and the Social Environment: Theory and Practice,* as well as a number of book chapters and papers.

Sarah E. Meyers-Ohki, BA, is a member of the Research Program on Children and Global Adversity directed by Dr. Betancourt at the François-Xavier Bagnoud Center for Health and Human Rights, Harvard School of Public Health. Her interests are in cross-cultural research on maternal and child health.

Eugenie Mukeshimana, BSW, is the founder and executive director of Genocide Survivors Support Network, a charitable organization created to provide services to survivors living in the United States. She was a young adult when the genocide broke in her native country, Rwanda, in 1994. After the genocide, she worked with refugees and returnees, mostly women and children. Mukeshimana's professional goal is to educate practitioners in social service agencies about the challenges immigrants face when they enter a world that knows little or nothing about them.

Christine Mushashi, BA, is a research coordinator on the Family Strengthening Intervention project led by the Research Program on Children and Global Adversity and Partners In Health. Ms. Mushashi is pursuing a master's degree in clinical psychology at Bircham International University.

Father Remigio C. Obol, MA, is the parish priest of Assumption Parish Awac in Gulu Archdiocese in northern Uganda. He is serving as chairman of the Diocesan Priests of the Gulu Archdiocese. Father Remigio is developing a program—Gulu Artilive Peace Artists—to help youths affected by armed conflict express themselves through music and dance. He likes reading and writing especially on peace, development, and violence and conflict prevention.

Stella Ojera, BA, is founder and director of Acholi Community Empowerment Network (ACEN) in Gulu, Uganda. ACEN was founded in 2004 with the mission of developing psychosocial support and income-generating activities for individuals and families rebuilding their lives during postconflict in northern

Uganda. Ms. Ojera's career has centered on research and program development for children affected by armed conflict.

Sara N. Stulac, MD, MPH, is the director of pediatrics and oncology programs for Partners In Health, and oversees work in Rwanda, Haiti, Malawi, and Lesotho. She is on faculty at the Division of Global Health Equity at Brigham and Women's Hospital, and at Harvard Medical School and Children's Hospital Boston. Dr. Stulac's areas of clinical and programmatic focus include pediatric HIV prevention and treatment, malnutrition, neonatology, pediatric oncology, and mental health.